VISUAL QUICKSTART GUIDE

APPLEWORKS 6

FOR MACINTOSH

Nolan Hester

 Peachpit Press

Visual QuickStart Guide
AppleWorks 6 for Macintosh
Nolan Hester

Peachpit Press
1249 Eighth Street
Berkeley, CA 94710
(800) 283-9444
(510) 524-2178
(510) 524-2221 (fax)

Find us on the World Wide Web at: http://www.peachpit.com

Peachpit Press is a division of Addison Wesley Longman

Copyright © 2000 by Nolan Hester

Editor: Nancy Davis
Production Coordinator: Lisa Brazieal
Compositor: David Van Ness
Cover Design: The Visual Group, Mimi Heft
Indexer: Emily Glossbrenner

ISBN: 0-201-70282-7

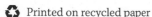 Printed on recycled paper

0 9 8 7 6 5 4 3 2 1

Printed and bound in the United States of America

To Mary for a life sheltered by leaves and light.

Special thanks to:
Nancy Davis who is simply the best editor one could ever ask for; David Van Ness for turnarounds so fast I never knew when he slept; Lisa Brazieal and Mimi Heft for their usual top-notch work and unfailing attention to the crucial production details; Emily Glossbrenner for the kind of thorough indexing that readers need but seldom encounter; Nancy Aldrich-Ruenzel for starting me on this work; and Laika, my study buddy, for making me stop—no matter what—for evening walks.

TABLE OF CONTENTS

PART II:	**HANDLING TEXT IN APPLEWORKS**	**97**

Chapter 5:	**Entering and Editing Text**	**99**

Chapter 6:	**Formatting Text**	**117**

Chapter 7:	**Creating and Using Tables**	**147**

Chapter 15: Painting   **355**

PART I

GETTING STARTED

USING
APPLEWORKS 6

Welcome to the Visual QuickStart Guide for
AppleWorks 6. Whether you bought it as a
stand-alone program or it came installed on
your new iMac or iBook, AppleWorks gives
you everything you need to create great-looking documents, drawings, presentations, and
more—all in a single, easy-to-use program. If
this is your first time using AppleWorks, you
can say good-bye to the head-scratching frustrations of other programs. If you've used earlier versions of the program, you already
know how quickly AppleWorks lets you get to
work. But before you dive in, be sure to read
on page 5 about the many improvements
made to AppleWorks.

Why AppleWorks?

Why use a dump truck when a pickup will do? That's part of the philosophy behind the all-in-one AppleWorks. It offers just about everything you could need—word processing, spreadsheets, charts, databases, graphics, and now a presentation module—in an easy, straightforward package. It does not have all the bells and whistles—and complications—of that other all-in-one program, Microsoft Office. But at less than $75, it's *much* cheaper. And it demands a lot less computer memory: 4 MB of RAM for AppleWorks vs. at least 7–10 MB for Office.

Best of all, AppleWorks comes packed with extras to help you create great-looking documents: 50 fonts (including four fonts for teaching cursive writing), 100 templates, and 25,000 pieces of clip art at the AppleWorks Web site. Hard to beat, easy to use: that's AppleWorks.

What's New in AppleWorks 6?

In creating AppleWorks 6, its designers wanted to improve the program without disorienting longtime users. While aspects of the new program have been completely retooled, other portions, such as the database module, have changed very little. In short, the designers weren't just looking for bragging rights: If an item worked well in version 5, they left it alone in version 6.

Still, there's plenty to brag about in AppleWorks 6, starting with a revamped interface that's much cleaner and easier to use. AppleWorks also now contains a dedicated presentation module that's very intuitive. Recognizing that Web browser programs have become our main way of accessing the Internet, AppleWorks has retired its old communications module. But the Web is very much a part of AppleWorks 6, as evidenced by the Clippings feature, which lets you grab art off the Web. And as long as you have an open Internet connection, you can share AppleWorks documents with other AppleWorks users without ever touching your browser.

There are many more tweaks, fixes, and major improvements. Here are some highlights:

Revamped interface

◆ **A streamlined Button Bar:** In previous versions of AppleWorks, the Button Bar was packed to the gills with icons, many of them cryptic. The new Button Bar, by default, contains only commonly used icons. However, it's easy to add as many icons as you want. AppleWorks contains dozens of icons for specific commands (**Figure 1.1**) or you can easily make your own. The Button Bar now includes scroll arrows so you can keep the bar small, yet move left or right to find out-of-sight icons. For more information, see *The Button Bar* on page 26.

◆ **A new Tools Palette:** All your tools now appear in a single floating palette (**Figure 1.2**). While previous versions of AppleWorks attached a task-specific tool-bar to every document, the Tools Palette in AppleWorks 6 simply dims any tools not available for a specific document type. The change, like so many AppleWorks 6 revisions, creates a much cleaner interface. For more information, see *The Tools Palette* on page 26.

◆ **The Starting Points Palette:** This new palette (**Figure 1.3**), which replaces the more limited New Document window of AppleWorks 5, works somewhat like the Bookmarks or Favorites popular in Web browsers. Equipped with a series of tabs, the Starting Points Palette enables you to quickly create different types of documents, find recently used documents, open templates, retrieve and post Web documents, and generate your own custom tabs. For more information, see *The Starting Points Palette* on page 28.

Figure 1.1 It's easy to customize the new Button Bar with dozens of command-specific icons.

Figure 1.2 The new Tools Palette puts all the AppleWorks tools in a single floating window.

Figure 1.3 The new tab-equipped Starting Points Palette replaces the New Document window of AppleWorks 5.

Figure 1.4 AppleWorks 6 makes it easy to retrieve thousands of high-quality art clippings from the AppleWorks Web site.

◆ **The Accents Palette:** This palette replaces the old color palette and puts in one place all the tools used for changing colors, patterns, textures (called wallpaper), gradients, and line styles. For more information, see *Working with Floating Palettes* on page 30.

◆ **The Clippings Palette:** This palette, which replaces the library of AppleWorks 5, provides a great way to organize and find art clippings, whether they're on your local hard drive or on the Web (**Figure 1.4**). While version 5 limited you to a single library, AppleWorks 6 lets you add as many clipping collections as you want. For more information, see *Working with Floating Palettes* on page 30 and *Using Clippings* on page 73.

WHAT'S NEW IN APPLEWORKS 6?

Presentation creation

◆ **A new presentations tool:** If you've been using Microsoft's ubiquitous slide presentation program, now you have a choice. AppleWorks's new presentation tool (**Figure 1.5**) is easier to use than PowerPoint and makes it simple to incorporate your AppleWorks documents into a professional multimedia presentation. For more information, see *Making Presentations* on page 381.

◆ **Master slides:** The presentation tool lets you create a uniform background and style for all the slides in a single presentation. For more information, see *To create a master slide* on page 385.

◆ **Multimedia effects and transitions:** You can integrate movies, sounds, and special transition effects right into your presentation. For more information, see *Adding Transitions, Movies, and Sounds* on page 391.

◆ **Generate notes:** Whether you need to make notes for yourself or handouts for the audience, AppleWorks makes it easy. For more information, see *To create slide notes* on page 401.

Figure 1.5 The new presentation tool lets you incorporate AppleWorks documents into multimedia slide shows.

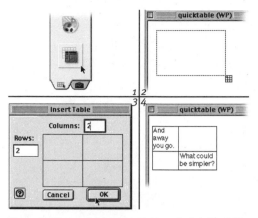

Figure 1.6 Four quick steps to tables: 1) click the Table Tool, 2) draw a frame in your document, 3) set the rows and columns, and 4) that's it.

Easier table creation

◆ **Spreadsheet work-around no longer needed:** Before AppleWorks 6, it was a pain to make a table. To put text in rows and columns, you first had to create a spreadsheet frame. Now, you just click the Table Creation Tool, draw a frame in your document, tell AppleWorks how many rows and columns you need, and you've got a table (**Figure 1.6**). For more information, see *Creating and Using Tables* on page 147.

◆ **Embed content:** Tables need not be limited to text. It's now possible to insert sounds, pictures, and even movies into table cells.

◆ **Customize any table element:** The appearance of cells, rows, columns, and lines can all be given custom text and color treatments.

Web friendly

◆ **Exports to HTML:** AppleWorks documents can be converted to Hypertext Markup Language (HTML), making it easy to use your work—including tables—to build Web pages.

◆ **Built-in retrieval of Web clippings:** The Clippings Palette lets you search through the more than 25,000 pieces of clip art stored on the AppleWorks Web site. For more information, see *Using Clippings* on page 73.

Other changes

◆ **Auto-Save** and **Auto-Recover:** The first automatically saves your documents as you work. The second protects your documents when your computer crashes. Together, they will save you a lot of heartache.

◆ **Ready for the future:** AppleWorks 6 isn't limited to running just on Mac OS 8 and 9; it's ready to run on Apple's forthcoming system software, OS X. That's because it fully supports Apple's so-called Carbon application programming interface.

◆ **Improved Mail Merge:** It's now much easier to merge database information into a form letter or spreadsheet. For more information, see *Creating, Form Letter Layouts with Mail Merge* on page 280.

Using this Book

The key to this book, like all of Peachpit's Visual QuickStart Guides, is that word *visual*. As much as possible, I've used illustrations with succinct captions to explain AppleWorks's major functions and options. Ideally, you should be able to quickly locate what you need by scanning the page tabs, illustrations, and captions. Once you find a relevant topic, the text provides the details and tips you need.

If you're new to AppleWorks, you'll find it easy to work your way through the book chapter by chapter. By the final pages, you'll know AppleWorks better than most of the folks who use it daily.

But if you've got an immediate AppleWorks problem or question that you need answered right now, the book makes it easy for you to dive right in and get help quickly. For those of you who find even a QuickStart Guide too slow, take a look at *AppleWorks Basics* on page 15 where the program's windows, menus, and context-sensitive palettes are explained with an extra serving of illustrations and screen shots.

Updates and feedback

For AppleWorks updates and patches, make a point of checking Apple's web site from time to time: www.apple.com/appleworks/

This book also has a companion site: www.peachpit.com/vqs/appleworks6 By the way, once the Windows version of AppleWorks is released, the site will include tips on the key differences from the Mac version. You're also welcome to write me directly at appleworks@waywest.net with your own tips or—heaven forbid—any mistakes you may have spotted.

AppleWorks Basics 2

If you hate to read computer books, this chapter's for you. By taking a brief look at the menus and palettes assembled here and the explanations of how they and various commands work, you'll get a quick overview of AppleWorks that will allow you to dive right in—if that's your style.

For readers who prefer a go-slow approach, this chapter's brief explanations also include page references to where in the book you'll find all the details you could want.

No matter which approach you prefer, this chapter provides a visual map for learning all the major functions within AppleWorks.

Menu Bar —— File Edit Format Text Outline Table Window ⊘ Help

Button Bar ——

Title Bar ——

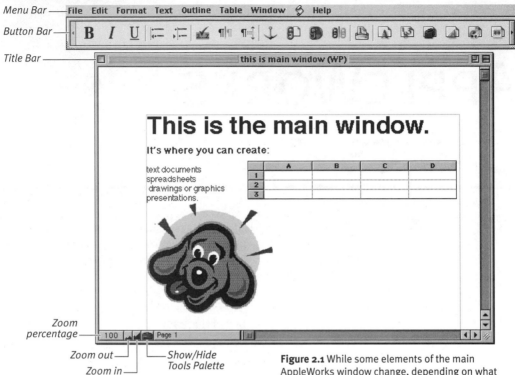

Zoom percentage —— 100

Zoom out —— Zoom in —— Show/Hide Tools Palette

Figure 2.1 While some elements of the main AppleWorks window change, depending on what you're doing, most remain relatively constant.

The Main Window

While some elements of the main AppleWorks window (**Figure 2.1**) change, depending on what you're doing, certain features remain relatively constant:

◆ **Menu Bar:** The AppleWorks Menu Bar is context sensitive, which simply means that the menus change as you switch from one type of document to another. For example, the Organize menu, visible when you're creating a text document, disappears when you open a database. For more on each menu, see *The Menus* on page 18.

Figure 2.2 The title bar includes an abbreviation that immediately tells you the document's type.

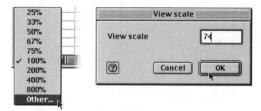

Figure 2.3 Selecting *Other...* in the pop-up menu in the main window (left) opens the View scale dialog box where you can type in a custom magnification (right).

◆ **Title Bar:** Besides displaying the title of the current document, the bar includes an abbreviation that immediately tells you the document's type (**Figure 2.2**). WP stands for a word processing document, SS stands for a spreadsheet, and so on. Each type of document is covered in detail in individual chapters.

◆ **Button Bar:** The Button Bar displays icons for common tasks. The icons change as you switch from one type of document to another. You can even add your own icons. Some folks find the Button Bar incredibly convenient. Others prefer to hide it, gain a bit of screen space, and use the menu commands instead. To hide or show the Button Bar, choose Window > Hide/Show Button Bar (Shift ⌘ X). For more information on the Button Bar, see page 26.

◆ **Zoom percentage, Zoom in, Zoom out:** Clicking the Zoom-out or Zoom-in controls in the main window allows you to shrink or magnify your view of the current AppleWorks document. Clicking on the Zoom percentage box triggers a pop-up menu where you can select a magnification view. Selecting *Other...* in the pop-up menu triggers the display of the View scale dialog box where you can type in a custom magnification (**Figure 2.3**).

◆ **Show/Hide Tools Palette:** Clicking on this icon allows you to hide or show the Tools Palette. Hiding the Tools Palette can be handy when you want to give the document itself as much screen space as possible. For more on the Tools Palette, see page 26.

THE MAIN WINDOW

The Menus

As mentioned earlier, the menus in
AppleWorks change as you switch from one
type of document to another (**Figure 2.4**).
The commands listed within a menu also
may change depending on your current document's type. The File, Edit, Format,
Window, and Help menus always appear in
the Menu Bar, while others such as Outline,
Organize, and Calculate only appear while
working within a few document types.

The File menu

As the name implies, all the commands
within the File menu control actions related
directly to file management (**Figure 2.5**).
The File menu appears no matter which document type you are using.

◆ **New, Open, Close, Save:** These first commands within the File menu operate much
as they do in all programs. For more information, see *Creating, Opening, and Closing
Documents* and *Saving and Reverting
Documents* on page 44 and 50.

◆ **Save As:** Use this command if you want
to save a document but want to change
its name, save a copy to another location,
save it as a template, or change its file format. For more information, see *Saving
and Reverting Documents* on page 50.

◆ **Show/Hide Starting Points:** This command lets you switch between showing or
hiding your Starting Points Palette. It's
handy when you need to temporarily gain
a bit of screen space for your documents.
The palette replaces the New Document
dialog box used in previous versions of
AppleWorks. For more information, see
The Starting Points Palette on page 28.

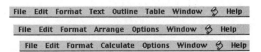

Figure 2.4 The AppleWorks menus change as you
switch from one type of document to another.

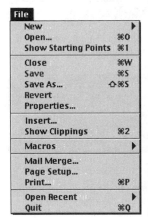

Figure 2.5 The File
menu controls actions
related directly to file
management.

◆ **Revert:** Use this command if you change your mind and do *not* want to save recent changes to a document. The command reverts the document to how it was before your most recent save—even if you are using Auto-Save. For more information, see *Saving and Reverting Documents* on page 50.

◆ **Properties:** Use this command to add comments or summary information on the current document.

◆ **Insert:** This command enables you to locate another file and insert its contents into your current AppleWorks document.

◆ **Show Clippings:** This command opens the Clippings Palette where you can store favorite images, objects, or bits of text—or search for them on the Web. Clippings replace the libraries used in previous versions of AppleWorks. For more information on clippings, see *Using Clippings* on page 73.

◆ **Macros:** Use the submenus under this command to record, play, or edit any macros you may have created. Macros—also called scripts—can save you from a lot of repetitive work by triggering a series of actions in one step. For more information, see *Creating Macros* on page 425.

◆ **Mail Merge:** Use this command to locate and insert a database file into the current AppleWorks document. Mail merge has been greatly improved in AppleWorks 6. For more information, see *Creating Form Letter Layouts with Mail Merge* on page 280.

(continued)

THE MENUS

◆ **Page Setup, Print:** These commands operate much as they do in all programs. For more information, see *Printing AppleWorks Documents* on page 434.

◆ **Open Recent:** Use this to quickly reach other AppleWorks documents that are closed but that you recently worked on. To change how many recent items are shown, choose Edit > Preferences. When the Preferences dialog box appears, use the *Topic* pop-up menu to choose *Files* and set the *Recent Items* preference.

◆ **Quit:** Use this command to exit AppleWorks. How did you ever guess?

The Edit menu

Many of this menu's commands—for example, Cut, Copy, and Paste—operate just as they do in other programs. The menu's other commands, however, change depending on which type of document you're working in (**Figure 2.6**). For more information on those commands, see the chapter covering the type of document you're using. If you haven't already used the Preferences command, take a moment now and you'll save yourself a lot of time and frustration. For more information, see *Setting Preferences* on page 453.

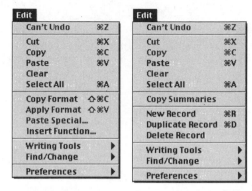

Figure 2.6 The Edit menu's first six commands remain constant, while the others change to reflect the type of document you're using.

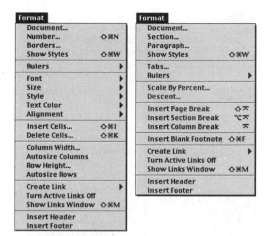

Figure 2.7 The Format menu appears no matter what type of document you're using, though the available commands vary.

The Format menu

The Format menu appears no matter what type of document you're using, though the available commands vary (**Figure 2.7**). Only a few of its commands are explained here. For details on every command, see the chapter covering the type of document you're working with.

◆ **Document** through **Show Styles:** Use this first group of commands to format an entire document, a particular section of the document, or just a paragraph. Show Styles opens the Styles Palette where you can apply an existing style to the selected text, or create a new style for it.

◆ **Tabs**, **Rulers:** Use both commands to display and set indents and tabs for your document. For more information, see *Formatting Text* on page 117.

◆ **Font** through **Alignment:** This group of commands give you direct control over the appearance of text in *non-text* documents, such as spreadsheets or drawings. The same commands for text documents appear under the context-sensitive Text menu.

◆ **Create Link** through **Show Links Window:** This group of commands let you create and manage links within the current document or to other documents, even those on the Web. Because the links work much like those on a Web page, it enables you to add interactivity to even non-Web pages. For more information, see *Creating Links and Web Pages* on page 405.

THE MENUS

The Text menu

The Text menu only appears when you're working with a text document (**Figure 2.8**). Though only four items deep, don't let its size fool you: Each item contains a submenu that gives you direct control over that aspect of the text.

Figure 2.8 Not surprisingly, the Text menu only appears when you're working with a text document.

The Outline menu

The Outline menu only appears when you're working with a text document (**Figure 2.9**). Its commands let you quickly create new topics, rearrange their order, and collapse or expand part or all of the outline. Two of the commands, *Move Left* and *Move Right*, also appear in the Button Bar whenever a text document is selected. For more information, see *Creating and Using Outlines* on page 178.

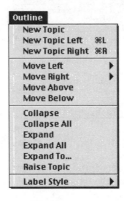

Figure 2.9 The Outline menu only appears when you're working with a text document.

The Table menu

The Table menu (**Figure 2.10**), new in AppleWorks 6, gives you quick and easy control when creating a table. The menu only appears when you're working with a text document. For more information, see *Creating and Using Tables* on page 147.

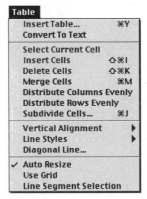

Figure 2.10 New in AppleWorks 6, the Table menu includes common commands for creating tables.

The Layout menu

The Layout menu only appears when you're working with a database document (**Figure 2.11**). Its available commands will change slightly, depending on what you're doing with the database. For more information on creating, sorting, and laying out databases, see *Working with Databases* on page 255.

Figure 2.11 The Layout menu only appears when you're working with a database document.

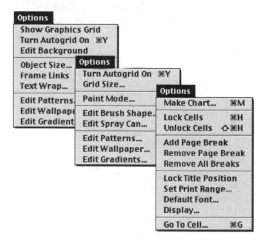

Figure 2.12 The Organize menu only appears when you're working with records in a database document.

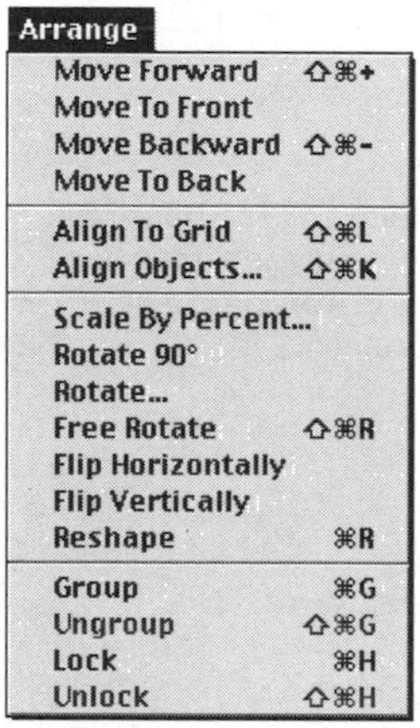

Figure 2.13 The Arrange menu only appears when you're creating a database layout, a drawing, or a presentation.

Figure 2.14 The contextual Options menu acts as a catchall for miscellaneous commands.

The Organize menu

The Organize menu only appears when you're working with records in a database document (**Figure 2.12**). Its commands let you find, hide, or sort individual records within your database. For more information, see *Working with Databases* on page 255.

The Arrange menu

The Arrange menu only appears when you're creating a layout for a database, or working with a drawing or presentation document (**Figure 2.13**). All three make extensive use of such graphic objects as rectangles, curves and arcs, or fields containing data. The Arrange commands give you control over positioning objects relative to each other.

The Options menu

The Options menu appears for all but text and database documents. The menu is completely contextual and, so, acts as a catchall for miscellaneous commands associated with each document type (**Figure 2.14**).

The Transform menu

The Transform menu only appears when you're working in a paint document (**Figure 2.15**). The last group of commands, *Fill* through *Darken*, also appear in the Button Bar whenever a paint document is selected.

The Calculate menu

The Calculate menu only appears when you're working with a spreadsheet (**Figure 2.16**). For more information, see *Creating Spreadsheets* on page 203.

The Window menu

This works much like the Window menu in most programs, enabling you to control what's visible on your desktop (**Figure 2.17**). The third group of commands are particularly handy for gaining screen space when you need it. The last grouping lists all currently open AppleWorks documents.

Transform
- Slant
- Stretch
- Add Perspective
- Resize
- Scale By Percent...
- Rotate 90°
- Rotate...
- Free Rotate ⇧⌘R
- Flip Horizontally
- Flip Vertically
- Fill
- Pick Up
- Invert
- Blend
- Tint
- Lighten
- Darken

Figure 2.15 The Transform menu only appears when you're working in a paint document.

Calculate
- Move...
- Fill Right ⌘R
- Fill Down ⌘D
- Fill Special...
- Sort... ⌘J
- Auto Sum
- Auto Average
- Calculate Now ⇧⌘=
- ✓ Auto-Calculate

Figure 2.16 The Calculate menu only appears when you're working with a spreadsheet.

Window
- New View
- Open Frame
- ✓ Page View ⇧⌘P
- Slide Show...
- Hide Button Bar ⇧⌘X
- Hide Tools ⇧⌘T
- Hide Accents ⌘K
- Hide Presentation Controls
- Tile Windows
- Stack Windows
- database example (DB)
- draw example (DR)
- paint example (PT)
- presentation example (PR)
- spreadsheet example (SS)
- ✓ this is main window (WP)

Figure 2.17 The Window menu's third group of commands are particularly handy for gaining screen space when you need it.

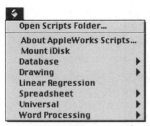

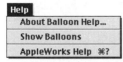

Figure 2.18
The Scripts menu lets you start scripts built into AppleWorks or ones you've created.

Figure 2.19 Use the Help menu to launch AppleWorks' built-in Help program.

Figure 2.20 The Help program lets you select a topic in the left-hand column or search for terms directly.

The Scripts menu

The Scripts menu lets you quickly trigger the scripts built into AppleWorks or any you've created yourself (**Figure 2.18**). Scripting takes a bit of time to learn, but it will save you hours in the long run. For more information, see *Using Scripts* on page 430. One heartbreaking note: Any scripts you created in previous versions of AppleWorks have to be recreated from scratch in version 6.

The Help menu

Use the Help menu to launch AppleWorks' Help program (**Figure 2.19**). Once the Help program appears (**Figure 2.20**), you can either select a topic in the left-hand column or type in a term and click *Search*.

THE MENUS

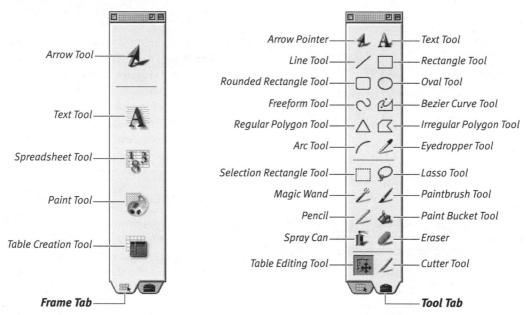

Figure 2.21 Tools now appear in their own palette with frame tools in the left tab and all other tools in the right tab.

The Floating Palettes

AppleWorks has several floating windows, or palettes, that put often-used commands and tools within handy reach. These include the Tools Palette, the Button Bar, the Starting Points Palette, the Accents Palette, and the Clippings Palette. (The more specialized Styles Palette is explained on page 170.) For more information, see *Working with Floating Palettes* on page 30.

The Tools Palette

AppleWorks tools now appear in their own palette (**Figure 2.21**). Use the Frame tab for creating frames within documents. The Tool tab contains all the drawing and painting tools. For more information on individual tools, see *Mixing Document Types* on page 60, *Creating and Using Tables* on page 147, *Drawing* on page 321 and *Painting* on page 355.

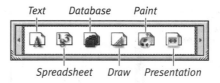

Figure 2.22 The icons in the Button Bar change with your document type.

The Button Bar

The Button Bar, previously crammed with icons, has been cleaned up in version 6 (**Figure 2.22**). It has new powers as well: the icons change as you shift document types to reflect common tasks (**Figures 2.23–2.28**). Left and right scroll arrows have been added to the bar, enabling you to reach icons that can't fit in the bar's palette. You also can delete or add icons. For more information, see *Working with Floating Palettes* on page 30 and *Customizing palette icons* on page 35.

THE FLOATING PALETTES

Bold   Underline   Demote   Show/Hide   Add   Link to   Print
                     Topic   Invisibles   Anchor Web Page

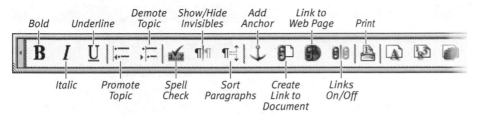

Italic   Promote   Spell   Sort   Create   Links
          Topic   Check   Paragraphs Link to   On/Off
                                          Document

Figure 2.23 When you're working in a text document, the Button Bar offers quick access to common word processing tasks.

Add Outside   Add Border Add Border Autosize   Make
Border to Cells to Top   to Bottom   Row   Chart

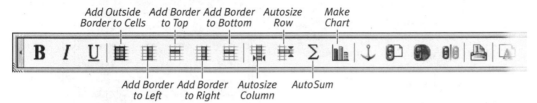

Add Border Add Border Autosize AutoSum
to Left   to Right   Column

Figure 2.24 For a spreadsheet, the Button Bar displays icons for creating borders, sizing cells, inserting an AutoSum function, and creating a chart.

Ascending   Add   Show All   List Mode
Sort   Record   Records

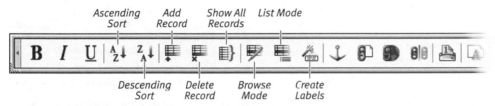

Descending   Delete   Browse   Create
Sort   Record   Mode   Labels

Figure 2.25 For databases, the Button Bar includes icons for sorting, adding, and deleting records, as well as switching modes and creating labels.

Wrap Text   Align
Around Object Objects

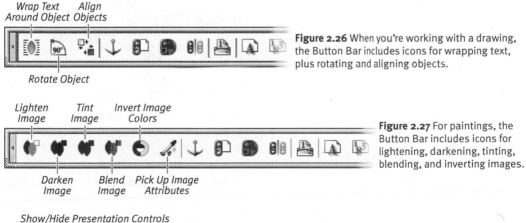

Figure 2.26 When you're working with a drawing, the Button Bar includes icons for wrapping text, plus rotating and aligning objects.

Rotate Object

Lighten   Tint   Invert Image
Image   Image   Colors

Figure 2.27 For paintings, the Button Bar includes icons for lightening, darkening, tinting, blending, and inverting images.

Darken   Blend   Pick Up Image
Image   Image   Attributes

Show/Hide Presentation Controls

Figure 2.28 When you're working with a presentation, the Button Bar gives you full control over the slide show.

Start Slide Show

The Starting Points Palette

The Starting Points Palette (**Figure 2.29**) replaces the New Document window used in AppleWorks 5, and it's been supercharged with many new features. A series of tabs help you quickly create different types of documents, find recently used documents, open templates, retrieve and post Web documents, or create a custom set of icons.

◆ **Basic:** This tab (**Figure 2.29**) appears by default when you launch AppleWorks or whenever no AppleWorks document is open. Click any of the six icons to create a document of that type.

◆ **Assistants:** Clicking this tab (**Figure 2.30**) reveals six icons for creating a variety of documents. Click any icon to launch that assistant. AppleWorks contains two other assistants reached via the menus. For more information, see *Using Assistants and Templates* on page 54.

◆ **Recent Items:** Clicking this tab (**Figure 2.31**) reveals the 10 most recently opened AppleWorks documents. That number, by the way, can be changed. See *Setting Preferences* on page 453.

◆ **Templates:** Click this tab (**Figure 2.32**) to discover one of the best things about AppleWorks—the incredible number of labor-saving templates built right into the program. You also can create your own templates. For more information, see *Using Assistants and Templates* on page 54.

◆ **Web:** Click this tab (**Figure 2.33**) to quickly reach Web pages stored on the Internet. For more information, see page 57.

◆ **+:** Clicking this tab lets you add your own custom tabs to the Starting Points Palette. For more information, see *Working with palette tabs* on page 39.

Figure 2.29 The Starting Points Palette, which replaces AppleWorks 5's New Document window, contains lots of new features.

Figure 2.30 The Starting Points *Assistants* tab contains six icons for creating a variety of documents.

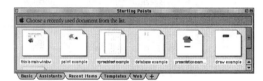

Figure 2.31 By default, the Starting Points *Recent Items* tab contains the 10 most recently opened AppleWorks documents.

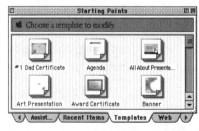

Figure 2.32 The Starting Points *Templates* tab contains a great number of labor-saving templates.

Figure 2.33 Use the Starting Points *Web* tab to quickly reach Web pages stored on the Internet.

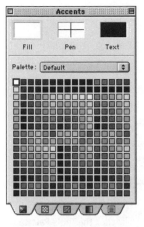

Figure 2.34 The Accents Palette includes tools used in text, drawing, and painting documents.

Figure 2.35 The Clippings Palette, which replaces the AppleWorks 5 libraries, provides a central location for all your art clippings.

The Accents Palette

The Accents Palette (**Figure 2.34**) pulls together a number of tools used in text, drawing, and painting documents. For more information, see *Changing Text Color* on page 121 and *Drawing* on page 321, and *Painting* on page 355.

The Clippings Palette

The Clippings Palette (**Figure 2.35**) replaces the libraries used in version 5 of AppleWorks. It provides a great way to organize and find all your art clippings, whether they're on your local hard drive or on the Web. For more information, see *Using Clippings* on page 73.

THE FLOATING PALETTES

Working with Floating Palettes

AppleWorks gives you lots of freedom in setting up the floating palettes. You can hide them, reposition them, and resize them. Palette tabs can be moved around or hidden as well. You can even reconfigure their default settings. It may take a while to discover the best combination for your own work, so feel free to experiment.

Using contextual menus in palettes

All five floating palettes contain a contextual menu, which is triggered with a (Ctrl)-click within the palette (**Figures 2.36–2.40**). Aside from the exceptions noted below, the choices within contextual menus are fairly similar:

◆ **Help:** Selecting this opens AppleWorks's built-in help program.

◆ **Add Tab:** Available only for Starting Points and Clippings, this choice lets you create your own tabs for customized content. For more information, see *Working with palette tabs* on page 39.

◆ **Remove Button, Place divider after button**, **Customize Button Bar:** Available only for the Button Bar (**Figure 2.37**), these choices let you delete or add buttons and customize their organization. For more information, see *Customizing palette icons* on page 35.

◆ **Switch To** and **Hide Tabs:** If you elect to hide a palette's tabs, using *Switch To* enables you to move from tab to tab even when they are hidden (**Figure 2.41**).

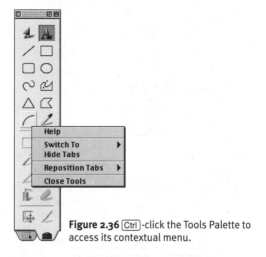

Figure 2.36 (Ctrl)-click the Tools Palette to access its contextual menu.

Figure 2.37 (Ctrl)-click the Button Bar to access its contextual menu.

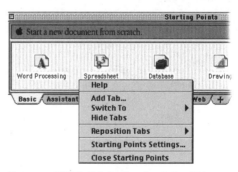

Figure 2.38 (Ctrl)-click the Starting Points Palette to access its contextual menu.

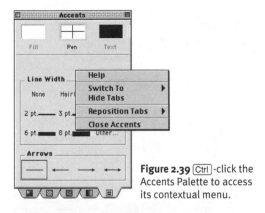

Figure 2.39 Ctrl -click the Accents Palette to access its contextual menu.

Figure 2.40 Ctrl -click the Clippings Palette to access its contextual menu.

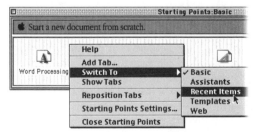

Figure 2.41 Use the contextual menu's *Switch To* command to find tab content even when the tabs themselves are hidden.

◆ **Reposition Tabs:** This choice lets you put the palette's tabs where they're most convenient. For more information, see *Working with palette tabs* on page 39.

◆ **Starting Points Settings:** Use this Starting Points Palette choice (**Figure 2.38**) to set the display size for the palette's thumbnail icons. For more information, see *Customizing palette icons* on page 35.

◆ **Clippings Settings:** Use this Clippings Palette choice (**Figure 2.40**) to set how AppleWorks searches for clippings, how much space (cache) your computer sets aside for clippings, and the display size for clipping thumbnails. For information on the thumbnail display size, see *Customizing palette icons* on page 35. For more information on the other clipping settings, see *Using Clippings* on page 73.

◆ **Delete Clipping:** Use this Clippings Palette choice (**Figure 2.40**) to delete a clipping that you've selected within the palette.

◆ **Sort:** Use this Clippings Palette choice (**Figure 2.40**) to sort how your clippings are displayed. For more information, see *Using Clippings* on page 73.

◆ **Close:** Use this choice to close the selected palette. When the selected palette is docked and its title bar hidden, this is the only way to close the palette.

To move among the floating palettes:

1. Whether you're working within a document or in a palette, press Option Tab. A palette will become highlighted.

2. Repeat the command as many times as necessary to move to the desired palette.

WORKING WITH FLOATING PALETTES

Docking palettes

By default, AppleWorks docks the Button Bar at the top of the screen and the Tools Palette on the left side. But if you find it easier, for example, to dock the Starting Points Palette at the top and the Tools Palette along the bottom, then do it. The Accents Palette is the only one of the five that cannot be docked.

To undock a palette:

1. Move your cursor up the edge of a docked palette until the arrow becomes a hand (**Figure 2.42**).

2. Click and hold the cursor as you drag the palette to where you want it located. Release the cursor and the palette will become freestanding with a title bar.

To dock a palette:

1. Move your cursor up the edge of a free-standing palette until the arrow becomes a hand.

2. Click and hold the cursor as you drag the palette back to its original position along the edge of the screen.

3. When the title bar disappears, release the cursor and the palette will redock.

Figure 2.42 To undock a palette, grab the edge and drag toward the middle of your screen until a title bar appears.

Figure 2.43 To open or close the Tools Palette, choose Window > Show Tools or Window > Hide Tools.

Figure 2.44 You also can click the toolbox icon at the bottom of any AppleWorks document to show or hide the Tools Palette.

Figure 2.45 To open or close the Button Bar, choose Window > Show Button Bar or Window > Hide Button Bar.

Showing or hiding floating palettes

True to form, AppleWorks lets you customize your screen by showing or hiding the floating palettes, which is very handy in managing your available screen space.

To show or hide the Tools Palette:

◆ Choose Window > Show Tools or Window > Hide Tools ((Shift)(⌘)(T)) (**Figure 2.43**). The palette will appear or disappear, depending on your choice.

◆ You also can click the toolbox icon in the lower-left corner of any AppleWorks document to show or hide the Tools Palette (**Figures 2.44**).

◆ You also can close the palette with a (Ctrl)-click within the palette and choose *Close Tools* when the pop-up menu appears (**Figure 2.36**).

To show or hide the Button Bar:

◆ Choose Window > Show Button Bar or Window > Hide Button Bar ((Shift)(⌘)(X)) (**Figure 2.45**). The bar will appear or disappear, depending on your choice.

◆ You also can close the palette with a (Ctrl)-click within the palette and choose *Close Button Bar* when the pop-up menu appears (**Figure 2.37**).

To show or hide the Starting Points Palette:

◆ Choose File > Show Starting Points or File > Hide Starting Points (⌘1) (**Figure 2.46**). The palette will appear or disappear, depending on your choice.

◆ You also can close the palette with a Ctrl-click within the palette and choose *Close Starting Points* when the pop-up menu appears (**Figure 2.38**).

To show or hide the Accents Palette:

◆ Choose Window > Show Accents or Window > Hide Accents (⌘K) (**Figure 2.47**). The palette will appear or disappear, depending on your choice.

◆ You also can close the palette with a Ctrl-click within the palette and choose *Close Accents* when the pop-up menu appears (**Figure 2.39**).

To show or hide the Clippings Palette:

◆ Choose File > Show Clippings or File > Hide Clippings (⌘2) (**Figure 2.48**). The palette will appear or disappear, depending on your choice. For more information on clippings, see *Using Clippings* on page 73.

◆ You also can close the palette with a Ctrl-click within the palette and choose *Close Clippings* when the pop-up menu appears (**Figure 2.40**).

Figure 2.46 To open or close the Starting Points Palette, choose File > Show Starting Points or File > Hide Starting Points.

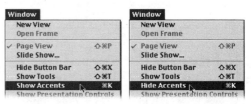

Figure 2.47 To open or close the Accents Palette, choose Window > Show Accents or Window > Hide Accents.

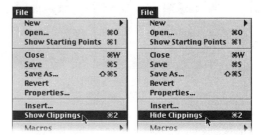

Figure 2.48 To open or close the Clippings Palette, choose File > Show Clippings or File > Hide Clippings.

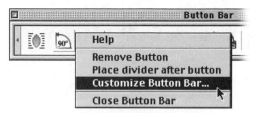

Figure 2.49 To add Button Bar icons, [Ctrl]-click in the bar and choose *Customize Button Bar*.

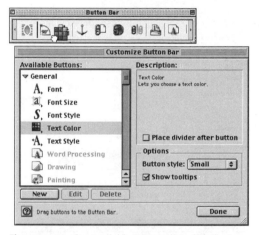

Figure 2.50 In the *Available Buttons* list, click the icon you want and drag it into the bar.

Figure 2.51 To remove Button Bar icons, [Ctrl]-click on the icon in the bar and choose *Remove Button* from the pop-up menu.

Customizing palette icons

It's easy to customize the Button Bar with your most used commands by adding or removing icons. By default, the Button Bar's icons are set large, while those for the Starting Points and Clippings are set to medium. Making them smaller gives you more working room. For some users, however—young kids, for example—you may actually want to bump up the Starting Points and Clippings icons to the large setting.

To add Button Bar icons:

1. [Ctrl]-click in the Button Bar and choose *Customize Button Bar* from the pop-up menu (**Figure 2.49**).

2. When the Customize Button Bar dialog box appears, scroll through the *Available Buttons* list until you find the icon you want to add.

3. Click within the list on the icon you want to add and drag it into the Button Bar (**Figure 2.50**). When the icon appears in the Button Bar, release your cursor and the icon will be added.

4. Click *Done* to close the Customize Button Bar dialog box.

To remove Button Bar icons:

◆ [Ctrl]-click on the icon in the Button Bar and choose *Remove Button* from the pop-up menu (**Figure 2.51**). Release the cursor and the icon will be removed.

To rearrange Button Bar icons:

1. Click on the Button Bar icon you want to move (top, **Figure 2.52**).

2. While still clicking on the icon with your cursor, drag it to its new position. A black bar will mark the insertion point (middle, **Figure 2.52**).

3. Release the cursor and the icon will appear in its new position (bottom, **Figure 2.52**).

To change the size of Button Bar icons:

1. Choose Edit > Preferences > Button Bar (**Figure 2.53**).

2. When the Customize Button Bar dialog box appears, use the *Button style* drop-down menu to select the desired size (**Figure 2.54**).

3. Click *Done* and the buttons will change size.

✔ Tip

■ To use AppleWorks' tooltips to identify buttons in the Button Bar (**Figure 2.55**), just check *Show tooltips* in the Customize Button Bar dialog box in step 2 (**Figure 2.54**).

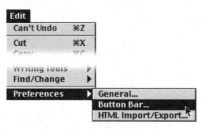

Figure 2.52 To rearrange Button Bar icons, click the icon and, while keeping the cursor pressed, move the icon to its new position.

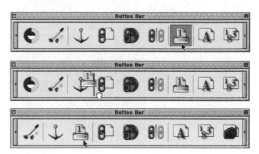

Figure 2.53 To change the size of Button Bar icons, choose Edit > Preferences > Button Bar.

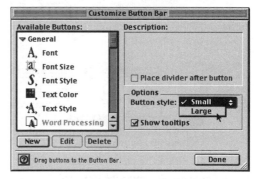

Figure 2.54 Use the Customize Button Bar dialog box to control icon sizes and to turn on tooltips.

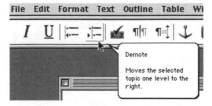

Figure 2.55 AppleWorks' tooltips help you identify the functions of Button Bar icons.

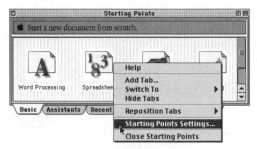

Figure 2.56 To change the size of Starting Points icons, [Ctrl]-click in the palette and choose *Starting Points Settings*.

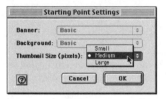

Figure 2.57 Change icon sizes with the *Thumbnail Size* pop-up menu in the Starting Points Settings dialog box.

Figure 2.58 To change the size of Clippings thumbnails, [Ctrl]-click in the palette and choose *Clippings Settings*.

Figure 2.59 Change thumbnail sizes with the *Thumbnail size* pop-up menu in the Clippings Settings dialog box.

To change the size of Starting Points icons:

1. [Ctrl]-click within the Starting Points Palette and when the pop-up menu appears, choose *Starting Points Settings* (**Figure 2.56**).

2. When the Starting Points Settings dialog box appears, use the *Thumbnail Size* pop-up menu to choose a size (**Figure 2.57**).

3. Click *OK* and the buttons in the Starting Points Palette will change size.

To change the size of Clippings thumbnails:

1. [Ctrl]-click within the Clippings Palette and when the pop-up menu appears, choose *Clippings Settings* (**Figure 2.58**).

2. When the Clippings Settings dialog box appears, use the *Thumbnail size* pop-up menu to choose a size (**Figure 2.59**).

3. Click *OK* and the buttons in the Clippings Palette will change size.

WORKING WITH FLOATING PALETTES

Resizing floating palettes

Only the two most-used floating palettes—the Button Bar and Starting Points—can be resized. If you need more screen space, simply turn the other palettes on and off as you need them.

To resize the Button Bar or Starting Points:

1. Click and drag the hashed corner of the Starting Points Palette or Button Bar to the desired size (**Figure 2.60**).

2. Once you've sized the palette to your liking, release your cursor (**Figure 2.61**).

✔ Tip

- It takes a bit of practice to click on the hashed area in the lower-right corner of either palette. It's all too easy to overshoot the area and, instead, wind up clicking the desktop. But if you click too far inside the palette, your cursor becomes a hand, which is for dragging the entire palette.

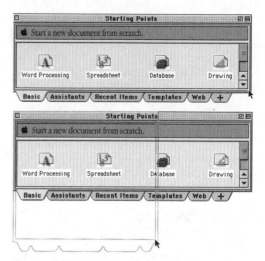

Figure 2.60 To resize the Button Bar or Starting Points palettes, click and drag the hashed corner.

Figure 2.61 Release the cursor once you've resized the palette.

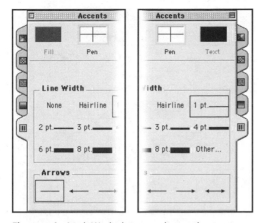

Figure 2.62 AppleWorks lets you choose the most convenient position for your palette tabs.

Figure 2.63 To move tabs, Ctrl-click the palette and choose *Reposition Tabs*.

Figure 2.64 The tabs will move to their new position after you've made a choice in the submenu.

Working with palette tabs

By default, palettes with tabs—the Starting Points, Tools, Accents, and Clippings—place them across the bottom. However, you can reposition the tabs to suit your screen set up (**Figure 2.62**).

Reducing the size of your palettes gives you more screen space, but may hide some of the Starting Points and Clippings tabs. Fortunately, AppleWorks lets you flip through the tabs to find the one you need. You also can create new tabs to better organize either palette.

To reposition tabs:

1. Ctrl-click in either the Starting Points, Tools, Clippings, or Accents palettes and choose *Reposition Tabs* from the pop-up menu (**Figure 2.63**). Your choices will vary depending on where the tabs are currently.

2. Make a choice from the submenu, release the cursor, and the tabs will be repositioned (**Figure 2.64**).

WORKING WITH FLOATING PALETTES

To flip through tabs:

1. If not all of the tabs for the Starting Points or Clippings palettes are visible, click the right-hand tab (marked by an arrow) (top, **Figure 2.65**). The tabs will shift to the left, revealing the first hidden tab (middle, **Figure 2.65**).

2. Continue clicking the tab with the arrow until you reach the tab you want. To move back to the left, click the palette's left arrow tab (bottom, **Figure 2.65**).

✔ Tips

■ If there are no more hidden tabs in a particular direction, the arrow on that side's tab will be dimmed (middle, **Figure 2.65**).

■ To rename a tab, double-click it and give it a new name in the dialog box that appears.

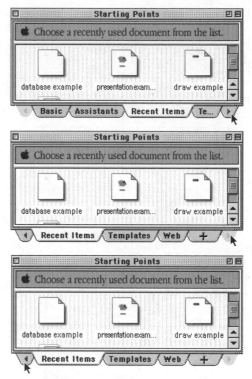

Figure 2.65 To find palette tabs not currently visible, click the right or left arrow.

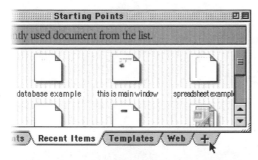

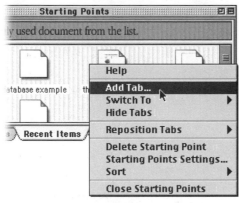

Figure 2.66 To add palette tabs, click the ⊞ tab (top); or Ctrl-click in the palette and choose *Add Tab* (bottom).

Figure 2.67 When the Add Tab dialog box appears, name your new tab and click *Add*.

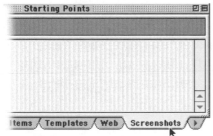

Figure 2.68 Once a new tab is added, you can begin adding content.

To add tabs:

1. Click the far-right ⊞ tab (top, **Figure 2.66**).

   or

   Ctrl-click in the palette and choose *Add Tab* from the pop-up menu (bottom, **Figure 2.66**).

2. When the Add Tab dialog box appears, type in a name for your new tab and click *Add* (**Figure 2.67**). A new tab with no contents will be added to the palette (**Figure 2.68**). For information on adding content to a tab, see *Using Clippings* on page 73.

WORKING WITH DOCUMENTS

3

The basics of creating, opening, closing, and saving AppleWorks documents work like most programs. However, in creating a new file, AppleWorks doesn't force you to create a single-type document. Instead, you can mix various document types (e.g., database, drawing, and spreadsheet) within the same document using what AppleWorks calls frames. For more information, see *Mixing Document Types* on page 60.

AppleWorks 6 includes two new features that definitely will make life easier: Auto-Save and Auto-Recover. Auto-Save lets you determine exactly how often AppleWorks saves your documents, while Auto-Recover protects your documents when your computer crashes. For more information on setting the Auto-Save interval, see *Setting Preferences*, on page 453.

Creating, Opening, and Closing Documents

By default, AppleWorks makes any new document a new word-processing document. However, you can set AppleWorks's preferences so that pressing ⌘N will create whatever type of document you most commonly need. For more information, see *Setting Preferences* on page 453.

To create a new document:

1. Choose File > New and use the sub-menu to select the type of document you want to create (**Figure 3.1**).

   or

   Click the *Basic* tab in the Starting Points Palette and choose one of the six document-type icons (**Figure 3.2**).

2. A blank document will appear, with its type indicated by a two-letter abbreviation within parentheses (**Figure 3.3**).

✔ Tips

■ If you're creating a text (word processing) document, you can use the keyboard command: ⌘N.

■ You're not limited to single-type documents. By using frames, you can create a mixed-type document. For more information, see *Mixing Document Types* on page 60.

Figure 3.1 To create a new document, choose File > New and use the sub-menu to select a document type.

Figure 3.2 You also can create a new document by clicking the Starting Points *Basic* tab and choosing one of six document-type icons.

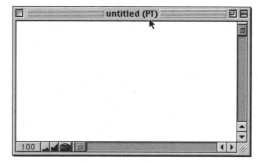

Figure 3.3 When the new document appears, the title bar includes a two-letter abbreviation indicating its type (in this case, *PT* for a paint document).

Figure 3.4 To open an existing document, choose File > Open (⌘O).

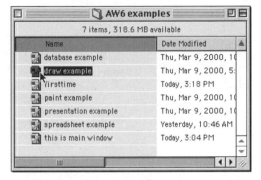

Figure 3.5 You also can open an AppleWorks existing document by double-clicking it within an open folder.

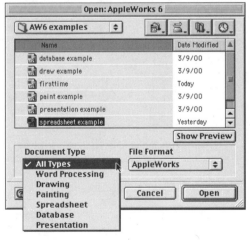

Figure 3.6 When the Open dialog box appears, navigate to the document you want. To narrow your search, use the *Document Type* and *File Format* pop-up menus.

To open an existing document:

1. Choose File > Open (⌘O) (**Figure 3.4**).
   or
   Double-click an AppleWorks document within an open folder (**Figure 3.5**).

2. When the Open dialog box appears, use your folder icons to navigate to the document you want. To narrow your search, you may use the *Document Type* and *File Format* pop-up menus (**Figure 3.6**). The selected document will open.

Closing a document

Because FileMaker automatically saves your data, closing a file is simple. You can close a file several different ways.

To close a document:

◆ Choose File > Close (⌘W) (**Figure 3.7**).

or

◆ Click the close box in the left corner of the document's title bar (**Figure 3.8**).

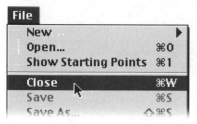

Figure 3.7 To close a document, choose File > Close (⌘W).

Figure 3.8 You also can close a document by clicking the icon in the top-left corner.

Importing and Exporting Documents

Unless you've never used a computer before, you probably have existing documents that you'd like to use within AppleWorks. To do that, you'll need to import them into AppleWorks. Fortunately, that's very easy for documents created with earlier versions of AppleWorks.

You also can easily save your AppleWorks 6 documents so that they can be read in older versions of AppleWorks or even Microsoft Word. Finally, you also can save Mac versions of AppleWorks documents so that they can be read by Windows versions of AppleWorks.

To import older AppleWorks documents:

1. Choose File > Open (⌘O).

2. When the Open dialog box appears, use your folder icons to navigate to the document you want. To narrow your search, you may use the *Document Type* and *File Format* pop-up menus. Click *Open* and the older AppleWorks document will open just as if it was an AppleWorks 6 document.

✔ Tip

■ Don't worry when your old AppleWorks documents display the new AppleWorks 6 icon instead of the old AppleWorks icon. AppleWorks 6 displays all AppleWorks documents with the new icon, no matter which version was used to create them.

Working with Microsoft Word documents

Microsoft Word has long been the most used word-processing program for Macintosh and Windows. For that reason alone, you will inevitably need to either open a document originally created on Word or save an AppleWorks document to Word. Neither program can read the other's native format, but they both can read RTF (Rich Text Format) files. By saving AppleWorks or Word documents to RTF, you can pass them back and forth while preserving most of the original formatting. For more information, see *Saving and Reverting Documents* on page 50.

To import Microsoft Word documents:

1. Using Microsoft Word, open the Word document that you want to import into AppleWorks (**Figure 3.9**).

2. Choose File > Save As (**Figure 3.10**).

3. When the Save As dialog box appears, use the *Save File as Type* pop-up menu to select *Rich Text Format* (**Figure 3.11**).

4. Name the document, navigate to the folder where you want it saved, and click *Save* (**Figure 3.12**).

Figure 3.9 Before exporting to AppleWorks: The document as it appears in Microsoft Word.

Figure 3.10 To save a copy of a document or change its format, choose File > Save As ([Shift][⌘][S]).

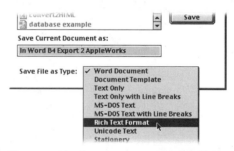

Figure 3.11 Use the pop-up menu to select *Rich Text Format*.

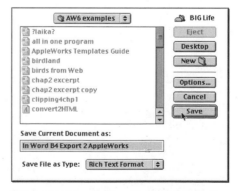

Figure 3.12 Name the document, navigate to the folder where you want it saved, and click *Save*.

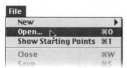

Figure 3.13 Having saved the Word document as a Rich Text Format file, switch to AppleWorks and choose File > Open.

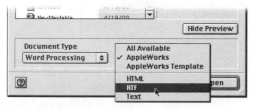

Figure 3.14 Use the two pop-up menus to select *Word Processing* and *RTF*.

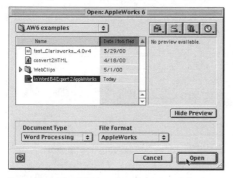

Figure 3.15 The RTF version of the Word document as it appears in AppleWorks's Open dialog box.

Figure 3.16 A Converting File dialog box will appear briefly...

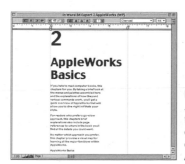

Figure 3.17 ...and then the former Word document will open in AppleWorks.

5. Now switch to AppleWorks and choose File > Open (**Figure 3.13**).

6. When the Open dialog box appears, use the two pop-up menus to select *Word Processing* and *RTF* (**Figure 3.14**).

7. Navigate to the folder where you saved the Word document in step 4, click to select that document, and click *Open* (**Figure 3.15**). A Converting File dialog box will appear briefly and then the document will open in AppleWorks (**Figures 3.16** and **3.17**).

✔ Tip

■ As you can see in **Figure 3.17**, if the Word document was created on a Mac with different fonts than those on the Mac running AppleWorks, available fonts automatically replace the missing fonts.

Saving and Reverting Documents

Saving and Reverting are similar in that both let you preserve your work. Saving preserves your current work while Reverting takes you back a step to how your work was *before* the most-recent save.

To save a document:

1. Choose File > Save (⌘Ⓢ) (**Figure 3.18**).

2. When the Save dialog box appears (**Figure 3.19**), type a title into the *Name* window. Choose where you want to store the document by navigating through the dialog box's folder icons. By default, the document will be saved in the AppleWorks file format. If you want to change the file type, say for exporting the document, use the *File Format* pop-up menu to select another file type. You also have the option to save the file as a template by clicking the *Template* radio button. For more information, see *Using Assistants and Templates* on page 54.

3. Once you've picked your file name, destination, and file type, click *Save*. The document will be saved and Auto-Save will automatically save it from that point on.

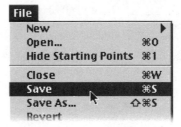

Figure 3.18 To save a document, choose File > Save (⌘Ⓢ).

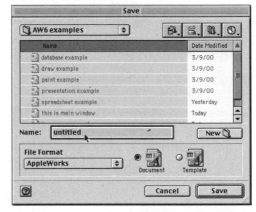

Figure 3.19 When the Save dialog box appears, name the document, choose where to save it, and click *Save*.

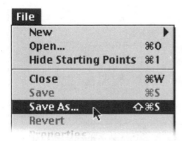

Figure 3.20 To change a document's format or save a copy, choose File > Save As ([Shift][⌘][S]).

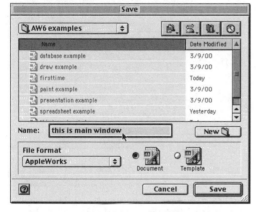

Figure 3.21 When the Save dialog box appears, replace the document's existing name with a new one, and click *Save*.

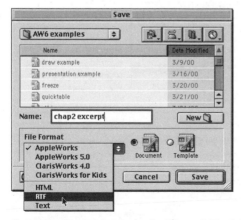

Figure 3.22 To save documents for Microsoft Word, use the *File Format* pop-up menu to chose *RTF*.

To save a copy of a document:

1. Choose File > Save As ([Shift][⌘][S]) (**Figure 3.20**).

2. When the Save dialog box appears, the document's existing name will appear in the *Name* window (**Figure 3.21**). Type in a new name and choose where you want to store the document by navigating through the dialog box's folder icons.

3. Once you've picked your file name, destination, and file type, click *Save*. The document will be saved.

To save documents for Microsoft Word:

1. Using AppleWorks, open the document you want to export to Microsoft Word.

2. Choose File > Save As ([Shift][⌘][S]) (**Figure 3.20**).

3. When the Save dialog box opens, use the *File Format* pop-up menu to choose *RTF* (**Figure 3.22**). Give the file a name, navigate to the folder where you want to save it, and click *Save*. The file will be saved in a format readable by Microsoft Word.

To save documents for older AppleWorks versions:

1. With the document open, choose File > Save As ([Shift][⌘][S]) (**Figure 3.20**).

2. When the Save dialog box opens, use the *File Format* pop-up menu to chose *AppleWorks 5.0, ClarisWorks 4.0*, or *ClarisWorks for Kids* (**Figure 3.23**). Give the file a name, navigate to the folder where you want to save it, and click *Save*. The file will be saved in a format readable for the version of AppleWorks you chose.

To save Mac documents for AppleWorks for Windows:

1. If you're working on a Mac and plan to open an AppleWorks document in Windows, first choose File > Save As ([Shift][⌘][S]).

2. When the Save As dialog box appears, type *.cwk* at the end of the file name and click *Save* (**Figure 3.24**). The document can now be opened with the Windows version of AppleWorks.

To revert a document:

1. Choose File > Revert (**Figure 3.25**).

2. A dialog box will appear asking if you really want to revert to the last-saved version of the document (**Figure 3.26**). Click *OK* and the document will revert.

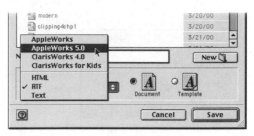

Figure 3.23 To save AppleWorks 6 documents for earlier versions of AppleWorks, use the *File Format* pop-up menu.

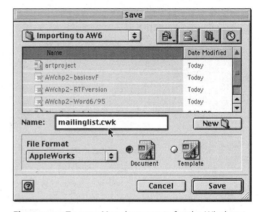

Figure 3.24 To save Mac documents for the Windows version of AppleWorks, add *.cwk* to the end of the file name.

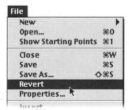

Figure 3.25 If you do *not* want to save your most recent changes, choose File > Revert.

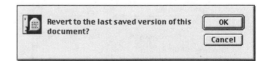

Figure 3.26 When a dialog box appears asking if you really want to revert to the last-saved version, click *OK*.

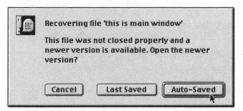

Figure 3.27 To quit AppleWorks, choose File > Quit (⌘Q).

Figure 3.28 If your computer crashes, AppleWorks's Auto-Recover will ask you upon restart which version of your document to save.

To quit AppleWorks:

◆ Choose File > Quit (⌘Q) (**Figure 3.27**).

✔ Tip

■ If you don't quit AppleWorks properly (for example, your machine crashes), the next time you open an AppleWorks document, the program's Auto-Recover will kick in. An alert dialog box will appear asking which version you want to save (**Figure 3.28**). Generally, you should choose *Auto-Saved* unless you're dead sure you manually saved the document moments before it crashed, in which case choose *Last Saved*.

QUITTING APPLEWORKS

Using Assistants and Templates

You can save yourself a lot of time by using the AppleWorks assistants and templates to help you create good-looking documents. The program comes with six assistants, which are designed to guide you through the creation of common document types. Two other assistants—one for adding footnotes to documents and another for creating mailing labels—are covered separately on pages 140 and 278.

AppleWorks' templates give you two routes to creativity. Use them to create documents that exactly mimic the templates. Or use the templates as inspiring departure points for customized documents of your own.

To use an assistant:

1. If it's not visible, open the Starting Points Palette (⌘1).

2. When the Starting Points Palette appears, click the *Assistants* tab (**Figure 3.29**).

3. Click one of the six icons to launch an assistant.

4. A dialog box will appear with step-by-step instructions (**Figure 3.30**).

5. As you complete each step, click the highlighted button to reach the next step (**Figure 3.31**). The assistant will walk you through the rest of the steps until the task is completed.

Figure 3.29 To use an assistant, click the Starting Points *Assistants* tab and choose one of the six icons.

Figure 3.30 Once you launch an assistant, a dialog box will appear with step-by-step instructions.

Figure 3.31 As you work through the assistant steps, click the highlighted button to reach the next step.

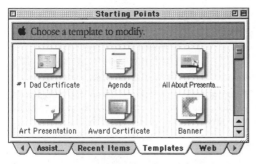

Figure 3.32 To create a template-based document, click any of the icons within the Starting Points *Templates* tab.

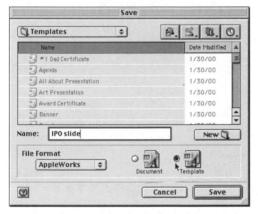

Figure 3.33 To turn a document into a template, click the *Template* radio button in the Save As dialog box.

To create a template-based document:

1. If it's not visible, open the Starting Points Palette (⌘1).

2. When the Starting Points Palette appears, click the *Templates* tab (**Figure 3.32**).

3. Click any of the icons to open a template.

4. Once the template opens, change the content to meet your needs. When you're satisfied, choose File > Save As (Shift⌘S), and give it a new name.

To create a new template:

1. Once you've created a document that you want to save as a template, choose File > Save As (Shift⌘S).

2. When the Save As dialog box appears, type a title into the *Name* window.

3. Click the dialog box's *Template* radio button and the AppleWorks Templates folder will automatically open (**Figure 3.33**).

4. Click *Save* and your template will be stored with the program's other templates (and appear in the Starting Points *Templates* tab the next time you open it).

To change an existing template:

1. Open the Starting Points Palette (⌘1) and click the *Templates* tab (**Figure 3.32**).

2. Once the template opens, change the content to meet your needs. When you're satisfied, choose File > Save As (Shift⌘S).

3. When the Save As dialog box appears, click the dialog box's *Template* radio button and the AppleWorks Templates folder will automatically open.

4. Type into the *Name* window the exact name as the original template had and click *Save*.

5. An alert dialog box will appear asking to confirm that you want to replace the original template (**Figure 3.34**). If you're sure, click *Replace* and the customized template will overwrite the original template.

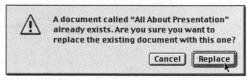

Figure 3.34 When you customize an existing template, an alert dialog box will warn you that it will replace the original template.

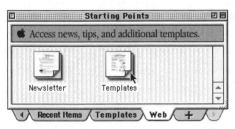

Figure 3.35 To download more AppleWorks templates, connect to the Internet *before* you click *Templates* in the *Web* tab.

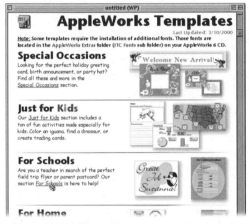

Figure 3.36 An untitled AppleWorks document will display general categories for AppleWorks's online templates.

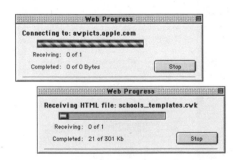

Figure 3.37 Once you click the link for a desired template category, two Web Progress dialog boxes track the download.

Downloading templates from the AppleWorks Web site

AppleWorks's Web site offers more than 150 additional templates running the gamut from field trip flyers to math lessons. Downloading them from the Web, however, can be a bit tricky so first read *No browser necessary?* on page 86 to save yourself some frustration.

To download AppleWorks templates:

1. If you have an always-on link to the Internet, such as a cable modem, DSL (Digital Subscriber Line), or a dedicated hardwire connection, you're all set. If you have a dial-up connection, connect now to the Internet.

2. Open the Starting Points Palette (⌘1), click the *Web* tab, and then click the *Templates* icon (**Figure 3.35**). In a moment, an untitled AppleWorks document will open, displaying general categories for the online AppleWorks templates (**Figure 3.36**). Remain connected to the Internet and look through the categories. Once you find a desired category, click the link.

3. Two Web Progress dialog boxes will appear in sequence. The first one connects you to AppleWorks's main server. Once the server determines what you're seeking, the category template is downloaded (**Figure 3.37**).

(continued)

4. Once you find the individual template that meets your needs, decide whether you want it in *US Letter* or *A4* format and click the appropriate link (**Figure 3.38**). A new Web Progress dialog box will appear as that particular template is downloaded (**Figure 3.39**).

5. Once the template is downloaded, the Web Progress dialog box will disappear, and the template will appear in an untitled AppleWorks document (**Figure 3.40**). If the template is not what you need, repeat steps 2–4 until you find the right template.

6. Once you download the desired template, choose File > Save (⌘S).

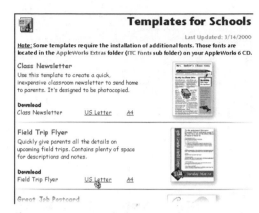

Figure 3.38 Once you find a template you want, click the appropriate format link: *US Letter* or *A4*.

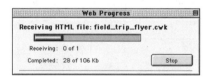

Figure 3.39 Yet another Web Progress dialog box appears as the individual template is downloaded.

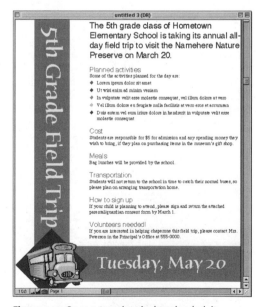

Figure 3.40 Once a template is downloaded, it appears in an untitled AppleWorks document, which you must save to use.

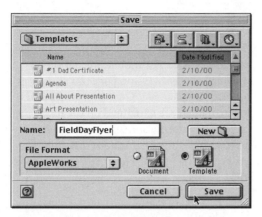

Figure 3.41 When saving a template, be sure to select the *Template* button.

Figure 3.42 After you've downloaded and saved an online template, it appears in the Starting Points *Templates* tab.

7. When the Save dialog box appears, navigate to the Templates folder (AppleWorks 6\Starting Points\Templates) and type a title into the *Name* window. Most importantly, choose the *Template* button (otherwise it will be saved as an ordinary AppleWorks document) and click *Save* (**Figure 3.41**). The template will be saved—as you can see by clicking the *Templates* tab in the Starting Points Palette (**Figure 3.42**).

8. Once you are done, disconnect from the Internet if you are using a dial-up connection.

Mixing Document Types

It's natural to want to mix different types of material—text, spreadsheets, databases, illustrations—in the same document. As an all-in-one suite of tools, AppleWorks makes that easy to accomplish (**Figure 3.43**). In fact, there are at least four ways to mix document types: creating frames, inserting files, inserting clippings, and using the drawing tools to work directly in non-graphic documents. Each method has its advantages and limitations. For more information on drawing, see *Drawing* on page 321 and *Painting* on page 355. Creating frames and inserting files are explained on the following pages. For information on *Using Clippings*, see page 73. Tables, which also use frames, are covered separately in *Creating and Using Tables* on page 147.

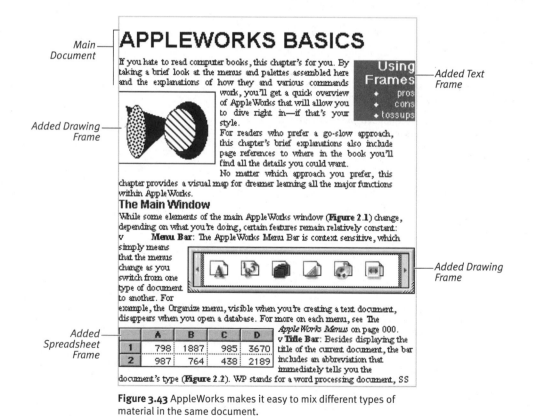

Figure 3.43 AppleWorks makes it easy to mix different types of material in the same document.

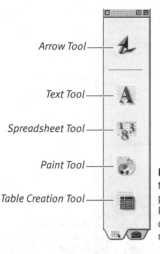

Arrow Tool

Text Tool

Spreadsheet Tool

Paint Tool

Table Creation Tool

Figure 3.44 Use the Frame tab, part of the Tools Palette, for creating and moving frames.

Figure 3.45 Floating frames initially float on top of the document's content.

Figure 3.46 Floating frames can be moved *behind* the document's main content.

Figure 3.47 Floating frames also let you wrap surrounding text around the frame.

Using Frames

Apple likens frames to "mini-documents" inside your main document. The Frame tab, part of the Tools Palette, acts as command central for creating and moving frames (**Figure 3.44**). Frames can accommodate text, spreadsheets, paintings, or tables.

As you shift, for example, from working in a text frame to a spreadsheet frame, AppleWorks's menus and Button Bar display the commands and tools needed for working in that particular type of frame. Although you can add borders to frames, they are generally left unmarked and simply let AppleWorks keep track of your mix of document types.

There are two types of frames: floating frames and inline frames. Each serves a different purpose. As the name suggests, floating frames initially float on top of the document's content (**Figure 3.45**). Unlike inline frames, floating frames can be moved behind the main content (**Figure 3.46**) or have text wrap around them (**Figure 3.47**). Wrapping text lets you create a separate text frame within a word-processing document, which can be very handy when laying out different stories in a newsletter. For more information, see *Wrapping Text Around Frames and Objects* on page 194.

USING FRAMES

Unlike a floating frame, an inline frame's content appears right "in line" with the rest of the document's text (**Figure 3.48**). Type in more words just before the inline frame and the frame will move to the right, just as if it were a bit of text (**Figure 3.49**). Inline frames can only be placed inside word-processing documents or in the text of database *layouts*.

Because word-processing documents accept both types for frames, you can easily change a floating frame to an inline frame and vice versa. For more information, see *Changing frame types* on page 65.

To show the frame tools:

◆ Choose Window > Show Tools ([Shift][⌘][T]).

or

Click the toolbox icon in the lower-left corner of any AppleWorks document and then click the Frame tab once the Tools Palette appears (**Figure 3.50**).

Figure 3.48 Unlike a floating frame, an inline frame appears "in line" with the document's text.

Figure 3.49 Adding words before an inline frame moves the frame to the right, just as if it were a bit of text.

Figure 3.50 To reach the frame tools, click the toolbox icon in the lower-left corner of any AppleWorks document (top) and then click the Frame tab in the Tools Palette (bottom).

Figure 3.51. Make sure the Frame tab of the Tools Palette is visible.

Figure 3.52
An AppleWorks
document before
any frames are
created.

Figure 3.53 To draw a frame, click in the document (left), drag to draw the frame (middle), and release the cursor to insert it into the document (right).

To create a frame:

1. Make sure the Frame tab of the Tools Palette is visible (**Figure 3.51**) and open the document in which you want to create a frame (**Figure 3.52**).

2. In the Frame tab, click the frame tool for the type of document you want to add: text, spreadsheet, painting, or table. (A variation is explained in *Creating Frames of the Same Type as the Document* on page 64.)

3. In the document, click where you want the frame to begin (left, **Figure 3.53**).

4. Drag the cursor to draw the frame (middle, **Figure 3.53**), and release the cursor. The new frame will appear in the document, floating atop the document's original content (right, **Figure 3.53**).

(continued)

USING FRAMES

5. Select the new frame by clicking *outside* the frame or by clicking the Arrow Tool in the Frame tab (**Figure 3.54**). Once the frame's selected, you can:

Add content to the new frame based on its document type (text, spreadsheet, painting, or table).

or

Reposition the frame. See *To move a floating frame* on page 67.

or

Leave the frame floating and place it *behind* the document's original content frame. For more information, see *Rearranging floating frames* on page 68.

or

If the document's original content is text, leave the frame floating and make the text flow around the new frame. For more information, see *Wrapping Text Around Frames and Objects* on page 194.

or

If you are working in a word-processing document or the layout mode of a database, you can turn the floating frame into an inline frame. For more information, see *Changing frame types* on page 65.

✔ Tip

■ Each frame tool uses a different cursor (**Figure 3.55**), but no matter which tool you select in step 2, the process for creating the frame is the same.

Figure 3.54 Select a frame by clicking the Arrow Tool in the Frame tab.

Figure 3.55 Each frame tool uses a unique cursor for creating frames (clockwise from top left): text, spreadsheet, table, and painting.

Creating Frames of the Same Type as the Document

To create a frame of the *same* type as the document you're working in, you need to press (Option) before you begin dragging the cursor in step 4 on page 63. Examples of this would include putting a text frame in a text document or a spreadsheet frame in a spreadsheet.

Creating a text frame within a text document can be used for simple items such as sidebars (upper right, **Figure 3.43** on page 60) or for more decorative effects (**Figure 3.56**).

Although you cannot create a painting frame within a painting, you can use the drawing tools to create a similar layered effect.

Figure 3.56 By arranging text frames within a text document, you can create layered effects.

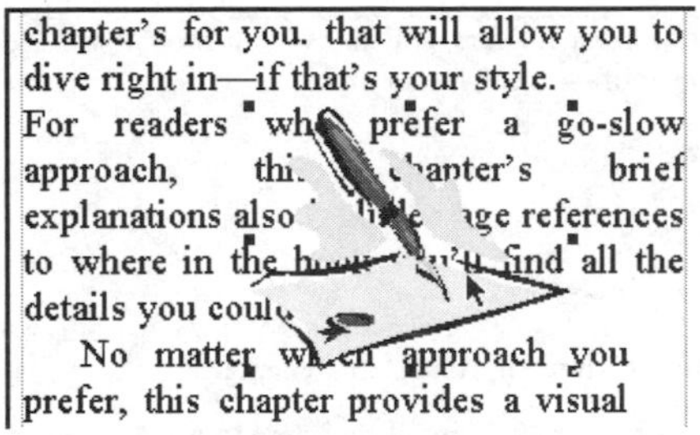

chapter's for you. that will allow you to
dive right in—if that's your style.
For readers who prefer a go-slow
approach, this chapter's brief
explanations also include page references
to where in the book you'll find all the
details you could want.

No matter which approach you
prefer, this chapter provides a visual

Figure 3.57 To change a floating frame to an inline frame, first click it to select it.

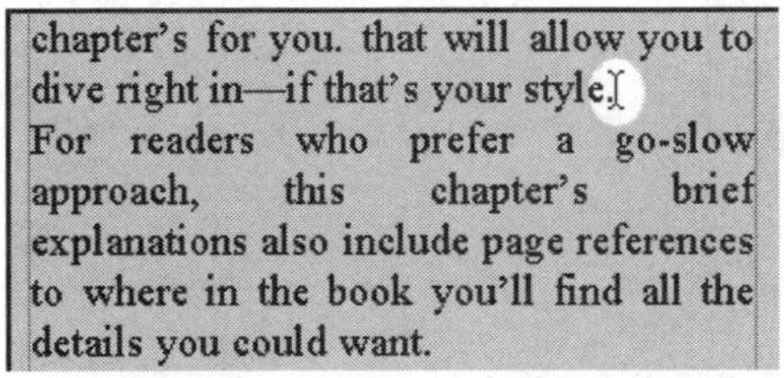

chapter's for you. that will allow you to
dive right in—if that's your style.
For readers who prefer a go-slow
approach, this chapter's brief
explanations also include page references
to where in the book you'll find all the
details you could want.

Figure 3.58 After cutting the frame, click in the text and the cursor will appear as an I-beam.

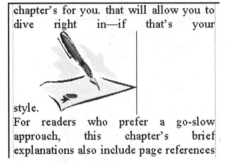

chapter's for you. that will allow you to
dive right in—if that's your
style.
For readers who prefer a go-slow
approach, this chapter's brief
explanations also include page references

Figure 3.59 Choose Edit > Paste and the frame reappears as inline with the text.

Changing frame types

If you are working in a word-processing document or the layout mode of a database, you can change a floating frame to an inline frame, or vice versa.

To change a floating frame to an inline frame:

1. Click on the floating frame to select it (**Figure 3.57**).

2. Choose Edit > Cut (⌘X) and the frame will be removed from the text.

3. Click in the text where you want the inline frame to appear. The cursor will appear as an I-beam (**Figure 3.58**).

4. Choose Edit > Paste (⌘V). The frame will reappear lined up with the text as an inline frame (**Figure 3.59**).

To change an inline frame to a floating frame:

1. Click once on the inline frame. The cursor will turn into an arrow with a small box and the frame will be marked with a dashed line and black box in the lower-right corner (**Figure 3.60**).

2. Choose Edit > Cut ((⌘)(X)) and the frame will be removed from the text.

3. Click the Arrow Tool in the Frame tab (**Figure 3.61**). Do not click in the document itself.

4. Choose Edit > Paste ((⌘)(V)). The frame will reappear, but this time as a floating frame, marked by eight black handles (**Figure 3.62**).

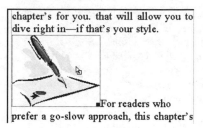

Figure 3.60 To change an inline frame to a floating frame, first select it.

Figure 3.61 After cutting the frame, click the Frame tab's Arrow Tool.

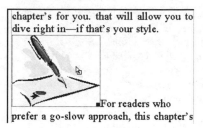

chapter's for you. that will allow you to dive right in—if that's your style.

For readers who prefer a go-slow approach, this chapter's brief explanations also include page references

Figure 3.62 Choose Edit > Paste and the frame reappears as a floating frame.

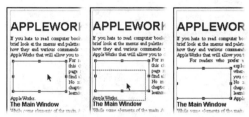

Figure 3.63 To move a floating frame, first click the Frame tab's Arrow Tool.

Figure 3.64 Click the frame, drag it to its new position, and release the cursor.

Moving frames

Only floating frames can be repositioned. Inline frames cannot be moved around since they have, in effect, become part of the document's text. To move the contents of an inline frame, first convert the frame to a floating frame.

To move a floating frame:

1. Click the Arrow Tool in the Frame tab (**Figure 3.63**).

2. Click on the frame you want to move (left, **Figure 3.64**).

3. Drag the frame to its new position (middle, **Figure 3.64**). Release the cursor and the frame will move to the new location (right, **Figure 3.64**).

✔ Tips

■ For more precise positioning of a frame, select the frame and then use your keyboard arrows to move it.

■ While **Figure 3.64** shows an empty frame, you can move a frame with content just as easily.

Rearranging floating frames

By default, floating frames float on top of the main document's contents. However, you can rearrange them, treating the floating frames like layers. If you have multiple floating frames, you can stack them with front, back, and in-between layers.

To rearrange floating frames:

1. Click the floating frame to select it (**Figure 3.65**).

2. Choose Arrange > Move To Back (**Figure 3.66**). The selected frame will move to the back, allowing the main document's content to float on top of the frame (**Figure 3.67**).

✔ Tip

■ If you have multiple floating frames, you can select each one and use the Arrange Menu's various Move Forward, Move To Front, Move Backward, and Move To Back commands (**Figure 3.66**) to create front, back, and in-between layers. Combine layered frames with text wraps for a variety of layout options (**Figure 3.68**).

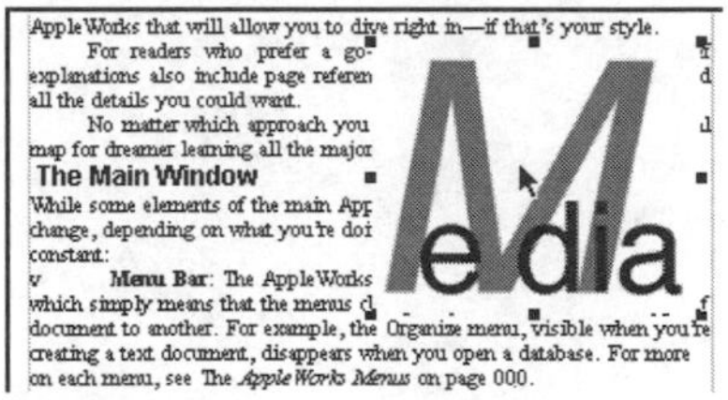

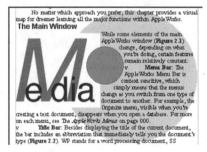

Figure 3.65 To rearrange a floating frame, first select it.

Figure 3.66 Use the Arrange menu to change the front-to-back position of the floating frame relative to the document.

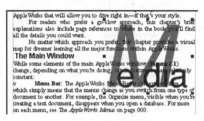

Figure 3.67 By moving the floating frame to the back, the text appears on top of the logo.

Figure 3.68 You can combine layered frames with text wraps for a variety of layout options.

Inserting files into documents

Existing files—assuming their format is compatible with AppleWorks—can be inserted directly into your document. You can insert the file as a floating frame or an inline frame, depending on the destination document's type. In general, inline frames can only be used in text documents or the layout mode of databases. For details, see **Table 3.1**, *How source files are inserted into AppleWorks documents*, below.

Table 3.1

How source files are inserted into AppleWorks documents				
DESTINATION DOCUMENT TYPE	**FILE SOURCE TYPE:** **TEXT**	**SPREADSHEET**	**DATABASE**	**IMAGE/MOVIE**
Text	Inline Frame, Floating Frame	Top-left cell* (Data, formulas)	Inline Frame, Floating Frame	Inline Frame, Floating Frame
Spreadsheet	Top-left cell (Data, results)	Top-left cell (Data, formulas)	Top-left cell (Data, formulas)	Floating Frame
Database *Browse Mode*	New records (Fields mark tabs, Records mark line returns)	Top-left cell* (Data, formulas)	New records (Fields mark tabs, Records mark line returns)	Field**
Layout Mode	Inline Frame, Floating Frame	Top-left cell* (Data, formulas)	Inline Frame, Floating Frame	Inline Frame, Floating Frame
Image		Top-left cell* (Data, formulas)		Floating Frame

*First create spreadsheet frame   **First create a multimedia field

To insert a file as a floating frame:

1. Click anywhere in the document into which you want to insert the file. (You cannot control exactly where the insertion will appear, but you can move the frame after it's inserted.)

2. Click the Arrow Tool in the Frame tab to eliminate the I-beam cursor (**Figures 3.69** and **3.70**).

3. Choose File > Insert (**Figure 3.71**).

4. When the Open dialog box appears, navigate to the file you want and click *Insert* (**Figure 3.72**). The file will be inserted into the document as a floating frame, which you can then move or rearrange as needed (**Figure 3.73**).

✔ Tips

- To insert the file as a floating frame, you must click the Arrow Tool in step 2. Otherwise, you'll wind up with an inline frame.

- To make it easier to find one file among many, use the *File Format* pop-up menu in step 4 (**Figure 3.72**) to reduce the number of files appearing in the Open dialog box.

- In step 4, click the *Show Preview* button if you want to see the file's contents before making the insert.

Figure 3.69 Before inserting a file as a floating frame, click the Arrow Tool.

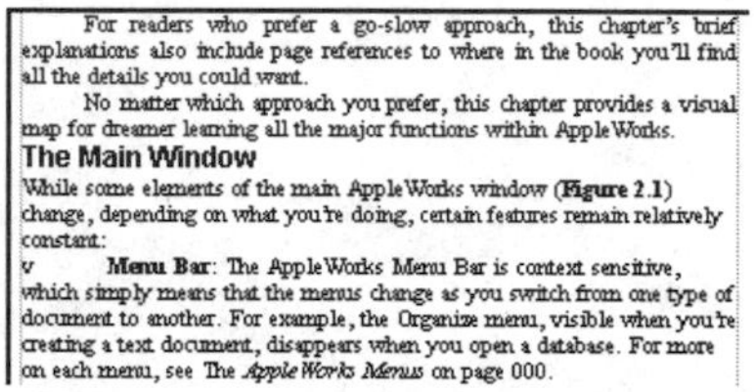

Figure 3.70 If you want to insert a floating frame, the cursor should *not* be visible in the document.

Figure 3.71 To insert a file, choose File > Insert.

Figure 3.72 Use the Open dialog box to navigate to the file and click *Insert*.

Figure 3.73 The inserted file will float in its own frame on top of the document content.

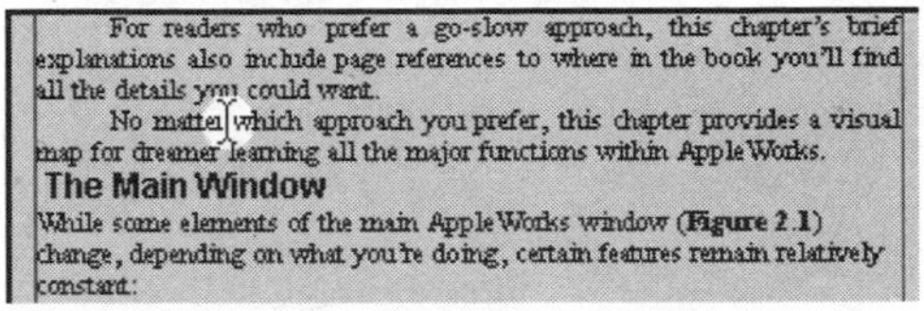

For readers who prefer a go-slow approach, this chapter's brief explanations also include page references to where in the book you'll find all the details you could want.

No matter which approach you prefer, this chapter provides a visual map for dreamer learning all the major functions within AppleWorks.

The Main Window

While some elements of the main AppleWorks window (**Figure 2.1**) change, depending on what you're doing, certain features remain relatively constant:

Figure 3.74 To insert a file as an inline frame, make sure the cursor appears as an I-beam within the text.

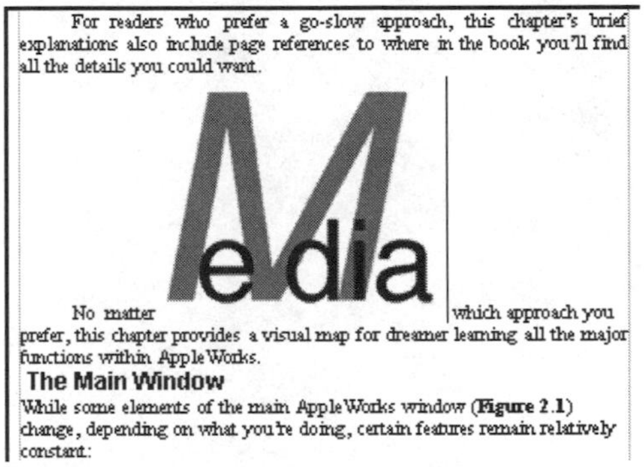

For readers who prefer a go-slow approach, this chapter's brief explanations also include page references to where in the book you'll find all the details you could want.

No matter which approach you prefer, this chapter provides a visual map for dreamer learning all the major functions within AppleWorks.

The Main Window

While some elements of the main AppleWorks window (**Figure 2.1**) change, depending on what you're doing, certain features remain relatively constant:

Figure 3.75 The inserted file appears inline with the document's main text.

To insert a file as an inline frame:

1. Click in the document where you want the file inserted. The cursor will appear as an I-beam (**Figure 3.74**)

2. Choose File > Insert (**Figure 3.71**).

3. When the Open dialog box appears, navigate to the file you want and click *Insert* (**Figure 3.72**). The file will be inserted into the document as an inline frame (**Figure 3.75**).

USING CLIPPINGS

Figure 4.1 AppleWorks automatically installs a variety of images in the Clippings Palette.

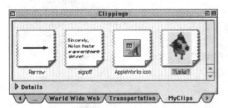

Figure 4.2 You can add your most-used items, including text and images, to the Clippings Palette.

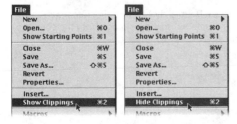

Figure 4.3 To show or hide the Clippings Palette, use the File menu or press ⌘②.

Clippings, which supersede the libraries used in AppleWorks 5, enable you to quickly add your most-used items to documents. Organized within the Clippings Palette, clippings can include images, bits of text, Web addresses, frames, aliases to items on remote servers—to name just a few items. AppleWorks automatically installs a variety of images in the palette (**Figure 4.1**), but you also can add your own most-used items (**Figure 4.2**).

If you are an AppleWorks or ClarisWorks veteran, you'll want to dig right into this chapter since clippings give AppleWorks 6 greatly expanded capabilities compared with its predecessors. If you're new to AppleWorks, you may want skip this chapter for now until you have mastered the program's more basic aspects.

To show or hide the Clippings Palette:

◆ To show the Clippings Palette, choose File > Show Clippings (⌘②). Repeat the command to hide the palette—something you'll do often since it always floats on top of your documents (**Figure 4.3**).

Finding Local Clippings

The Clippings Palette's Search tab lets you find AppleWorks local clippings already stored on your own computer or Web clippings at the AppleWorks Web site. Since AppleWorks automatically installs a decent set of clippings on your computer, start with *To find local clippings* below to get a feel for how the often-confusing Clippings Palette works. For finding Web-based clippings, see *To add clippings from the AppleWorks Web site* on page 83.

To find local clippings:

1. Make sure the Clippings Palette is visible (⌘②) and click on the Search tab (the first one on the left).

2. Type a word or words (just spaces, no commas) into the *Search* window and click the *Search* button (**Figure 4.4**). (Do *not* check the *Search Web Content* box.) In a moment, thumbnail versions of clippings that match your search term will appear in the Search tab's window (**Figure 4.5**).

3. If you have an AppleWorks document open, you can double-click the thumbnail and a higher-resolution version of the clipping will be pasted automatically into the document (**Figure 4.6**). If you want more control over how a clipping is placed in your document, see *Inserting Clippings* on page 76.

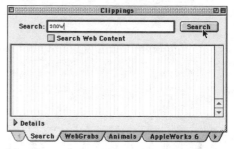

Figure 4.4 To find clippings stored on your computer, type a word in the *Search* window and click the *Search* button. Make sure the *Search Web Content* box is *not* checked.

Figure 4.5 Clippings matching your search terms appear in the Search tab's window.

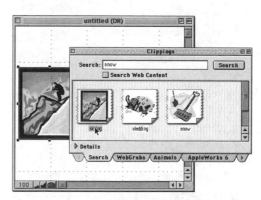

Figure 4.6 Double-click the clipping thumbnail and a higher-resolution version is pasted into the open document.

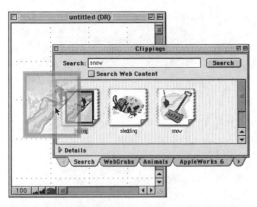

Figure 4.7 You also can click and drag a clipping into your AppleWorks document.

Figure 4.8 Each clipping installed by AppleWorks includes associated keywords.

✔ Tips

■ You also can click and drag a clipping into your AppleWorks document (**Figure 4.7**).

■ What is AppleWorks's secret in finding local clippings that match your search term, no matter what the clipping actually is named? Each clipping installed by AppleWorks includes associated keywords (**Figure 4.8**). For more information on adding your own keywords to images, see step 6 of *To add local items to the Clippings Palette* on page 79.

Inserting Clippings

Once you find a clipping that meets your needs, you can insert it into any AppleWorks document. Just as you can when inserting files, you have the choice of inserting clippings as *floating* or *inline* frames. For more information on the difference, see *Using Frames* on page 61.

To insert a clipping:

1. Open your document and if the Clippings Palette is not visible, choose File > Show Clippings (⌘2). Also open the Tools Palette (Shift⌘T) and click on the Frame tab.

2. If you want the clipping to appear in a *floating* frame, click the Arrow Tool in the Frame tab (left, **Figure 4.9**).

   or

   If you want the clipping to appear in an *inline* frame, click in the document text where you want the clipping inserted. The cursor will appear as an I-beam (right, **Figure 4.9**).

3. By default, the Clippings Palette opens to the Search tab (**Figure 4.10**). If you already know under which tab the desired clipping is stored, click that tab (**Figure 4.11**) or flip through the tabs until you find something you like. For more information on searching clippings, see *Finding Local Clippings* on page 74.

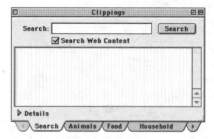

Figure 4.9 To insert a clipping into a *floating* frame, click the Arrow Tool in the Frame tab (left). To insert it as an *inline* frame, click in the document text so the cursor appears as an I-beam (right).

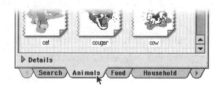

Figure 4.10 By default, the Clippings Palette opens to the Search tab, which is empty until you perform a search.

Figure 4.11 If you know where a clipping is stored, click that tab to open it.

INSERTING CLIPPINGS

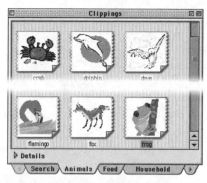

Figure 4.12 When the desired clippings tab appears, type the first few letters of the clippings name and it will be selected automatically.

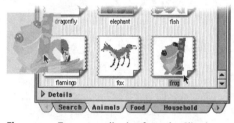

Figure 4.13 To move a clipping from the Clippings Palette, click and drag it to the open document. A semi-transparent icon of the clipping will guide your progress.

Figure 4.14 A clipping inserted as a *floating* frame appears on top of the document content.

Figure 4.15 A clipping inserted as an *inline* frame appears as part of the document's content.

4. When the desired clippings tab appears, you can use the scroll bar to reach the desired clipping. If you know the name of the clipping, click inside the tab's window and type just the first few letters of the clipping name. The window will automatically scroll to the desired item and highlight it (**Figure 4.12**).

5. Click and drag the clipping (**Figure 4.13**) into the document. Depending on your choice in step 2, the clipping will appear in the document as a floating frame (**Figure 4.14**) or an inline frame (**Figure 4.15**).

Adding Clippings

You have two sources to tap when adding items to the Clippings Palette: local items on your own computer or items on the Web. Clipping candidates on your own computer, that is *local* items, include anything you use regularly. For more information, see *To add local items to the Clippings Palette* on page 79.

If you've upgraded from AppleWorks 5, or its predecessor ClarisWorks, you have another local source of clippings: library items. For more information, see *To add AppleWorks 5 libraries* on page 81.

Adding clippings from AppleWorks's Web site is not particularly intuitive and often awkward. In its favor, the AppleWorks's site has an astounding number of good-quality clippings. Schools and families with always-on Internet connections will find it a bit easier to use than dial-up users. For more information, see *To add clippings from the AppleWorks Web site* on page 83. Be sure to read *No browser necessary?* on page 86 and the *Tips* on page 85 beforehand to avoid some common pitfalls.

Adding clippings from other Web sites shares some of the same frustrations of downloading clippings from the AppleWorks Web site. For more information, see *To create tabs for Web clippings* on page 89.

Figure 4.16 To add text (left) or an image (right) to the Clippings Palette, first select it.

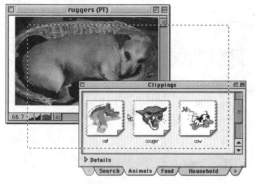

Figure 4.17 As you drag a selection to the Clippings Palette tab, a dashed outline will help guide you.

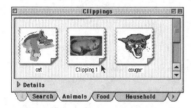

Figure 4.18 The selected item will be added to the tab and automatically given a generic name, such as *Clipping 1*.

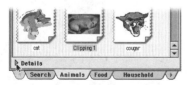

Figure 4.19 To give a clipping a distinctive name, click the item in the tab window, then click the *Details* arrow.

To add local items to the Clippings Palette:

1. Choose File > Show Clippings (⌘②).

2. Open the document containing the text or image you want to add to the Clippings Palette and select it (**Figure 4.16**).

3. Click the Clippings Palette tab to which you want to add the item, and drag the selected item into the tab window. A dashed outline of the selection will help guide you (**Figure 4.17**). The selected item will be added to the tab and automatically given a generic name, such as *Clipping 1* (**Figure 4.18**).

4. To give the clipping a distinctive name, click the item in the tab window, then click the arrow next to *Details* in the palette's lower-left corner (**Figure 4.19**).

(continued)

5. When the *Details* panel appears, use the *Name* text window to rename the clipping (**Figure 4.20**). Press Enter and the clipping will be renamed. Depending on how the clippings are sorted, their order may change instantly. You may need to scroll down the tab window (or type a few letters of its new name) to find the renamed item (**Figure 4.21**).

6. If you like, you can type a few words into the *Keyword* text window within the *Details* panel to help you find the clipping in a later search (**Figure 4.21**). This can be done later as well by selecting a clipping and clicking the *Details* arrow.

✔ Tips

- By default, clippings are displayed alphabetically in each tab. To change the sorting order, Ctrl-click the tab and make a choice from the submenu (**Figure 4.22**). The tab's clippings will be resorted accordingly.

- In step 6, you do not need to use any special characters to separate multiple keywords. Just type in each keyword followed by a single space.

Figure 4.20 When the *Details* panel appears, use the *Name* text window to rename the clipping.

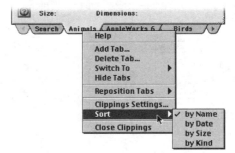

Figure 4.21 You can add a few words in the *Keyword* text window to help you find the clipping in a later search.

Figure 4.22 To change the order of clippings in a tab, Ctrl-click the tab and make a choice from the submenu.

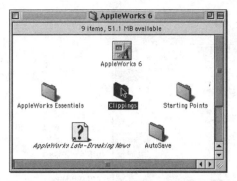

Figure 4.23 To add AppleWorks 5 libraries, first open the Clippings folder inside AppleWorks 6's main folder...

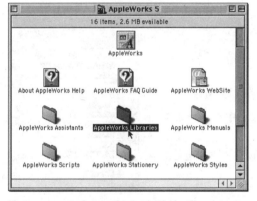

Figure 4.24 ...and open the AppleWorks Libraries folder inside the main AppleWorks 5 folder.

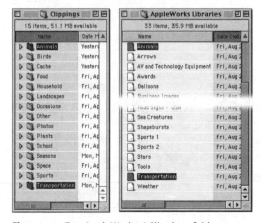

Figure 4.25 Two AppleWorks 6 Clippings folders (left)—*Animals* and *Transportation*—have the same names as files in the AppleWorks (5) Libraries folder (right).

Adding AppleWorks 5 Libraries

If you've built up a collection of AppleWorks 5 or ClarisWorks 5 library items—or just want to transfer the ones that came with either program—turning them into AppleWorks 6 clippings is pretty simple. There's just one wrinkle: Two of the AppleWorks 5 library items have the same names as AppleWorks 6 clipping folders. If you simply copy the library files to the Clippings folder (and ignore the Alert dialog box that appears), you'll wind up overwriting both folders. The solution, as explained below, is to change the names of those library items.

To add AppleWorks 5 libraries:

1. Open the Clippings folder inside AppleWorks 6's main folder, then open the AppleWorks Libraries folder inside the main AppleWorks 5 folder (**Figures 4.23** and **4.24**). Two Clippings folders—*Animals* and *Transportation*—have the same names as files in the AppleWorks Libraries folder (**Figure 4.25**).

(continued)

2. Select the AppleWorks 5 *Animals* file and give it a new name, then do the same thing for the *Transportation* file (**Figure 4.26**).

3. Select the files and folders within the AppleWorks Libraries folder you want to use, then drag them to the AppleWorks 6 Clippings folder (**Figure 4.27**). Once the files are copied, the tabs in the Clippings Palette will include your original AppleWorks 6 clippings and items copied from the AppleWorks 5 libraries (**Figure 4.28**).

✔ Tips

■ A lock icon appears on Clippings Palette tabs imported from AppleWorks 5 (right, **Figure 4.28**). Items in locked tabs cannot be deleted from the Clippings Palette (or even through the Finder). You can delete the entire tab, but not individual items, so you might want to weed out your AppleWorks 5 libraries before you copy them to AppleWorks 6.

■ *Folders* stored within the AppleWorks Libraries folder must be opened if you want to copy their contents to the AppleWorks 6 Clippings folder. Otherwise, you wind up with a tab named for the folder but it will be empty.

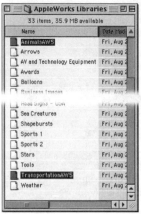

Figure 4.26 To avoid overwriting the AppleWorks 6 Clippings folders, rename the AppleWorks 5 *Animals* and *Transportation* files.

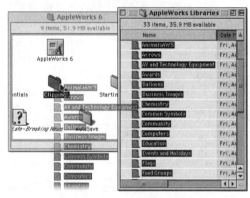

Figure 4.27 To add the AppleWorks (5) Libraries, click and drag them to the AppleWorks 6 Clippings folder.

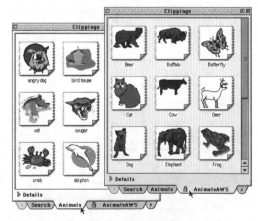

Figure 4.28 The Clippings Palette tabs now include the original AppleWorks 6 clippings (left) and the AppleWorks 5 libraries (right).

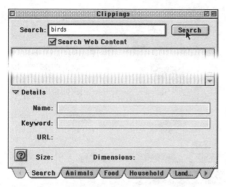

Figure 4.29 After connecting to the Internet, use the Search tab to add clippings from the AppleWorks Web site.

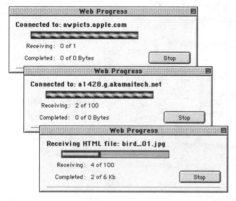

Figure 4.30 When you connect to AppleWorks's online clippings, three Web Progress dialog boxes will appear in sequence.

To add clippings from the AppleWorks Web site:

1. Choose File > Show Clippings (⌘2).

2. If you have an always-on link to the Internet, such as a cable modem, DSL (Digital Subscriber Line), or a dedicated hardwire connection, you're all set. If you have a dial-up connection, connect now to the Internet. Also take a look at *No browser necessary?* on page 86.

3. Once you're connected, click the Search tab in the Clippings Palette. Type a word or words (just spaces, no commas) into the *Search* window, check the *Search Web Content* box, and click the *Search* button (**Figure 4.29**).

4. Three Web Progress dialog boxes will appear in sequence (**Figure 4.30**). The first one connects you to AppleWorks's main server. Once the server determines what you're seeking, the second dialog box appears as you are switched to a server closer to your location to speed the download. The third dialog box appears once thumbnails of clippings begin downloading to your computer.

5. Once the clipping thumbnails are downloaded, the Web Progress dialog boxes will disappear, and the Search tab's window will display thumbnails of images that match your search terms.

(continued)

ADDING CLIPPINGS FROM APPLEWORKS

6. Remain connected to the Internet and look through the thumbnails. When you find one you want to use:

Double-click it in the Search tab window (**Figure 4.31**) and a higher-resolution version of the image will be downloaded and appear in your open document (**Figures 4.32** and **4.33**).

or

Click it in the Search tab window and drag it to another Clipping Palette tab (**Figures 4.34** and **4.35**). A higher-resolution version of the image will be downloaded and appear in the targeted tab (**Figures 4.36**).

7. If you don't find an image to your liking or need more images, start another online search by repeating steps 3–6. Once you are done, disconnect from the Internet if you are using a dial-up connection.

Figure 4.31 To place a clipping in an open document (left), double-click the Clippings Palette thumbnail (right).

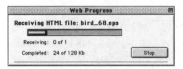

Figure 4.32 Once you find a clipping to use, a higher-resolution version of the image is downloaded.

Figure 4.33 After the download is done, the image appears in the open document (left).

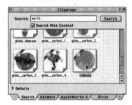

Figure 4.34 To download a higher-resolution clipping to another tab, select the thumbnail in the Search tab...

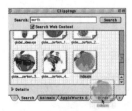

Figure 4.35 ...and drag it to another Clippings Palette tab. A semi-transparent icon will guide you.

Figure 4.36 A higher-resolution version of the image is downloaded to the other Clippings Palette tab.

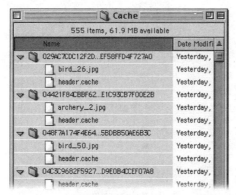

Figure 4.37 Can't find clippings from a previous search? Look inside AppleWorks's *Cache* folder and open those weirdly named folders.

Figure 4.38 A purple ribbon marks the corner of new clippings downloaded since your last online search.

✔ Tips

- If you start another online clippings search before dragging the previous search results into documents or to other Clippings Palette tabs, all the clippings disappear from the Search tab window. While they seem to have been lost, you'll find them inside AppleWorks's main folder. Look for the Cache folder inside the Clippings folder, then open the weirdly numbered folders (**Figure 4.37**). You can then drag the clippings into an AppleWorks document or to a Clippings Palette tab.

- The purple ribbon on the corner of some clippings indicates that the clipping is new since your last download (**Figure 4.38**). Don't worry, the ribbon doesn't appear on the actual clipping. It's just a reminder for you.

- When dragging items from the Clippings Palette's Search tab into a document, it's best to move only a few items at a time. If you grab them all at once, AppleWorks or your computer may crash. It will help *some* to bump up AppleWorks's memory setting if your computer has enough RAM. For more information, see *Allocating Memory* on page 452.

(continued)

- When using the Clippings Palette to download items from the AppleWorks Web site you cannot see what general categories of clippings there are before starting your keyword-based search. Do yourself a favor: Use your Web browser to at least get a listing of the clipping categories. You'll find it at: http://awpicts.apple.com (there's no www in the address) (**Figure 4.39**). You can then use the listing to find a folder that sounds promising before switching back to AppleWorks's Search tab to download items. AppleWorks's keyword approach does have the advantage of pulling clippings from *multiple* folders. But using your browser beforehand to look at the index will give you an overview of what's available.

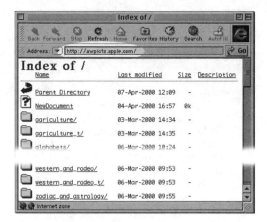

Figure 4.39 You can use your Web browser to get a listing of the available categories for AppleWorks's online clipping.

No browser necessary?

AppleWorks touts its ability to download Web clippings and templates without needing a Web browser. That's true in theory. For people using dial-up Internet connections, it may not be.

A dial-up clipping or template search will stall—even if you are connected to the Internet—unless you also have your Web browser open. The reason is a little checkbox inside a control panel that handles your online connections (**Figure 4.40**). If that box is checked (as it is by default), your online connection remains inactive unless triggered by an application like your browser. AppleWorks itself can't trigger that connection, so Apple recommends that everyone *not* check this box. That can

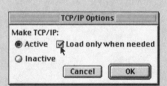

Figure 4.40 Don't touch that dial? Read this sidebar first.

be a problem for dial-up users. If you change that setting, your browser will start reconnecting to the Internet *after* you've logged off as it tries to download banner ads or animated images for any Web page on your screen. Some email messages with embedded Web images also will send your browser scurrying online. With an always-on connection, this is not a problem. But dial-up users will find themselves fighting with their browser as it keeps reconnecting to the Web.

The solution? Dial-up users should leave that control panel alone and just open your browser when you use AppleWorks to search for Web clippings or templates. (You don't need to enter an address in the browser, just launch it and switch back to AppleWorks.) Users with always-on connections may want to change the setting. For how to do it, see *Changing the TCP/IP Setting* on page 458.

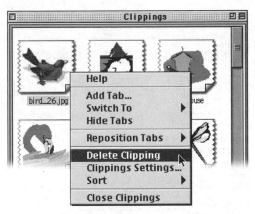

Figure 4.41 To delete selected clippings, Ctrl-click and choose *Delete Clipping* in the pop-up menu.

Deleting clippings

You can delete clippings one by one or you can select a group and delete them all. If you're really cleaning house or just want to tidy up the Clippings Palette, see *Hiding, disabling, and deleting tabs* on page 94.

To delete clippings:

1. Click on the Clippings Palette tab and select the clipping you want to delete by clicking it once. To select multiple items, press Shift while clicking each item.

2. Ctrl-click and when the pop-up menu appears, choose *Delete Clipping* (**Figure 4.41**). The selected clippings will be deleted.

Managing Clipping Tabs

The more you use AppleWorks the more the Clippings Palette will begin to resemble a pack rat's nest. Fortunately, you have several ways to control the clutter by creating new clipping tabs, deleting unused tabs, and hiding less-used tabs.

Creating clipping tabs

If you are adding a bunch of new clippings, it helps sometimes to create a new tab for them. Or you can add tabs to recategorize clips in your existing tabs. If you are creating a tab for images stored on the *Web*, creating the tab and downloading the images to that tab are part of the same process.

To create tabs for local clippings:

1. Choose File > Show Clippings (⌘2).

2. Click the Clipping Palette's ▶ tab until you reach the last tab (the **+** tab), and click that tab (**Figure 4.42**).

3. When the Add Tab dialog box appears, type in a *Tab Name* (**Figure 4.43**).

4. If the items you want to add are stored on your computer (as opposed to the Web), leave the *Location* drop-down menu set to *My Computer* and click *Add*. A new empty tab will appear (**Figure 4.44**).

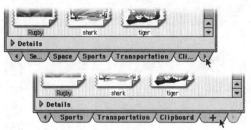

Figure 4.42 To create a new tab, use the arrow tab (top) to reach the + tab (bottom).

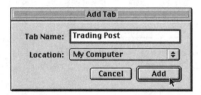

Figure 4.43 When the Add Tab dialog box appears, type in a *Tab Name*.

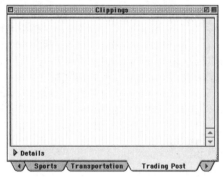

Figure 4.44 The Clippings Palette displays an empty window after a new tab is created.

Figure 4.45 After connecting to the Internet, create a new tab for *Web* clippings by typing in a URL and clicking *OK*.

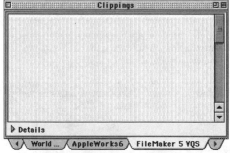

Figure 4.46 When a new tab for *Web* clippings is created (top), AppleWorks begins downloading images from the Web address (bottom).

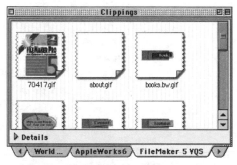

Figure 4.47 Once the download is done, the Web page's images appear in the tab.

To create tabs for Web clippings:

1. If you have an always-on link to the Internet, go to step 2. If you have a dial-up connection, connect now to the Internet. Also take a look at *No browser necessary?* on page 86.

2. Choose File > Show Clippings (⌘②).

3. Click the Clipping Palette's ▶ tab until you reach the last tab (the **+** tab) and click that tab (**Figure 4.42**).

4. When the Add Tab dialog box appears, type in a *Tab Name* and use the *Location* drop-down menu set to choose *Internet Based*. When the *URL* window appears in the Edit Tab dialog box, type in the full address, including the protocol (e.g., http or ftp), and click *OK* (**Figure 4.45**).

5. The new empty tab will be added to the Clippings Palette and a Web Progress dialog box will appear as AppleWorks connects to the URL entered in step 4 (**Figure 4.46**).

6. The Web Progress dialog box will update as each image at the targeted URL is downloaded. Once the download is complete, the dialog box will disappear and the Web images will appear in the tab (**Figure 4.47**).

7. If you want to download images from another URL, repeat steps 3–6. Once you are done, disconnect from the Internet if you are using a dial-up connection.

CREATING TABS

✔ Tips

- The clipping collection at AppleWorks's Web site offers thumbnail and higher resolution versions of the same image. Because other Web sites are not set up as clipping connections, however, only one version of each image downloads.

- Most Web images are protected by copyright. Don't download and use other people's images without permission. (I used images of my own books in this example.)

- In **Figure 4.47** only the first image has a ribbon over its corner. That's because the other images had been downloaded previously to the adjacent AppleWorks 6 tab.

- The next time you use AppleWorks to search for online clippings, it will automatically check all the URLs you've associated with tabs and download only new images on those pages (**Figure 4.48**). If you are online, you can trigger this manually by Ctrl-clicking on the tab and choosing *Reload Tab* from the drop-down menu (**Figure 4.49**).

Figure 4.48 Each time you use AppleWorks to search for online clippings, it automatically checks *all* the URLs you've linked to clipping tabs.

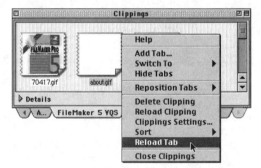

Figure 4.49 If you are online, you can check manually for *new* Web images by Ctrl-clicking the tab and choosing *Reload Tab*.

CREATING TABS

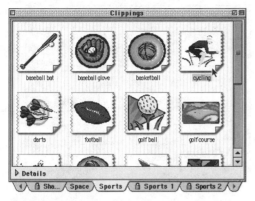

Figure 4.50 To move a clipping from one tab to another, first select it.

Figure 4.51 Use the arrow tabs to shift the destination tab into view along the edge of the Clippings Palette.

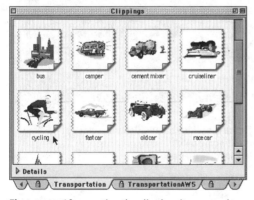

Figure 4.52 After pasting the clipping, it appears in the destination tab.

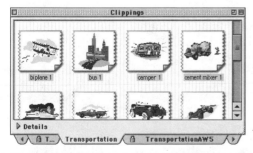

Figure 4.53 Clippings *copied* to another tab will have a number added to each name.

Moving clippings to other tabs

AppleWorks gives you three routes for getting clippings on your computer from one Clippings Palette tab to another: cutting and pasting, copying and pasting, and a click-and-drag method. The click-and-drag move, however, requires a sure hand so as to not overrun the destination tab.

To cut and paste or copy and paste clippings to another tab:

1. Click the Clippings Palette tab where the clipping you want to move is stored.

2. Click on the clipping you want to move (**Figure 4.50**). If you want to select multiple clippings, press (Shift) first and then click on each clipping.

3. To cut (and later paste) the clipping(s), choose Edit > Cut (⌘X). To copy the clipping(s), choose Edit > Copy (⌘C).

4. Use the arrow tabs to shift the destination tab into view along the edge of the Clippings Palette (**Figure 4.51**).

5. Click inside the tab window and choose Edit > Paste (⌘V). The clipping(s) will be pasted into the new tab (**Figure 4.52**). Copied clipping(s) will display a number at the end of the name (**Figure 4.53**).

To drag clippings to another tab:

1. Click the Clippings Palette tab where the clipping you want to move is stored (**Figure 4.50**).

2. Click on the clipping you want to move. If you want to select multiple clippings, press (Shift) first and then click on each clipping.

3. Drag the selected clipping(s) over the tab where you want to move it. A semi-transparent version of the clipping(s) will help you guide the cursor (**Figure 4.54**). If the destination tab is not visible, drag the clipping(s) onto either of the Clippings Palette's arrow tabs until the destination tab appears (**Figure 4.55**).

4. Release your cursor and the clipping(s) will be moved.

Figure 4.54 When you click and drag a clipping to another tab, a semi-transparent icon guides your progress.

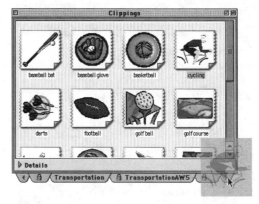

Figure 4.55 If the destination tab is not visible, drag the clipping onto the arrow tab until the destination tab scrolls into view.

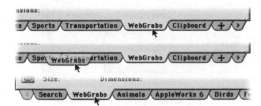

Figure 4.56 To reorder the clipping tabs, click and drag a tab to a new spot and release the cursor.

Reordering clipping tabs

AppleWorks displays new Clippings Palette tabs in the order you create them and adds them to the *right* end of the tabs, next to the Clipboard and + tabs. The Search tab meanwhile sits on the far *left*. If you want to quickly move some online clippings to particular tabs, you end up doing a lot of clicking and dragging. One solution is to reorder the tabs to suit your work style.

To reorder clipping tabs:

1. Click to select the tab you want to move (top, **Figure 4.56**).

2. Click and drag the tab toward its new spot in the tabs. A semi-transparent version of the tab will mark your progress (middle, **Figure 4.56**).

3. When you reach the desired spot, release the cursor and the tab will be repositioned (bottom, **Figure 4.56**).

Hiding, disabling, and deleting clipping tabs

Jargon alert: AppleWorks uses the term "hiding tabs" in two different ways. Hiding can mean tucking out of sight *all* the Clippings Palette's tabs. It also sometimes refers to making a *single* tab disappear, a trick that AppleWorks also calls *disabling* a tab. To keep it all straight, this book uses hiding only when referring to hiding *all* the tabs.

Disabling a tab makes it disappear from the Clippings Palette but AppleWorks leaves an identically named folder—with every clipping tucked safely inside—on your computer. Deleting a tab does exactly what it sounds like: It puts the tab and all its contents in the Trash. The steps for disabling or deleting a tab are very similar, so pay particular attention in step 2 of either process.

To hide or show all the clipping tabs:

◆ To simultaneously hide all the Clippings Palette's tabs, (Ctrl)-click anywhere in the palette and choose *Hide Tabs* from the drop-down menu (**Figure 4.57**). All the tabs will disappear.

◆ If none of the Clippings Palette's tabs is visible, (Ctrl)-click on the palette and choose *Show Tabs* from the drop-down menu (**Figure 4.58**). All the palette's tabs will reappear.

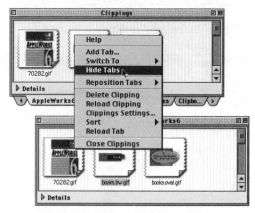

Figure 4.57 To hide all the Clippings Palette's tabs, (Ctrl)-click in the palette and choose *Hide Tabs* (top). All the tabs disappear (bottom).

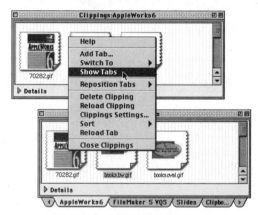

Figure 4.58 To show all the Clippings Palette's tabs, (Ctrl)-click in the palette and choose *Show Tabs* (top). All the tabs reappear (bottom).

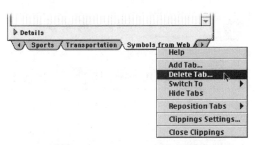

Figure 4.59 To disable *or* delete a clipping tab, Ctrl-click and choose *Delete Tab*.

Figure 4.60 When the alert dialog box appears, click *Disable Tab* to remove the tab but leave its content on your computer.

Figure 4.61 When you disable *or* delete a selected tab (**Figure 4.59**), it no longer appears along the edge of the Clippings Palette.

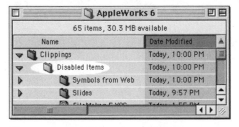

Figure 4.62 Disabling a tab puts it and its contents in AppleWorks's Disabled Items folder.

To disable a clipping tab:

1. Ctrl-click the tab you want to *disable* and choose *Delete Tab* from the drop-down menu (**Figure 4.59**).

2. When the alert dialog box appears, click *Disable Tab* (**Figure 4.60**). The selected tab will be removed from the Clippings Palette and placed in the *Disabled Items* folder within AppleWorks's main folder (**Figures 4.61** and **4.62**).

To delete a clipping tab:

1. Ctrl-click the tab you want to *delete* and choose *Delete Tab* from the drop-down menu (**Figure 4.59**).

2. When the alert dialog box appears, click *Move To Trash* (**Figure 4.63**). The tab and its contents will be removed from the Clippings Palette and placed in the Trash (**Figures 4.61** and **4.64**).

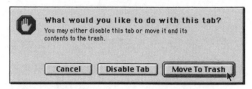

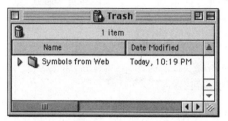

Figure 4.63 If you want to get rid of the tab and its contents, click *Move To Trash*.

Figure 4.64 *Deleting* a tab puts it in the Trash.

PART II

HANDLING TEXT IN APPLEWORKS

ENTERING AND EDITING TEXT

5

What could be simpler than text? You type and words appear on the screen. True enough. Still, AppleWorks gives you lots of control over turning that text into a good-looking document. From setting margins to adding line breaks, from searching your text to automatically inserting page numbers, there's plenty to learn. So read on.

Creating Word-processing Documents

Whenever you create a word-processing document, AppleWorks automatically sets the margins based on its default settings: a one-inch margin for the top, sides, and bottom. The text ruler's default setting is to show inches with eight subdivisions. These settings can easily be changed, though unfortunately only one document at a time. For information on adding columns, headers, and footnotes, see *Formatting Text* on page 117. For information on setting your document's page size, see *Printing AppleWorks Documents* on page 434.

To create a word-processing document:

1. Choose File > New > Word Processing (**Figure 5.1**).

   or

   Click the *Basic* tab in the Starting Points Palette and choose the *Word Processing* icon (**Figure 5.2**).

   or

   Use the keyboard command: ⌘N.

   A blank untitled document will appear, with *(WP)* in the title bar to indicate that it is an unsaved word-processing document (**Figure 5.3**).

3. Choose File > Save As (Shift⌘S) (**Figure 5.4**).

4. When the Save dialog box appears (**Figure 5.5**), type a title for the document into the *Name* window, navigate to the folder where you want it stored, and click *Save*. The document will be saved and Auto-Save will automatically save it from that point on. You're now ready to begin entering text into the document.

Figure 5.1 To create a word-processing document, choose File > New > Word Processing (⌘N).

Figure 5.2 You also can create a new word-processing document using the Starting Points' *Basic* tab.

Figure 5.3 The *(WP)* in the title bar indicates this is a word-processing document.

Figure 5.4 To save your document the first time, choose File > Save As (Shift⌘S).

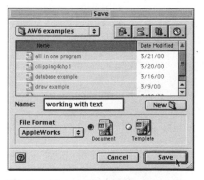

Figure 5.5 Type a title into the *Name* window and click *Save*.

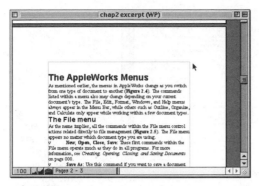

Figure 5.6 To change the settings for a document, first open it.

Figure 5.7 The second step in changing document settings is to choose Format > Document.

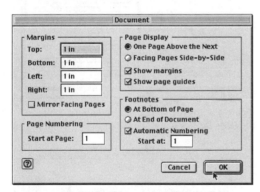

Figure 5.8 When the Document dialog box appears, use the *Margins* panel to set the margin widths.

Figure 5.9 To accommodate bindings, check the *Mirror Facing Pages* box and the *Left* and *Right* choices will become *Inside* and *Outside*.

To change document settings:

1. Open your word-processing document (**Figure 5.6**), then choose Format > Document (**Figure 5.7**).

2. When the Document dialog box appears (**Figure 5.8**), use the four text windows in the *Margins* panel to set your desired margin widths.

3. If your document will be in a binder, check the *Mirror Facing Pages* box within the *Margins* panel. The *Left* and *Right* choices will become *Inside* and *Outside*, enabling you to create a wider inside margin to accommodate the binding (**Figure 5.9**).

(continued)

CHANGING DOCUMENT SETTINGS

4. Use the *Page Display* panel to control whether pages are shown *One Page Above the Next* (vertically) (**Figure 5.10**) or as *Facing Pages Side-by-Side* (horizontally) (**Figure 5.11**).

5. If you want to hide the white area bordering your page (the margins) or the pale line denoting the margin (the page guide), uncheck the *Show margins* or *Show page guides* boxes in the *Page Display* panel.

6. Once you've made your choices, click *OK* and the changes will be applied to the active document (**Figure 5.12**).

✔ Tip

■ While each of the *Margins* text windows includes an abbreviation for the units being used (e.g., *in* for inches), don't worry about preserving that text (**Figure 5.8**). Just type in your numbers and AppleWorks will apply the proper unit based on your ruler settings (see following page).

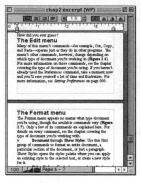

Figure 5.10 The *One Page Above the Next* choice in the *Page Display* panel shows pages vertically.

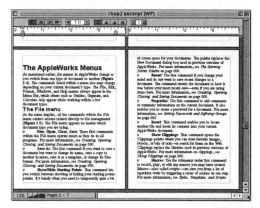

Figure 5.11 The *Facing Pages Side-by-Side* choice in the *Page Display* panel shows pages horizontally.

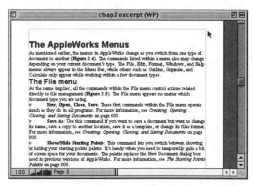

Figure 5.12 New margin settings applied to the same document that appears in Figure 5.6.

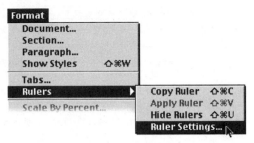

Figure 5.13 To change the text ruler settings, choose Format > Rulers > Ruler Settings.

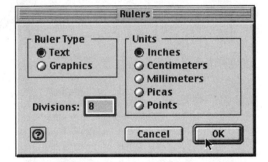

Figure 5.14 Click one of the radio buttons in the *Units* panel of the Rulers dialog box if you don't want to use the default *Inches*.

Figure 5.15 To hide the text ruler, choose Format > Rulers > Hide Rulers ((Shift)(⌘)(U)). Repeat the command to show it again.

To change the text ruler settings:

1. Choose Format > Rulers > Ruler Settings (**Figure 5.13**).

2. When the Rulers dialog box appears, click one of the radio buttons in the *Units* panel if you don't want to use the default *Inches* (**Figure 5.14**).

3. If you want to change the number of divisions for your chosen unit of measurement, enter a number in the *Divisions* text window.

4. Once you've made your choice, click *OK* and the active document's text ruler will reflect the change.

✔ Tip

■ Changing the ruler settings only affects the active document. Any other word-processing documents, whether open or closed, must be changed individually.

To hide or show the text ruler:

◆ To hide the normally visible text ruler, choose Format > Rulers > Hide Rulers ((Shift)(⌘)(U)) (**Figure 5.15**). The ruler will disappear.

◆ To show the text ruler, choose Format > Rulers > Show Rulers (also (Shift)(⌘)(U)) and the ruler will reappear.

USING THE TEXT RULER

Entering and Editing Text

Entering text in AppleWorks works similarly to typing in any word-processing program. When your typing reaches the right edge of the document window, the text automatically wraps to the next line. Similarly, you use the cursor to select text, which then can be moved or copied or pasted elsewhere.

To enter text:

1. Click your cursor where you want to enter text on the page. A vertical bar will mark the insertion spot.

2. Start typing and the text will appear at the insertion spot (**Figure 5.16**).

To move the text cursor:

1. Use your mouse or the arrow keys to move the cursor where you want to insert text. An I-beam will mark the cursor's screen location (top, **Figure 5.17**).

2. Click at the insertion point and the vertical bar will move to that spot (bottom, **Figure 5.17**). You're ready to begin typing at the new spot.

✔ Tip

■ If you see an arrow instead of an I-beam, you're not in word-processing mode. Click the text tool in the Tools Palette, then click back inside your document and the cursor will appear as an I-beam (**Figure 5.18**).

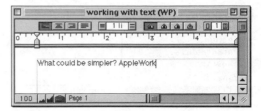

Figure 5.16 A vertical bar marks your insertion spot in the text.

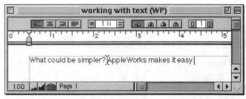

Figure 5.17 Within a word-processing document an I-beam replaces your cursor arrow (top). Click where you want to add text and the insertion bar will move to the new spot (bottom).

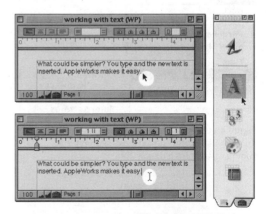

Figure 5.18 If your cursor appears as an arrow, you're not in word-processing mode (top). Click the text tool in the Tools Palette (right), click again in the document, and the cursor will be an I-beam (bottom).

Figure 5.19 To select text, drag your cursor to highlight it.

Figure 5.20 To delete the text, select it, and press [Delete], and the selection will be cut.

Figure 5.21 To move text, click and drag the highlighted text to its new location.

Figure 5.22 When you release the cursor, the text will move to the new location.

To select text:

1. Position your cursor at the beginning or end of the text you want to select.

2. Click and drag your cursor to select the text, which will become highlighted (**Figure 5.19**).

3. You now can copy the selected text (⌘C) or cut it (⌘X) for pasting elsewhere (⌘V).

To delete text:

1. Position your cursor at the beginning or end of the text you want to select.

2. Click and drag your cursor to select the text, which will become highlighted (**Figure 5.19**).

3. Press [Delete] and the text will be deleted (**Figure 5.20**).

To move text:

1. Select the text you want to move.

2. Click and drag the highlighted text to its new location (**Figure 5.21**).

3. Release the cursor and the text will be moved to the new spot (**Figure 5.22**).

✔ Tip

■ You can also use keyboard commands to accomplish the same thing: Select the text, cut it (⌘X), click where you want to move it, and paste it in place (⌘V).

SELECTING, DELETING, MOVING TEXT

To undo an action:

◆ Choose Edit > Undo or press ⌘Z. The previous action will be undone.

To redo an action:

◆ Choose Edit > Redo or again press ⌘Z (**Figure 5.23**). The previous action will be reapplied.

✔ Tip

■ Both the *Undo* and *Redo* choices under the Edit menu change, depending on the previous action (**Figure 5.24**).

Figure 5.23 To redo an action, choose Edit > Redo or press ⌘Z.

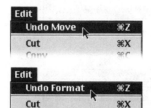

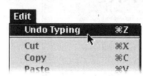

Figure 5.24 The *Undo* choices under the Edit menu change, depending on the previous action.

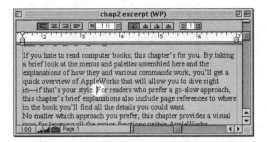

Figure 5.25 To add a paragraph, click in the text where you want the break to appear.

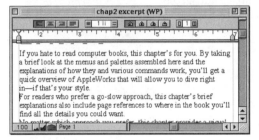

Figure 5.26 Press (Return) and a paragraph break will be inserted in the text.

To add a line break to text:

◆ Click your cursor where you want a line break to appear in the text and press (Shift)(Return). A line break will be inserted.

✔ Tip

■ To remove a line break, place the cursor at the beginning of the line right after the break and press (Delete). The break will be removed.

To add a paragraph:

1. Click your cursor where you want a paragraph break to appear in the text (**Figure 5.25**).

2. Press (Return) and a paragraph break will be inserted into the text (**Figure 5.26**).

Showing line break and paragraph marks

Depending on your work style, AppleWorks lets you display or hide the symbols that mark the location of line breaks and paragraphs within the text.

To show or hide line break and paragraph marks:

◆ Press ⌘;. The text will display all line break and paragraph return marks (**Figure 5.27**). To hide the marks, repeat the keyboard command and the marks will disappear.

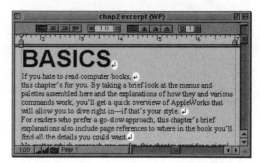

Figure 5.27 To show line breaks and paragraph marks in your text, press ⌘;.

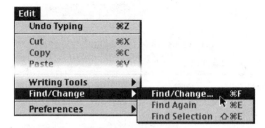

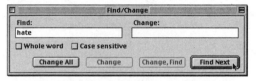

Figure 5.28 To find or replace text, first choose Edit > Find/Change > Find/Change (⌘F).

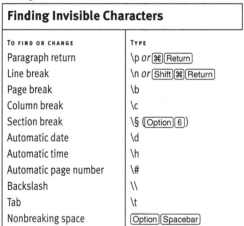

Figure 5.29 In the Find/Change dialog box, type into the *Find* text window the word you're seeking.

Table 5.1

Finding Invisible Characters	
TO FIND OR CHANGE	**TYPE**
Paragraph return	\p *or* ⌘ Return
Line break	\n *or* Shift ⌘ Return
Page break	\b
Column break	\c
Section break	\§ (Option 6)
Automatic date	\d
Automatic time	\h
Automatic page number	\#
Backslash	\\
Tab	\t
Nonbreaking space	Option Spacebar

Finding and Replacing Text

Whether you use the Find Text command by itself to hunt down a particular word or combine it with the Replace Text command to fix a document-wide error, these two commands are word-processing workhorses.

To find text:

1. Choose Edit > Find/Change > Find/Change (⌘F) (**Figure 5.28**).

2. When the Find/Change dialog box appears, type into the *Find* text window the word you're seeking (**Figure 5.29**).

3. Check the *Whole word* box if you want to find individual words (e.g., *hate*) rather than other words that may contain that text (e.g., *hateful*). Check the *Case sensitive* box if that will help you narrow your search.

4. Once you've made your choices, click *Find Next*. The word will be highlighted in your document. You can then choose to edit or replace it.

✔ Tip

- Don't limit yourself to just looking for words. You can use the Find command to hunt down punctuation marks or even invisible characters, such as paragraph returns. For more information, see **Table 5.1**.

To replace text:

1. Choose Edit > Find/Change > Find/Change (⌘F) (**Figure 5.28**).

2. When the Find/Change dialog box appears, type into the *Find* text window the word you're looking for (**Figure 5.29**).

3. Check the *Whole word* box if you want to find individual words (e.g., *hate*) rather than other words that may contain that text (e.g., *hateful*). Check the *Case sensitive* box if that will help you narrow your search.

4. Type the new word you want to use into the *Change* text window and click *Find Next* (**Figure 5.30**).

5. When the search item is found and high-lighted in your document, you can choose to skip it and look for the next instance by clicking *Find Next* again; make the replacement and move to the next instance by clicking *Change, Find*; replace only that instance by clicking *Change*; or automatically change every instance by clicking *Change All* (**Figure 5.31**). Click the button of your choice and the changes will be made.

✔ Tip

■ If you're certain you want to automatically find and change every instance of an item, click *Change All* in step 3. The changes, which cannot be undone, will be made without asking you to confirm each replacement.

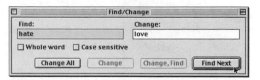

Figure 5.30 Type the new word you want to use into the *Change* text window and click *Find Next*.

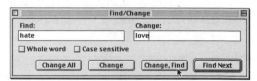

Figure 5.31 Once the search item is found, the Find/Change dialog box offers you a choice of four different actions.

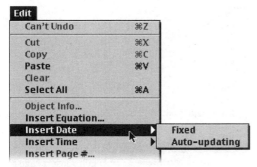

Figure 5.32 To insert a date, choose Edit > Insert Date and choose *Fixed* or *Auto-updating* from the submenu.

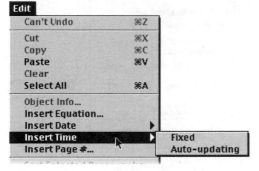

Figure 5.33 To insert a time, choose Edit > Insert Time and choose *Fixed* or *Auto-updating* from the submenu.

Inserting Dates, Times, and Page Numbers

AppleWorks includes a handy way to automatically insert the date, time, or page number. You have the option of having the date and time fixed or automatically updated. You also have your choice of five date formats. For more information, see *Setting Preferences* on page 453.

To insert a date:

1. Click where you want the date to appear in your text.

2. Choose Edit > Insert Date and choose *Fixed* or *Auto-updating* from the submenu (**Figure 5.32**). The current date will be inserted. If you choose *Fixed*, the date will not change again. If you choose *Auto-updating*, the date will change each time the document is opened.

To insert a time:

1. Click where you want the time to appear in your text.

2. Choose Edit > Insert Time and choose *Fixed* or *Auto-updating* from the submenu (**Figure 5.33**). The current time will be inserted. If you choose *Fixed*, the time will not change again. If you choose *Auto-updating*, the time will change each time the document is opened.

To insert a page number:

1. Click where you want the page number to appear in your text.

2. Choose Edit > Insert Page # (**Figure 5.34**).

3. When the Insert Page Number dialog box appears, use the *Representation* pop-up menu to choose a number format, and click *OK* (**Figure 5.35**). The number will be inserted and will change as you add or delete pages from the document.

✔ Tips

■ If you want to insert a *non-changing* page number, press (Option) during step 2.

■ If you want a page number to appear on every page, you'll need to first create a header or footer and insert the page number marker there. For more information, see *Creating Headers, Footers, and Footnotes* on page 140.

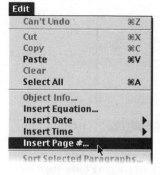

Figure 5.34 To insert a page number, choose Edit > Insert Page #.

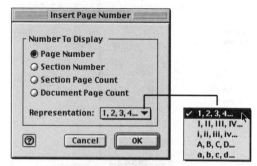

Figure 5.35 Use the pop-up menu in the Insert Page Number dialog box to choose a number format.

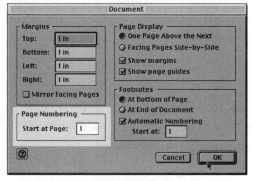

Figure 5.36 To set a starting page number for a document, choose Format > Document.

Figure 5.37 Use the *Start at Page* text window to set your document's beginning page number.

Setting where page numbering starts

Your document's page numbers do not have to start with "1," a handy option if you're creating a sequentially numbered series of documents.

To set a starting page number:

1. With your word-processing document open, choose Format > Document (**Figure 5.36**).

2. When the Document dialog box appears, use the *Start at Page* text window in the Page Numbering area to set your beginning page number (**Figure 5.37**). Click *OK* and the numbering sequence will be applied to the document.

✔ Tip

■ AppleWorks also lets you divide documents into sections, each of which can have its own numbering sequence. For more information, see *To number sections* on page 133.

Inserting Equations

AppleWorks includes a separate application called the Equation Editor. The editor doesn't create functioning formulas. It just lets you set the specially formatted text sometimes needed in a formula, such as fractions. To create working formulas see *Creating Spreadsheets* on page 203 or *Defining Fields* on page 262.

To insert an equation:

1. Click in the AppleWorks document where you want an equation to appear (**Figure 5.38**).

2. Choose Edit > Insert Equation (**Figure 5.39**).

3. When the Equation Editor appears, use the drop-down menus to choose an option (top, **Figure 5.40**). Release your cursor and the option—with placeholders—will appear in the editor's window.

4. Type the numbers or characters you need into the placeholders (bottom, **Figure 5.40**).

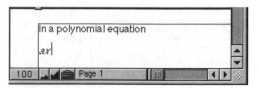

Figure 5.38 Click in the AppleWorks document where you want to add an equation element.

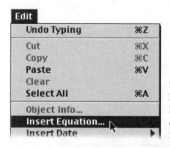

Figure 5.39 To insert an equation in your text, choose Edit > Insert Equation.

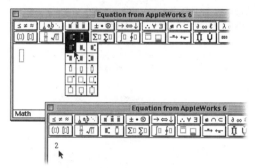

Figure 5.40 Use the Equation Editor's drop-down menus to choose a format option (top), which will be inserted into the editor's window (bottom).

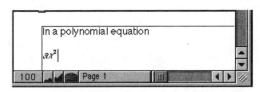

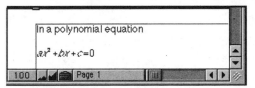

Figure 5.41 When you close the Equation Editor, the equation format appears in the AppleWorks document (top), where you can finish entering the rest of the equation (bottom).

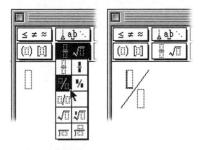

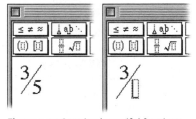

Figure 5.42 Creating beautiful fractions is as simple as picking a format from the drop-down menus and replacing the placeholders with your numbers (clockwise from top left).

5. Close the Equation Editor and the option chosen in step 3 will appear in the AppleWorks document (top, **Figure 5.41**). Continue using the editor until you finish building your formula (bottom, **Figure 5.41**).

✔ Tips

■ You don't have to be a rocket scientist to find the Equation Editor useful: It creates typographically beautiful fractions (**Figure 5.42**).

■ Unfortunately, AppleWorks does not include any pop-up tips to explain the functions in the Equation Editor's main window. If you need help, ask a math major.

FORMATTING TEXT

In formatting text, you'll find that the text ruler offers a handy way to quickly apply many of the most commonly used text commands discussed in the following pages (**Figure 6.1**). If the text ruler is not visible, choose Format > Rulers > Show Rulers. Also remember that AppleWorks includes button icons for most text commands (**Figure 6.2**). To add text-related icons to the Button Bar, see *Customizing palette icons* on page 35.

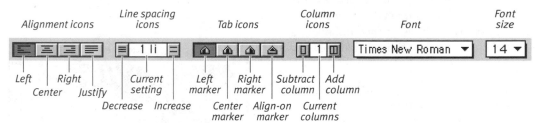

Figure 6.1 The text ruler lets you quickly apply many of the most commonly used text commands.

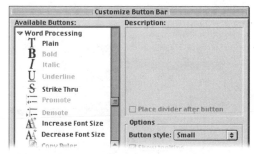

Figure 6.2 AppleWorks also includes icons for the most common text commands. You can add any of them to the Button Bar.

Changing Fonts and Text Styles

AppleWorks includes all the standard font and style tools that you'd expect to find in a dedicated word-processing program. By the way, AppleWorks automatically adds 10 additional fonts to your computer when you first install the program. If that's not enough for you, 50 fonts in all are included on the installation CD. For more information, see *Installing AppleWorks* on page 443.

To change fonts:

1. Select the text whose font you want to change (**Figure 6.3**).

2. Choose Text > Font and choose a font from the submenu (**Figure 6.4**). Release your cursor and the new font will be applied to the selected text (**Figure 6.5**).

✔ Tips

- You also can change the selected text by using the Font menu in the text ruler or Ctrl-clicking, choosing *Font*, and making a choice from the submenu that appears (**Figure 6.6**).

- If the font submenu does not appear when you choose Text > Font, you probably have a type utility program that conflicts with AppleWorks. Try turning off your font programs one at a time until you determine which one conflicts with AppleWorks.

Figure 6.3 To change a font, select the text you want to change.

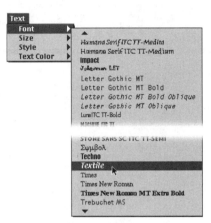

Figure 6.4 Choose Text > Font and choose a font from the submenu. The submenu's length will depend on how many fonts you have installed.

Figure 6.5 Once you've chosen a new font, it's applied to the selected text.

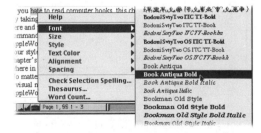

Figure 6.6 You also can change the selected text's font by Ctrl-clicking.

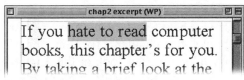

Figure 6.7 To change text size, first select the text.

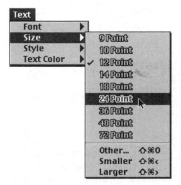

Figure 6.8 Choose Text > Size and pick a size from the submenu.

Figure 6.9 The selected text after the size change has been applied.

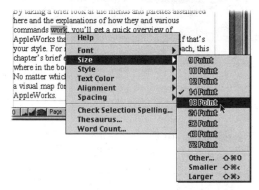

Figure 6.10 You also can change the selected text's size by [Ctrl]-clicking.

To change text size:

1. Select the text whose size you want to change (**Figure 6.7**).

2. Choose Text > Size and choose a size from the submenu (**Figure 6.8**). Release your cursor and the new size will be applied to the selected text (**Figure 6.9**).

✔ Tip

■ You also can change the selected text by [Ctrl]-clicking, choosing *Size*, and making a choice from the submenu that appears (**Figure 6.10**).

To change text style:

1. Select the text whose style you want to change (**Figure 6.11**).

2. Choose Text > Style and pick a style from the submenu (**Figure 6.12**). Release your cursor and the new style will be applied to the selected text (**Figure 6.13**).

✔ Tips

- You also can change the selected text by Ctrl-clicking, choosing *Style*, and making a choice from the submenu that appears (**Figure 6.14**).

- You also can change the selected text by clicking one of the *Bold*, *Italic* or *Underline* icons in the Button Bar (**Figure 6.15**).

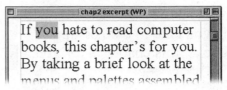

Figure 6.11 To change text style, first select the text you want to change.

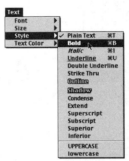

Figure 6.12 Choose Text > Style and pick a style from the submenu.

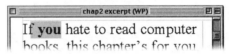

Figure 6.13 The selected text after the new style has been applied.

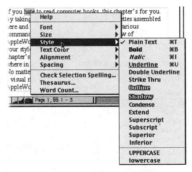

Figure 6.14 You also can change the selected text's style by Ctrl-clicking.

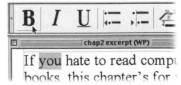

Figure 6.15 You also can change the selected text by clicking one of the icons in the Button Bar.

Figure 6.16 To apply a new color, first select the text you want to change.

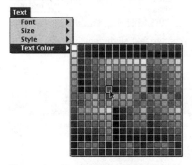

Figure 6.17 Choose Text > Text Color and select a color from the palette that appears.

Figure 6.18 The selected text after the new color has been applied.

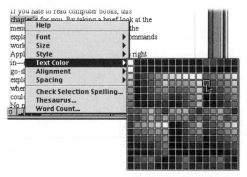

Figure 6.19 You also can change the selected text's color by Ctrl-clicking.

To change text color:

1. Select the text whose color you want to change (**Figure 6.16**).

2. Choose Text > Text Color and select a color from the palette that appears (**Figure 6.17**). Release your cursor over the color you want and it will be applied to the selected text (**Figure 6.18**).

✔ Tip

■ You also can change the selected text by Ctrl-clicking, choosing *Text Color*, and making a choice from the palette that appears (**Figure 6.19**).

To change text alignment:

1. Select at least one character or word within the paragraph you want to realign.

2. (Ctrl)-click, choose *Alignment*, and make a choice from the submenu that appears (**Figure 6.20**). Release your cursor and the new alignment will be applied.

✔ Tip

■ You also can change the alignment by clicking anywhere in the paragraph and then selecting one of the alignment icons in the text ruler (**Figure 6.21**).

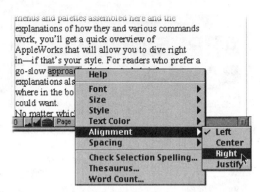

Figure 6.20 To change text alignment, (Ctrl)-click, choose *Alignment*, and make a choice from the submenu.

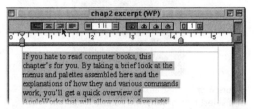

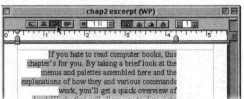

Figure 6.21 Since you can click anywhere in the paragraph, it's faster to change alignment using the icons in the text ruler.

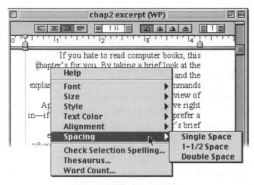

Figure 6.22 To change line spacing, Ctrl-click, choose *Spacing*, and make a choice from the submenu.

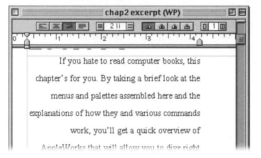

Figure 6.23 The selected text after the line spacing has been increased.

Changing line spacing

AppleWorks applies line spacing to an entire paragraph, which means you cannot change just three lines in a six-line paragraph. Instead, the change will apply to the whole paragraph.

To change line spacing:

1. If you want to change the line spacing in a single paragraph, click anywhere within the paragraph. To change more than one paragraph, use the cursor to select all of the text you want to change.

2. Click one of the line spacing icons in the text ruler to decrease or increase the spacing. Depending on your choice in step 1, the change will be applied to the single paragraph or to the text in all the paragraphs you selected.

✔ Tip

■ If you have highlighted text with your cursor, you also can Ctrl-click, choose *Spacing*, and make a choice from the submenu that appears (**Figure 6.22**). Release your cursor and the new line spacing will be applied to only that paragraph (**Figure 6.23**).

CHANGING TEXT ALIGNMENT AND LINE SPACING

Formatting Paragraphs

While you can use the paragraph indentation controls or the various text ruler icons to change individual aspects of a paragraph, AppleWorks also offers a way to change them all at once.

To set paragraph indentation:

1. Make sure the text ruler is visible (Format > Rulers > Show Rulers).

2. If you want to set indentation for a single paragraph, click anywhere in the paragraph. If you want to set indentation for several paragraphs of text, use your cursor to select them.

3. Click and drag any of the four indentation controls in the text ruler (top, middle, **Figure 6.24**). Release your cursor and the changes will be applied (bottom, **Figure 6.24**).

✔ Tip

- While the far-left indentation may look like a single control, it's actually two. Dragging the *top part* moves only the left margin; dragging the bottom part moves the margin *and* the first-line indentation.

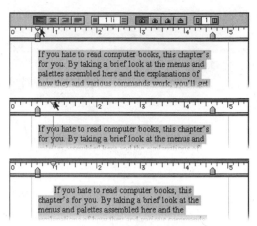

Figure 6.24 To change a paragraph's indentation, click on any of the four icons (top), drag it to a new spot (middle), and release the cursor (bottom).

Figure 6.25 To change multiple settings in a paragraph, click anywhere in the paragraph and choose Format > Paragraph.

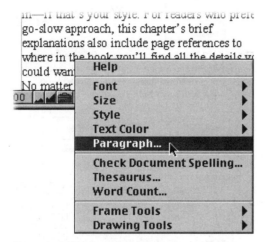

Figure 6.26 If you've selected a *single* paragraph, you also can change its settings by Ctrl-clicking and choosing *Paragraph*.

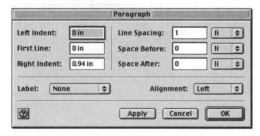

Figure 6.27 Use the *Left Indent, First Line* [Indent], or *Right Indent* text windows to change your paragraph's indentation.

To change multiple settings in a paragraph:

1. If you want to change the settings for a single paragraph, click anywhere in the paragraph. If you want to change the settings for several paragraphs of text, use your cursor to select them.

2. Choose Format > Paragraph (**Figure 6.25**).

   or

   If you've selected a *single* paragraph, you also can Ctrl-click and choose *Paragraph* (**Figure 6.26**).

3. When the Paragraph dialog box appears (**Figure 6.27**), enter new numbers to change the *Left Indent, First Line* [Indent], or *Right Indent.*

   (continued)

FORMATTING PARAGRAPHS

4. If you want to change the spacing between lines, enter a new number in the *Line Spacing* text window or select a new unit of measurement using the drop-down menu (**Figure 6.28**).

5. Enter new numbers in the *Space Before* or *Space After* text windows if you want to increase or decrease the white space above or below the paragraph. Again, use the drop-down menus to change the units used if you like (*Points* offers the smallest increments).

6. If in step 3 you chose to indent the first line, you can use the *Label* drop-down to add a symbol to mark each new paragraph (**Figure 6.28**).

7. If you want to preview the changes, click *Apply* (**Figure 6.29**). Once you're happy with your choices, click *OK*.

✔ Tip

■ If you change the settings in any of the indent text windows, do not try to preserve the "in" following the number. If you don't just delete it when you type in a new number, AppleWorks may complain that you've not entered an acceptable number. It shouldn't matter—but it does.

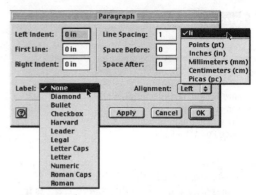

Figure 6.28 The drop-down menus for *Line Spacing*, *Space Before,* and *Space After* change the measuring units. The *Label* drop-down menu lets you mark paragraphs with a symbol.

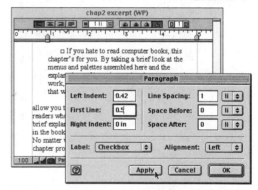

Figure 6.29 If you want to preview all your paragraph's changes, click *Apply.*

FORMATTING PARAGRAPHS

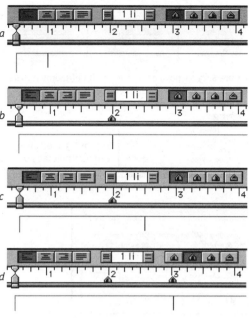

Figure 6.30 Default tab stops are set every half inch (a), but you can add a left margin tab to override that (b). However, half-inch tabs remain to the *right* of your custom tab (c), until you add more custom tabs (d).

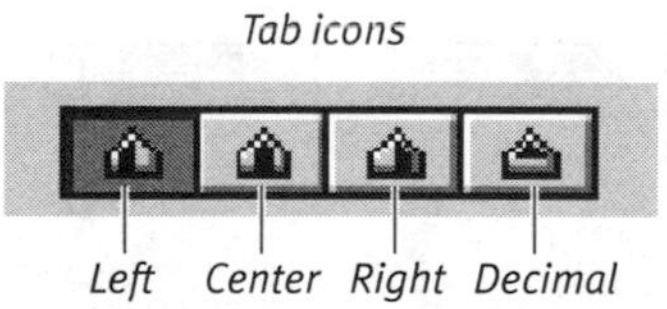

Tab icons

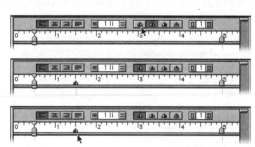

Left   Center   Right   Decimal

Figure 6.31
The text ruler includes four custom tab markers.

Figure 6.32 To set a custom tab, click one in the text ruler (top), drag it into position (middle), and release the cursor (bottom).

Setting Tabs

By default, AppleWorks sets tab stops at every half inch, as you'll see if you press [Tab] (a, **Figure 6.30**). If you place a left-tab marker two inches from the left margin, however, pressing [Tab] will automatically move your text cursor to that spot, skipping past what had been the first default position (b, **Figure 6.30**). To the *right* of your custom tab the every-half-inch tabs remain (c, **Figure 6.30**)—unless you add another custom tab (d, **Figure 6.30**).

To set a tab:

1. Make sure the text ruler is visible (Format > Rulers > Show Rulers).

2. If you want to apply the tabs to existing text, click anywhere in the paragraph; otherwise skip to step 3.

3. Click any one of the four tab icons (**Figure 6.31**), drag it to where you want it in the text ruler, and release your cursor. The new tab will be added (**Figure 6.32**).

✔ Tips

■ Tabs are applied to an entire paragraph. You can, however, create a different set of tab stops for each paragraph if you wish.

■ The decimal tab lets you align numbers by their decimal points, useful for arranging numbers in columns.

To reposition a tab:

◆ Click on the tab marker you want to reposition, drag it to a new spot on the text ruler, and the marker will move to its new position (**Figure 6.33**).

or

◆ Choose Format > Tabs (**Figure 6.34**) or just double-click any tab. Both actions will open a Tab dialog box for that particular tab (**Figure 6.35**). Type a new number into the *Position* text window or choose another tab type in the *Alignment* panel. Click *Apply* if you want to check how the new position looks, or *OK* if you're sure of your choice. The tab will move to the new position or change its type to reflect your choice.

To remove a tab:

◆ Click on the tab marker you want to remove, drag it off the text ruler, and the marker will disappear (**Figure 6.36**).

Creating tab fillers

Tab fillers, sometimes called tab leaders, enable you to have a repeating character fill in the space preceding a tab entry (**Figure 6.37**). They help readers match up items in widely separated columns, such as table of content entries.

To create a tab filler:

1. Double-click on the tab marker for which you want to create a filler.

2. When the Tab dialog box appears, select a radio button in the *Fill* panel and click *OK* (**Figure 6.38**). The fill character will appear in the area preceding the tab marker (**Figure 6.37**).

Figure 6.33 To move a tab, click on it (left), drag it to its new position (middle), and release the cursor (right).

Figure 6.34 You also can reformat tabs by choosing Format > Tabs.

Figure 6.35 To change a selected tab, make another choice in the *Alignment* panel or enter a new number in the *Position* text window.

Figure 6.36 To remove a tab, click on it (left), drag it off the text ruler (middle), and release the cursor (right).

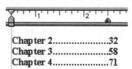

Figure 6.37 Tab fillers let you repeat a character to make matching column entries easier for the reader.

Figure 6.38 To create a tab filler, double-click the tab and use the *Fill* panel to choose a character to repeat.

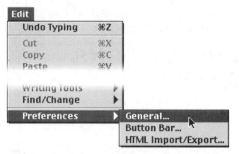

Figure 6.39 To show normally invisible characters, choose Edit > Preferences > General.

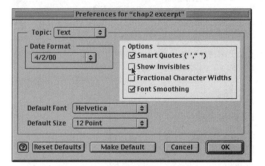

Figure 6.40 Check the *Show Invisibles* box within the *Options* panel, then click *OK*.

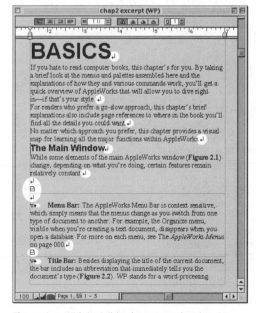

Figure 6.41 With invisible characters showing, it's easier to spot line, paragraph, and section breaks.

Creating Sections

Creating sections within your document enables you to give it different characteristics (such as columns) from adjacent portions of the document. AppleWorks also lets you number sections separately from your pages.

Sections give you intermediate formatting units that are bigger than paragraphs and smaller than entire documents. By defining sections within your document, you can quickly change things like alignment or line spacing for large blocks of text. Just remember that if you later merge two sections into a single section, the formatting within the old sections remains unchanged. In that sense, sections are no different from page breaks: If you remove a page break, the formatting on either side of the old page break does not change.

Showing or hiding invisible characters

Depending on what you're doing with a document, you may find it helpful to see normally invisible characters such as line breaks, paragraph markers, and section breaks.

To show invisible characters:

1. Choose Edit > Preferences > General (**Figure 6.39**).

2. When the document's Preferences dialog box appears, check the *Show Invisibles* box within the *Options* panel (**Figure 6.40**).

3. Click *OK* and once the dialog box closes the previously invisible characters will appear within the document (**Figure 6.41**).

To insert a section break:

1. Click your cursor where you want to start a new section (**Figure 6.42**).

2. Choose Format > Insert Section Break ((Option)(Enter)) (**Figure 6.43**).

3. A section break will be added to the document, indicated by a light gray horizontal line. Repeat steps 1–2 to mark the end of the section (**Figure 6.44**).

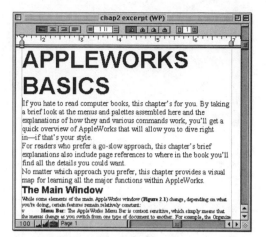

Figure 6.42 To insert a section break, click in the text where you want to start a new section.

Figure 6.43 Choose Format > Insert Section Break ((Option)(Enter)) to apply a break.

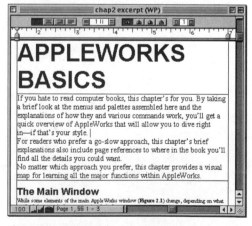

Figure 6.44 Light gray horizontal lines mark the breaks between sections.

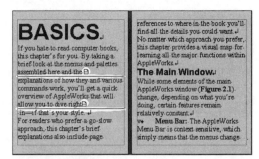

Figure 6.45 Click in the section whose style you want to change...

Figure 6.46 ...then choose Format > Section.

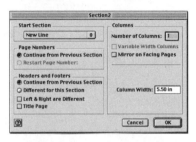

Figure 6.47 When the Section dialog box appears, *New Line* appears as the default section break in the *Start Section* panel.

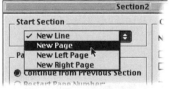

Figure 6.48 Use the *Start Section* drop-down menu to choose a new break style.

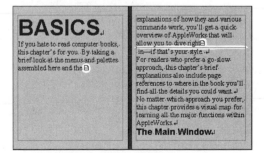

Figure 6.49 Changing the break style from *New Line* to *New Page* only affects the selected section.

Changing the type of section break

By default, new sections start on a new line. However, you can have a new section start on a new page or even specify that it start with a new left- or right-hand page. And, if you like, you can set a different type of break for any section.

To change the type of section break:

1. Click in the section where you want to change the type of break (**Figure 6.45**).

2. Choose Format > Section (**Figure 6.46**).

3. When the Section dialog box appears (**Figure 6.47**), use the *Start Section* drop-down menu to make a new choice (**Figure 6.48**).

4. Click *OK* and the new type of break will be applied to the current section and no others (**Figure 6.49**).

CREATING SECTIONS

To remove a section break:

1. Click your cursor at the very beginning of the section *following* the section break you want to eliminate (left, **Figure 6.50**).

2. Press [Delete]. The section break will be deleted and the two sections will become one (right, **Figure 6.50**). Both sections will retain their previous formatting, however.

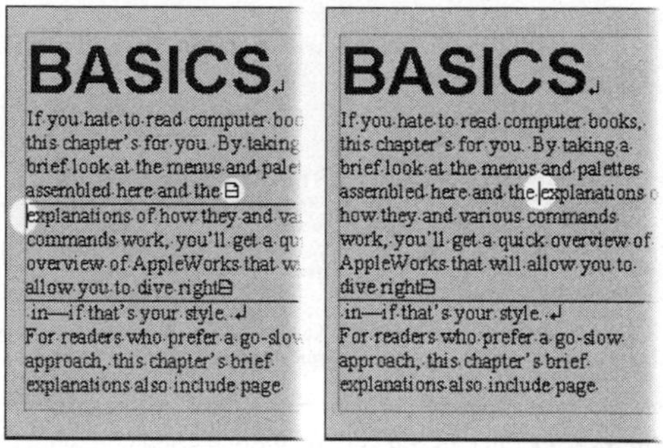

Figure 6.50 To remove a section break, click right after the section break you want to eliminate (left). Press [Delete], and the section break will be deleted (right).

Figure 6.51 To number sections, start with a document in which you've already created your sections.

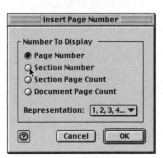

Figure 6.52 Click in the first section you want numbered and choose Edit > Insert Page #.

Figure 6.53 When the Insert Page Number dialog box appears, select *Section Number*.

Figure 6.54 Once you're done, the sections will be labeled in sequence.

Numbering sections

AppleWorks lets you number sections independently of a document's page numbers, which can be handy in formatting certain documents.

To number sections:

1. Start with a document in which you've already created your sections (**Figure 6.51**).

2. Click in the first section you want numbered and choose Edit > Insert Page # (**Figure 6.52**).

3. When the Insert Page Number dialog box appears, select *Section Number* (**Figure 6.53**).

4. If you want to use something other than standard numerals, use the *Representation* drop-down menu to choose another format.

5. Click *OK* and a number will be inserted into the current section.

6. Repeat steps 2–5 for every section you want to number. When you're done, the sections will be labeled in sequence (**Figure 6.54**).

✔ Tip

■ It would be nice if AppleWorks could automatically number all the sections in a document, but no such luck. Maybe in the next version.

Changing section attributes

AppleWorks makes it easy for you to change your mind about your settings for sections, columns, page numbers, or headers and footers. Use the Format > Section command to change a section's attributes any time.

To change section attributes:

1. Click anywhere within a section and choose Format > Section (**Figure 6.55**).

2. When the Section dialog box appears (**Figure 6.56**), use the *Start Section*, *Page Numbers*, *Headers and Footers*, or *Columns* panels to make your changes.

3. Once you make your changes, click *OK* and they will be applied to your document.

Figure 6.55 To change a section's attributes, click in the section and choose Format > Section.

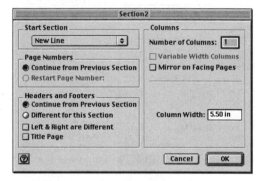

Figure 6.56 Once the Section dialog box appears, you can use the various panels to change multiple attributes for that section.

Figure 6.57 To divide a section into equal-width columns, click the add-column icon once.

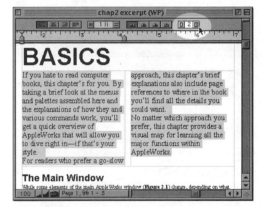

Figure 6.58 After clicking the add-column icon, the section will be divided into two equal-width columns—indicated by the "2."

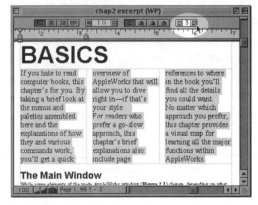

Figure 6.59 Click the add-column icon again, and the section divides into three equal-width columns.

Creating Columns

While you can format an entire document into columns, dividing it into different sections first will give you far more flexibility. For example, one section could have three columns of the same width while the next section could have two uneven columns. Used creatively, this ability lets you create a variety of great-looking layouts.

To add equal-width text columns:

1. Click anywhere in the text section to which you want columns applied and click the add-column icon once (**Figure 6.57**). The text will be divided equally into two columns, as indicated by the "2" in the middle of the text ruler's column icons (**Figure 6.58**).

2. To divide the text into three columns , click the add-column icon again and another column will be added (**Figure 6.59**). You can continue adding columns up to a maximum of nine columns.

✔ Tip

■ Unless you've broken your document into separate sections, the column formatting will be applied to the entire document. For more information, see *To insert a section break* on page 130.

To remove text columns:

1. Click anywhere in the text where you want to remove a column.

2. Click the remove-column icon (the left icon of the three column icons) in the text ruler (**Figure 6.60**). The number of text columns will be reduced by one (e.g., two columns will become one column, four columns will become three) (**Figure 6.61**).

3. Repeat step 2 until you've removed as many columns as you need.

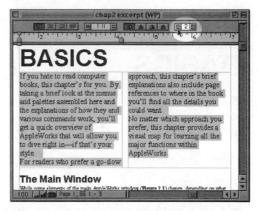

Figure 6.60 To remove text columns, click the icon on the left side of the text window displaying the number of columns.

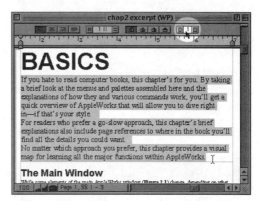

Figure 6.61 After removing the second column, the text reflows into a single column.

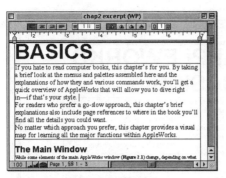

Figure 6.62 To add *unequal* text columns, first click anywhere in the section you want to change.

Figure 6.63 Choose Format > Section to create unequal text columns.

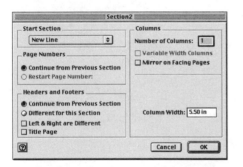

Figure 6.64 Once the Section dialog box appears, use the *Number of Columns* text window to set how many columns will be created.

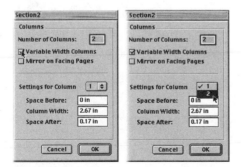

Figure 6.65 Left: Check the *Variable Width Columns* box and use the *Settings for Column* panel to set the first column. Right: Use the *Settings for Column* drop-down menu to switch to the next column and use the text windows to set its width and spacings.

To add unequal text columns:

1. Click anywhere within the targeted text (**Figure 6.62**).

2. Choose Format > Section (**Figure 6.63**) and the Section dialog box will appear (**Figure 6.64**).

3. Type how many columns you want into the *Number of Columns* text window and check the *Variable Width Columns* box (left, **Figure 6.65**).

4. In the *Settings for Column* section, use the *Space Before*, *Column Width*, and *Space After* text windows to set the width of your first column (left, **Figure 6.65**).

5. Once you're done setting your first column's width use the *Settings for Column* pop-up menu to select the second column (right, **Figure 6.65**).

(continued)

CREATING UNEVEN COLUMNS

6. Now use the *Space Before*, *Column Width*, and *Space After* text windows to set your second column's width.

7. Repeat steps 5–6 for however many columns you created. When you're done, click *OK* and the settings will be applied to the current section (**Figure 6.66**).

✔ Tips

■ If you want to resize the columns after they've been created, you'll have to reopen the Section dialog box. However, you can adjust the margins within each paragraph. For more information, see *To change multiple settings in a paragraph* on page 125.

■ You can use this same technique to create equal width columns but it's much easier to do that with the text ruler's column icons.

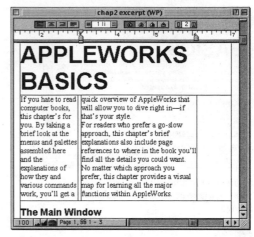

Figure 6.66 Creating uneven columns gives you layout options not available if you just stick to even widths.

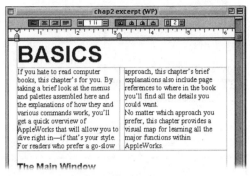

Figure 6.67 Before inserting a column break, text fills each column before flowing to the next.

Figure 6.68 To add a column break, choose Format > Insert Column Break ([Enter]).

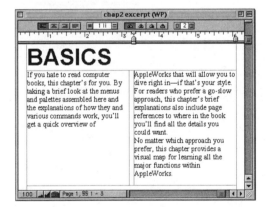

Figure 6.69 The column break bumps the text after "overview of" into the next column.

Inserting column breaks

Inevitably, there will be times when your text may break awkwardly across columns. By manually adding a column break, you can create a more natural text flow or a particular layout.

To add a column break:

1. Click your cursor where you want the text to flow into the next column (**Figure 6.67**).

2. Choose Format > Insert Column Break ([Enter]) (**Figure 6.68**). The text after where you clicked your cursor will be forced into the next column (**Figure 6.69**).

INSERTING COLUMN BREAKS

Creating Headers, Footers, and Footnotes

AppleWorks offers one of the easiest set of controls around for creating headers, footers, and footnotes. You can quickly add standard headers or footers to every page. Of, if you like, you can create different headers and footers for your document's first page and even- or odd-numbered pages.

To insert a header:

1. With your document open, choose Format > Insert Header (**Figure 6.70**).

2. Once the header appears in the document, you can add text, page numbers, or even graphics to the area (**Figure 6.71**).

✔ Tip

■ You also can insert fixed or auto-updating dates, times, or page numbers into headers or footers. For more information, see *Inserting Dates, Times, and Page Numbers* on page 111.

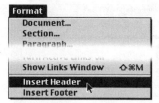

Figure 6.70 To insert a header, choose Format > Insert Header.

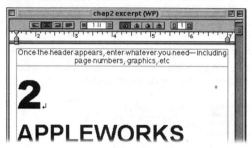

Figure 6.71 Once the header is inserted, you can add text, page numbers, or graphics.

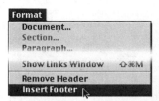

Figure 6.72 To insert a footer, choose Format > Insert Footer.

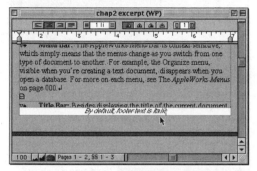

Figure 6.73 Just like headers, footers will accept text, automatic page numbers, or graphics.

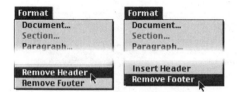

Figure 6.74 Choose Format > Remove Header or Format > Remove Footer and the selected area will be deleted.

To insert a footer:

1. With your document open, choose Format > Insert Footer (**Figure 6.72**).

2. Once the footer appears in the document, you can add text, page numbers, or even graphics to the area (**Figure 6.73**).

✔ Tip

■ You can easily change the default style of footers or headers. For more information, see *Using and Changing Styles* on page 170.

To remove a header or footer:

◆ Click within the header or footer you want to eliminate and choose Format > Remove Header or Format > Remove Footer (**Figure 6.74**). The header or footer will be deleted.

To create differing headers or footers:

1. Create your *first* header or footer as explained on pages 140 and 141. For the moment, this is your only footer or header so its *style* will be the same on every page—though if you're using auto-numbering, the numbers will be different (**Figure 6.75**).

2. Now click your cursor in the text where you want the second header or footer to appear, and choose Format > Insert Section Break (Option Enter). A section break will appear in the document.

3. Click your cursor in the new section and choose Format > Section (**Figure 6.76**).

4. When the Section dialog box appears (**Figure 6.77**), use the *Headers and Footers* panel to choose between *Continue from Previous Section*, which is the default, or *Different for this Section*.

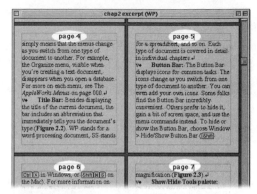

Figure 6.75 Before you create *different* headers or footers, you first create a standard header or footer, which appears on every page.

Figure 6.76 After inserting a new section, choose Format > Section.

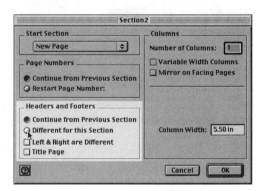

Figure 6.77 Once the Section dialog box appears, use the *Headers and Footers* panel to decide whether the new section's style should *Continue from Previous Section* or be *Different for this Section*.

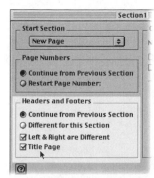

Figure 6.78 Even if you chose *Continue from Previous Section*, you can still create differing odd and even pages or a first-page-only header or footer.

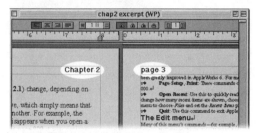

Figure 6.79 An example of differing left and right headers.

5. It seems a bit nonintuitive, but you can check the *Left & Right are Different* or *Title Page* boxes—even if you chose *Continue from Previous Section* in step 4 (**Figure 6.78**). The *Left & Right are Different* choice enables you, for example, to put titles on a document's left-hand pages and page numbers on the right-hand pages. The *Title Page* choice creates a first-page-only header or footer.

6. Once you make your choices, click *OK* and the additional headers or footers will be added to the document. At that point, click on the first instance of each new header or footer and add your graphics or text—including automatic page or section numbers (**Figure 6.79**).

7. If you want to add yet another differing header or footer, repeat steps 2–6 until you're done.

✔ Tips

- When adding extra headers or footers, make sure you click inside your main text. If you click within an existing header or footer, the Format > Section choice will not be available.

- Remember that you can quickly change your header or footer settings any time. For more information, see *Changing section attributes* on page 134.

Creating footnotes

AppleWorks gives you several options for formatting your footnotes. You can place them at the bottom of each page (the default setting) or at the end of a document. You also can choose to use something other than numbers to mark your footnotes. For more information, see *To set footnote options*.

To insert a footnote:

◆ Click in the document where you want a footnote reference to appear, then choose Format > Insert Blank Footnote ([Shift][⌘][F]) (**Figure 6.80**). A reference will be inserted into the body of your document and your cursor will appear at the end of the page where you can type in the footnote text (**Figure 6.81**).

✔ Tip

■ If the Insert Blank Footnote choice doesn't appear in the Format menu, it's because the document's preference is set to put footnotes at the end. For more information, see *To set footnote options* on the next page.

Figure 6.80 To add a footnote, click where you want a footnote reference to appear and choose Format > Insert Blank Footnote.

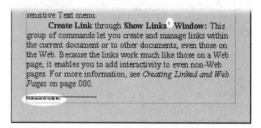

Figure 6.81 A reference will be placed in your document and your cursor will appear at the end of the page where you can type in the footnote text.

Figure 6.82 To change the footnote default, choose Format > Document.

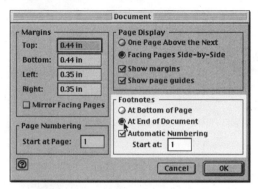

Figure 6.83 In the Document dialog box, use the *Footnotes* panel to change the default from footnotes appearing *At Bottom of Page* to *At End of Document*.

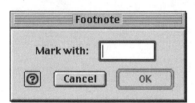

Figure 6.84 If you elect not to number your footnotes, a dialog box will ask you to type in the character you want used instead.

To set footnote options:

1. Click within your document and choose Format > Document (**Figure 6.82**).

2. When the Document dialog box appears, use the *Footnotes* panel to set whether footnotes appear *At Bottom of Page* or *At End of Document* (**Figure 6.83**).

3. If you want to reset the numerical sequence of the current footnote, type another number in the *Start At* text box.

4. By default, *Automatic Numbering* is checked. Uncheck the box if you want to use a character other than a numeral. The next time you choose Format > Insert Blank Footnote, a dialog box will appear asking you to type in the character you want used instead (**Figure 6.84**).

5. Click *OK* and new footnote options will be applied.

CREATING
AND USING TABLES

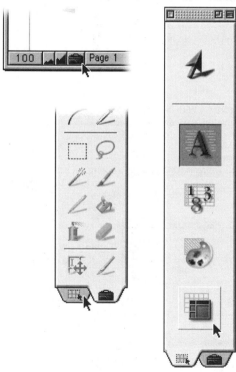

Figure 7.1 To reach the Table Tool (right), click the Tool icon (upper left), then click the Frame tab (lower left).

Table creation has become much easier in AppleWorks 6. You no longer have to bother with the awkwardness of creating a spreadsheet frame. Now it's a straightforward process of clicking the Table Tool and deciding how many rows and columns you need. AppleWorks 6 includes two other welcome table improvements: Table elements can have custom text and color treatments, and multimedia content can be embedded in table cells. If you plan to combine tables with other types of content—plain text, graphics, or spreadsheets—be sure to read *Mixing Document Types* on page 60.

Having the Table Tool available on your desktop, by the way, can speed up your work. To reach the tool, choose Window > Show Tools ([Shift][⌘][T]). Or click the toolbox icon in the lower-left corner of any AppleWorks document and then click the Frame tab once the Tools Palette appears (**Figure 7.1**).

Inserting Tables

AppleWorks offers two ways to insert tables into your documents. Experiment and use the method that works best for you.

To create a table:

1. Click the Table Tool in the Tools Palette (**Figure 7.2**).

2. Click and drag with the cursor to draw a table within your document (**Figure 7.3**), then release the cursor.

   or

   Choose Table > Insert Table ($\mathcal{H}$$\mathsf{Y}$) (**Figure 7.4**).

3. When the Insert Table dialog box appears, type in how many *Columns* and *Rows* you want within the table, and click *OK* (**Figure 7.5**). The table will appear within your document (**Figure 7.6**).

✔ Tip

■ If you are creating a table within a database, make sure you are in Layout mode ($\boxed{\mathsf{Shift}}$$\boxed{\mathcal{H}}$$\boxed{\mathsf{L}}$).

Figure 7.2 To create a table, click the Table Tool in the Tools Palette.

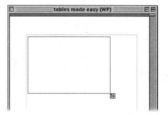

Figure 7.3 With the Table Tool activated, you can draw a table directly in your document.

Figure 7.4 You also can add a table by choosing Table > Insert Table.

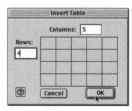

Figure 7.5 When the Insert Table dialog box appears, type in how many *Columns* and *Rows* you want and click *OK*.

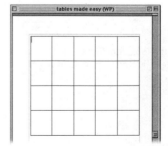

Figure 7.6 A blank table appears based on your entries in the Insert Table dialog box.

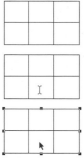

Figure 7.7 If nothing is already selected within the table (top), just click your cursor anywhere *inside* the table (middle), and the table will be selected (bottom).

Figure 7.8 If something is selected in the table (top), click your cursor *outside* the table and the entire table will be selected (bottom).

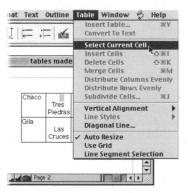

Figure 7.9 To select cells, click in the first cell (top), drag the cursor to highlight the cells you want (middle), and release the cursor (bottom).

Figure 7.10 You also can select a cell by double-clicking it and choosing Table > Select Current Cell.

Selecting and Moving Table Elements

Before you can do much work with a table or the individual cells within it, you first must make a selection. AppleWorks offers several ways to select tables and their individual elements.

To select an entire table:

◆ If nothing is already selected within the table, just click your cursor anywhere *inside* the table. The entire table will be selected—denoted by the eight small black boxes (handles) that appear around the edge of the table (**Figure 7.7**).

or

◆ If something is already selected in the table, click your cursor (which appears as a mini-table) anywhere *outside* the table. The entire table will be selected (**Figure 7.8**).

To select a cell or cells:

1. Click in the first cell you want to select (top, **Figure 7.9**).

2. Drag the cursor to highlight all of the cell or cells you want selected (middle, **Figure 7.9**). Release the cursor and the contents will be selected and ready for your next action (bottom, **Figure 7.9**).

✔ Tip

■ You also can select a cell by double-clicking inside it and choosing Table > Select Current Cell (**Figure 7.10**). But it is easier to use the click-and-drag method.

To select non-adjacent cells:

1. Click in the first cell you want to select and drag the cursor until the cell is high-lighted (top, **Figure 7.11**).

2. Press ⌘ and then click in the next cell you want to select. That cell also will become highlighted (bottom, **Figure 7.11**). Repeat until you've selected all the non-adjacent cells that you need.

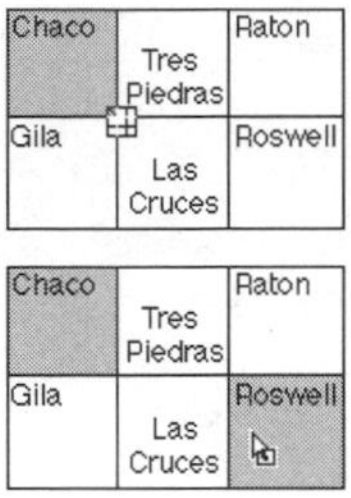

Selecting borders

There are two ways to select the lines, or borders, that define the cells in a table. You can select a border shared by several cells all at once, or you can select the borders of individual cells one by one. You can even combine both approaches by selecting a shared border and then selectively add individual cell borders to that selection.

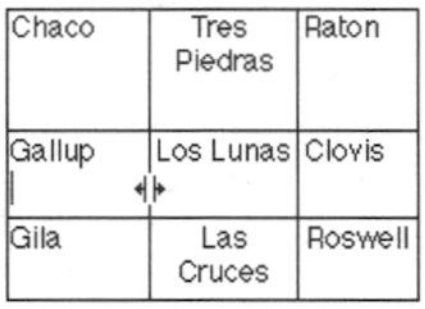

To select the borders of several cells at once:

1. Click anywhere inside the table, then move the cursor until it turns into a double-headed arrow over the table border you want to select (**Figure 7.12**).

2. Click and the entire line will be selected, indicated by that boundary line becoming dashed (top, **Figure 7.13**).

3. If you want to select another border as well, press Shift Option and click your cursor over the next line you want to select (bottom, **Figure 7.13**). For more information on changing borders once you've selected them, see *Changing Borders* on page 166.

Figure 7.11 To select non-adjacent cells, click the first cell and drag the cursor until it is highlighted (top). Press ⌘ and then click in the next cell you want selected (bottom).

Figure 7.12 To select a table border, click in the table and move the cursor over the border until it becomes a double-headed arrow.

Figure 7.13 Click the line, which becomes dashed (top). To select another line as well, press Shift Option and click over the next line (bottom).

Chaco	Tres Piedras	Raton
Gallup	Los Lunas	Clovis
Gila	Las Cruces	Roswell

Figure 7.14 To select a single cell's border, move the cursor until it becomes a double-headed arrow and press Option.

Chaco	Tres Piedras	Raton
Gallup	Los Lunas	Clovis
Gila	Las Cruces	Roswell

Chaco	Tres Piedras	Raton
Gallup	Los Lunas	Clovis
Gila	Las Cruces	Roswell

Figure 7.15 To select more than one cell's border, press Shift Option and click your cursor over the next border (top). Repeat until you've selected all the borders you need (middle, bottom).

Chaco	Tres Piedras	Raton
Gallup	Los Lunas	Clovis
Gila	Las Cruces	Roswell

Table 7.1

Moving from cell to cell

TO MOVE	PRESS
One cell left	⌘ ←
One cell right	⌘ →
One cell up	⌘ ↑
One cell down	⌘ ↓

To select the borders of individual cells:

1. Click once inside the cell whose border you want to select.

2. Move the cursor until it turns into a double-headed arrow over the border you want to select (**Figure 7.12**).

3. Press Option and the border beneath the arrow will become dashed (**Figure 7.14**).

4. If you want to select more borders, press Shift Option and click your cursor over the next border you want to select.

5. Repeat step 4 until you've selected all the borders you need (**Figure 7.15**). For more information on changing borders once you've selected them, see *Changing Borders* on page 166.

✔ Tips

■ If you select the wrong border by mistake, click on it again while pressing Shift Option and the border will be deselected.

■ You are not confined to selecting adjacent borders when using Shift Option.

Navigating within tables

You can move from cell to cell simply by clicking inside the new cell. But AppleWorks also offers a way to hop from cell to cell using the keyboard. For more information, see **Table 7.1**, *Moving from cell to cell.*

To move a table in a document:

1. Select the table, which will then display black boxes, or handles, around its edge (**Figure 7.16**).

2. Use your cursor to drag the table to where you want it, using the dashed outline that appears to guide your positioning (**Figure 7.17**).

   or

   Press your keyboard's arrow keys to move the table more precisely.

3. Release your cursor and the table will move to the new position (**Figure 7.18**).

To move a cell or cells:

1. Select the cell or cells you want to move (**Figure 7.19**).

2. Click and drag the cursor toward the destination cell or cells, which will be highlighted by a heavy border (**Figure 7.20**). Once the desired cell(s) become highlighted, release the cursor and the selected cells will be inserted in the destination (**Figure 7.21**).

✔ Tips

- When moving cells, the number of source cells must match the number of destination cells. For example, you cannot move four cells into just three cells or two cells into five.

- It is easy to drag cell content to a table in another *document*. Just open both documents and arrange them side by side on your screen.

- Be sure to select the entire cell before dragging it to another cell. It's easy, especially when working with cells containing graphics, to make the mistake of selecting just the graphic and not the entire cell (**Figure 7.22**).

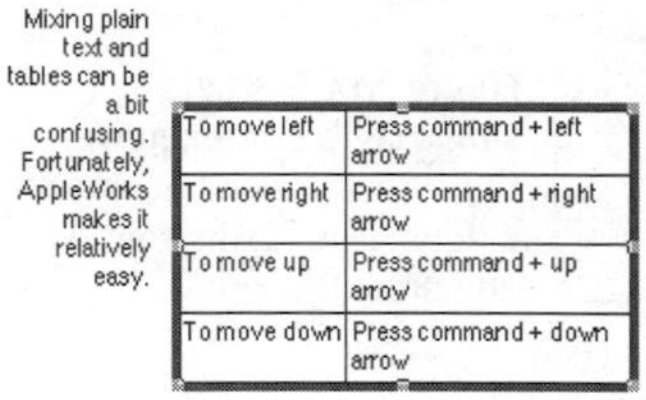

Figure 7.16
To move a table, select it so that black boxes, or handles, appear around its edge.

Figure 7.17
Drag the table where you want it, using the dashed outline to guide your positioning.

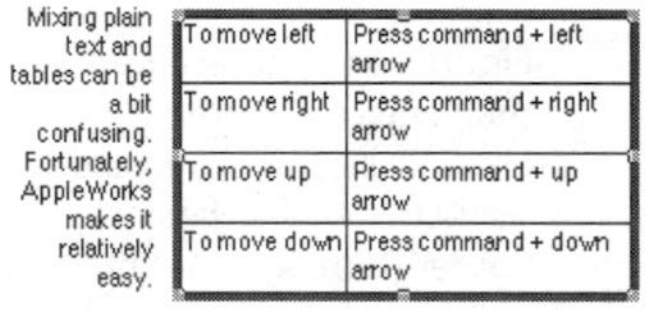

Figure 7.18
Release your cursor and the table lines up with the adjacent text.

Figure 7.19 To copy individual cells, first select them.

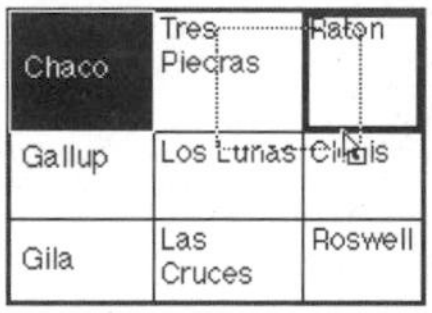

Figure 7.20 Click the source cell and drag it toward the destination, which will be highlighted by a heavy border.

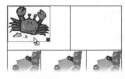

Figure 7.21 Release your cursor and the selected cells will be copied to the destination cells.

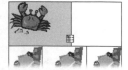

Figure 7.22 Make sure you copy the entire cell before trying to drag it. With a graphic, it's common to mistakenly select only the image (left) instead of the full cell (right).

Copying Table Items

Copying offers a way to quickly duplicate an entire table and all of its formatted borders and alignments. Once you've copied the table, you can then replace the contents in some or all of the cells, while retaining the formatting. Copying individual cells makes it possible to fill out a table with repeating items or to place their contents in another table.

To copy a table:

1. Select the entire table, then choose Edit > Copy (⌘C).

2. Click your cursor at the spot where you want to copy the table and choose Edit > Paste (⌘V). The table will be pasted into the new spot.

To copy a cell or cells:

1. Select the cell or cells you want to duplicate (**Figure 7.19**).

2. Click your cursor at the spot where you want to copy the table and choose Edit > Paste (⌘V). The copied contents will be pasted into the new cell or cells.

✔ Tip

■ When copying cells, the number of source cells must match the number of destination cells.

Inserting and Deleting Table Elements

AppleWorks will not let you insert or delete single cells. However, you can go back and change your table by inserting or deleting a row of cells, a column of cells, or an entire table. You also can retain cells while deleting just their *contents*.

To insert a row or column of cells:

1. Select the row or column next to where you want to insert a new row or column (**Figure 7.23**). (New rows are inserted *above* the selected row; new columns to the *left* of the selected column.)

2. Choose Table > Insert Cells ([Shift][⌘][I]) (**Figure 7.24**). Depending on what you selected in step 1, a new row or column of cells will be inserted (**Figure 7.25**).

✔ Tips

- You also can insert cells by making your selection, [Ctrl]-clicking, and choosing *Insert Cells* when the pop-up menu appears (**Figure 7.26**).

- If you don't see the Table menu in your menu bar, click twice inside the table.

- Yet another way to insert cells involves splitting existing cells. For more information, see *To split cells* on page 158.

Figure 7.23 Select the row or column next to where you want to insert a new row or column.

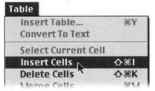

Figure 7.24 To insert a row or column, choose Table > Insert Cells.

Figure 7.25 A new row of cells will be inserted *above* the selected row.

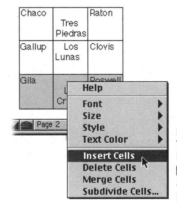

Figure 7.26 You also can insert cells by [Ctrl]-clicking and using the pop-up menu.

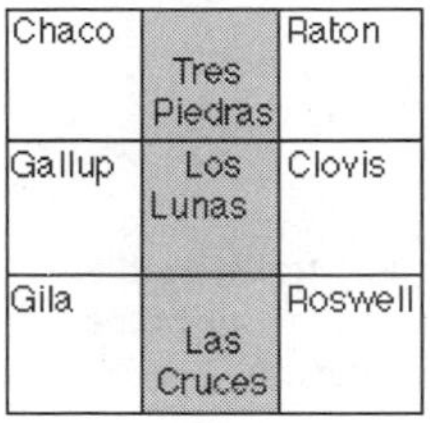

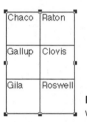

Figure 7.27 Select the row or column that you want to delete.

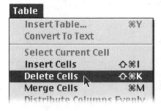

Figure 7.28 To delete a row or column, choose Table > Delete Cells.

Figure 7.29 The selected column will be deleted from the table.

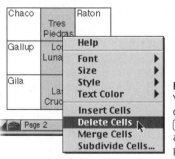

Figure 7.30 You also can delete cells by [Ctrl]-clicking and using the pop-up menu.

Figure 7.31 To leave the cells in place, select the cells (top), press [Delete], and only the content is deleted (bottom).

To delete a table:

1. To select the entire table, click your cursor *inside* the table if nothing is already selected. If something's already selected in the table, click your cursor *outside* the table.

2. Press [Delete] and the entire table will be deleted.

To delete a row or column of cells:

1. Select the row or column that you want to delete (**Figure 7.27**).

2. Choose Table > Delete Cells ([Shift][⌘][K]) (**Figure 7.28**). The selected row or column will be deleted (**Figure 7.29**).

✔ Tips

■ You also can delete cells by making your selection, [Ctrl]-clicking, and choosing *Delete Cells* when the pop-up menu appears (**Figure 7.30**).

■ By combining, or merging, existing cells, you also can reduce the number of cells in a table. For more information, see *To merge cells* on page 160.

To delete the contents of a cell, row, or column:

1. Select the cell, row of cells, or column of cells whose *content* you want to delete (top, **Figure 7.31**).

2. Press [Delete]. The content will be deleted, leaving blank cells where you can insert new content if desired (bottom, **Figure 7.31**).

INSERTING, DELETING TABLE ELEMENTS

Resizing Table Elements

Once you've created a table, you occasionally may need to adjust its overall size or the size of individual rows and columns to accommodate your content.

To resize a table by dragging:

1. Select the table.

2. Click on any of the table's eight handles (**Figure 7.32**) and drag it to the desired size, using the dashed line as a guide (**Figure 7.33**).

3. Release the cursor and the table will be resized (**Figure 7.34**).

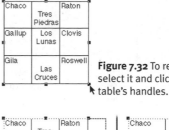

Figure 7.32 To resize a table, select it and click one of the table's handles.

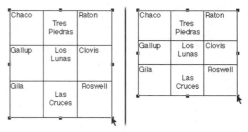

Figure 7.33 The click-and-drag method can be used to enlarge (left) or shrink (right) a table.

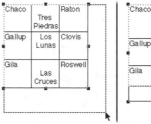

Figure 7.34 Release the cursor and the table will be resized.

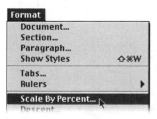

Figure 7.35
To resize a table by percentage, choose Format > Scale By Percent.

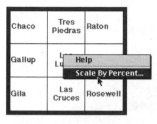

Figure 7.36
You also can resize by Ctrl-clicking the table and choosing *Scale By Percent* from the pop-up menu.

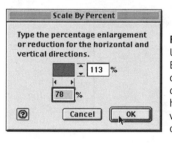

Figure 7.37
Use the Scale By Percent dialog box to change the horizontal and vertical scaling of the table.

Figure 7.38 To resize a row or column, move the cursor until it becomes a double-headed arrow (top), then click, and the border will turn into a dashed line (bottom).

Figure 7.39 Drag the border to its new position (top), release the cursor, and the resizing will be applied (bottom).

To resize a table by percentage:

1. Select the table.

2. Choose Format > Scale By Percent (**Figure 7.35**).

   or

   Ctrl-click the table and choose *Scale By Percent* when the pop-up menu appears (**Figure 7.36**).

3. When the Scale By Percent dialog box appears, use the number windows to change the horizontal and vertical scaling of the table (**Figure 7.37**). Click *OK* and the changes will be applied to the table.

To resize a row or column:

1. Move your cursor over a row or column border until the cursor becomes a double-headed arrow (top, **Figure 7.38**).

2. Click the cursor on the border, which will turn into a dashed line (bottom, **Figure 7.38**).

3. While pressing the cursor, drag the dashed border to its new position (top, **Figure 7.39**).

4. Release the cursor and the resizing will be applied to the cells on either size of the newly positioned border (bottom, **Figure 7.39**).

Splitting and Merging Cells

It's hard to know in advance how many cells you will need in a table. By letting you split (divide) or merge (combine) cells, AppleWorks helps you create tables on the fly. The program offers two ways to split cells, one menu based and the other tool based. Try both and use the one that feels most natural.

To split cells:

1. Select the cell or cells that you want to divide into more cells (**Figure 7.40**).

2. Choose Table > Subdivide Cells ($\mathcal{H}$ J) (**Figure 7.41**).

3. When the Subdivide Cells dialog box appears, it will display the existing divisions of your selection (top, **Figure 7.42**).

4. In the *Columns* and *Rows* text windows, enter the number of divisions you want the selection to have. The center diagram will change to reflect your choices (bottom, **Figure 7.42**).

5. When you're satisfied with your choice, click *OK* and the selection's cell or cells will be split (**Figure 7.43**).

✔ Tip

■ You also can split cells by making your selection, Ctrl-clicking, and choosing *Subdivide Cells* when the pop-up menu appears (**Figure 7.44**).

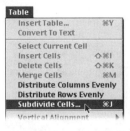

Figure 7.40 Select the cells you want to split into more cells.

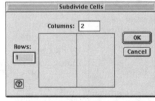

Figure 7.41 To split cells, choose Table > Subdivide Cells.

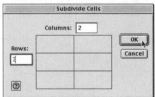

Figure 7.42 When the Subdivide Cells dialog box appears, it displays the existing divisions in your selection (top). Set how many *Columns* and *Rows* you want and the center diagram reflects the new setting (bottom).

Figure 7.43 The selected cells after being split.

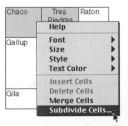

Figure 7.44 You also can split cells by Ctrl-clicking, and choosing *Subdivide Cells* from the pop-up menu.

Figure 7.45 To reach the Cutting Tool, click the Toolbox tab in the Tools Palette.

Chaco	Tres Piedras	Raton
Gallup	Los Lunas	Clovis
Gila	Las Cruces	Roswell

Figure 7.46 Drag the Cutting Tool across the cells you want to split and a dashed line will appear.

Chaco	Tres Piedras	Raton
Gallup	Los Lunas	Clovis
Gila	Las Cruces	Roswell

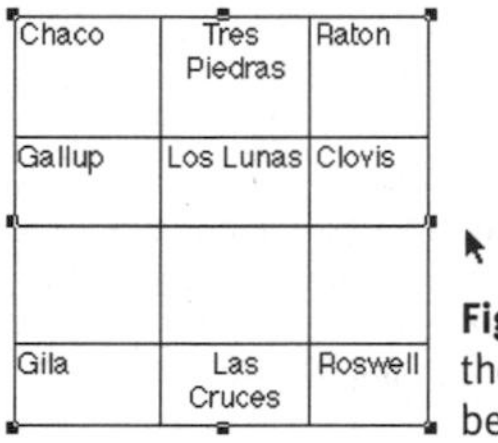

Figure 7.47 Click outside the table and the split will be applied.

To split cells with the Cutting Tool:

1. Click anywhere inside the table—once or twice, depending on the circumstances, until the table's black handles disappear. You do not have to click in the same cell or cells you want to split.

2. Click the Toolbox tab in the Tools Palette and then click the Cutting Tool (**Figure 7.45**).

3. Moving back to the AppleWorks document, your cursor will appear as a blade. Drag it across the cells you want to split and a dashed line will appear (**Figure 7.46**).

4. Click outside the table and the split will be applied, which is denoted by the dashed line becoming solid (**Figure 7.47**).

SPLITTING AND MERGING CELLS

To merge cells:

1. Select the cells you want combined, or merged, into a single cell (**Figure 7.48**).

2. Choose Table > Merge Cells (⌘M) (**Figure 7.49**).

3. The selected cells will merge and the contents of the two original cells will appear in the remaining single cell (**Figure 7.50**).

✔ Tip

■ You also can combine cells by making your selection, Ctrl-clicking and choosing *Merge Cells* when the pop-up menu appears (**Figure 7.51**).

Figure 7.48 Select the cells you want merged into a single cell.

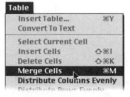

Figure 7.49 To merge cells, choose Table > Merge Cells.

Figure 7.50 Once the cells are merged, their contents are combined in the remaining cell.

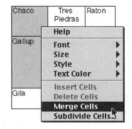

Figure 7.51 You also can combine cells by Ctrl-clicking and choosing *Merge Cells* from the pop-up menu.

Chaco	Tres Piedras	Raton		Chaco	Tres Piedras	Raton
Gallup	Los Lunas	Clovis		Gallup	Los Lunas	Clovis
Gila	Las Cruces	Roswell		Gila	Las Cruces	Roswell

Figure 7.52 Select the row (left) or columns (right) whose widths you want to even out.

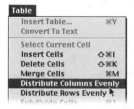

Figure 7.53 To make cells the same width, choose Table > Distribute Columns Evenly.

Chaco	Tres Piedras	Raton		Chaco	Tres Piedras	Raton
Gallup	Los Lunas	Clovis		Gallup	Los Lunas	Clovis
Gila	Las Cruces	Roswell		Gila	Las Cruces	Roswell

Figure 7.54 The widths of the selected cells after being distributed evenly.

Chaco	Tres Piedras	Raton		Chaco	Tres Piedras	Raton
Gallup	Los Lunas	Clovis		Gallup	Los Lunas	Clovis
Gila				Gila	Las Cruces	Roswell
	Las Cruces	Roswell				

Figure 7.55 Select the column (left) or rows (right) whose heights you want to even out.

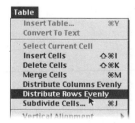

Figure 7.56 To make cells the same height, choose Table > Distribute Rows Evenly.

Evening up rows and columns

As you reformat tables, you may need to tidy things up from time to time. AppleWorks includes two commands—*Distribute Columns Evenly* and *Distribute Rows Evenly*—to make that easy.

To make cells the same width:

1. Select the cells with uneven widths (**Figure 7.52**).

2. Choose Table > Distribute Columns Evenly (**Figure 7.53**). The widths of the selected cells will be made the same (**Figure 7.54**).

To make cells the same height:

1. Select the cells with uneven heights (**Figure 7.55**).

2. Choose Table > Distribute Rows Evenly (**Figure 7.56**). The heights of the selected cells will be made the same (**Figure 7.57**).

Chaco	Tres Piedras	Raton		Chaco	Tres Piedras	Raton
Gallup	Los Lunas	Clovis		Gallup	Los Lunas	Clovis
Gila	Las Cruces	Roswell		Gila	Las Cruces	Roswell

Figure 7.57 The heights of the selected cells after being distributed evenly.

Changing and Formatting Cells

AppleWorks includes several commands to let you change the appearance of individual cells. The ability to align multiple cells at once is a real time saver. The ability to add diagonal lines to cells might seem an odd feature at first blush—until you realize how useful it is for highlighting out-of-date or cancelled items in a schedule or calendar.

Figure 7.58 To horizontally align the *content* of selected cells, click one of the alignment icons in the text ruler.

Figure 7.59 The contents of the selected cells now are all flush left.

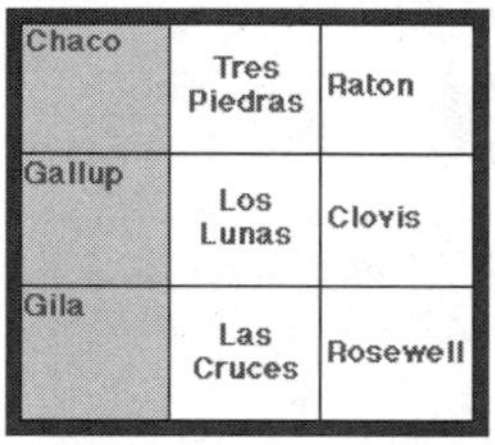

To horizontally align cell content:

◆ Make sure the text ruler is visible (Format > Rulers > Show Rulers). Select the cell or cells whose *content* you want to realign and click one of the alignment icons in the text ruler (**Figure 7.58**). The text will be realigned (**Figure 7.59**).

To vertically align cell content:

1. Select the cell or cells whose *content* you want to realign (**Figure 7.60**).

2. Choose Table > Vertical Alignment and make a choice from the submenu that appears (**Figure 7.61**). The content will be realigned (**Figure 7.62**).

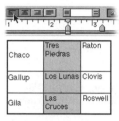

Figure 7.60 Select the cells whose *content* you want to vertically realign.

Figure 7.61 Choose Table > Vertical Alignment and make a choice from the submenu.

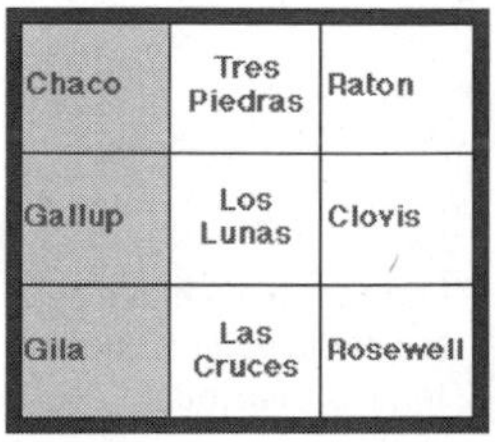

Figure 7.62 The contents of the selected cells now are all centered vertically.

Figure 7.63 Select the cell or cells where you want a diagonal line to appear.

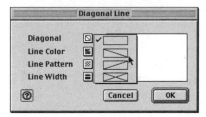

Figure 7.64 To add a diagonal line to the cell, choose Table > Diagonal Line.

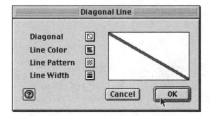

Figure 7.65 When the Diagonal Line dialog box appears, use the four drop-down menus to set the line's appearance.

Figure 7.66 Once you're happy with the line's preview, click *OK*.

Figure 7.67 The diagonal line option is handy when creating table-based calendars and schedules.

To add a diagonal line to cells:

1. Select the cell or cells where you want the line to appear (**Figure 7.63**).

2. Choose Table > Diagonal Line (**Figure 7.64**).

3. When the Diagonal Line dialog box appears, use the four drop-down menus to set how the line will appear (**Figure 7.65**).

4. Once you're satisfied with the preview of how the line will appear, click *OK* (**Figure 7.66**). The line will be applied to the selected cell or cells (**Figure 7.67**).

✔ Tip

■ If you want to remove the diagonal line, just select the cell, choose Table > Diagonal Line, and when the dialog box appears, use the *Diagonal* drop-down menu to pick the no-line option.

ADDING DIAGONAL LINES TO CELLS

Changing background colors or patterns

AppleWorks's Accents Palette includes a wide variety of colors and patterns that you can use to create good-looking tables. You can change the background color for a single cell, a group of cells, or those of the entire table.

To change background colors:

1. Make sure the Accents Palette is visible by choosing Window > Show Accents (⌘K) (**Figure 7.68**).

2. Select the cell, cells, or entire table whose background you want to change (**Figure 7.69**).

3. Click the Accents Palette's *Fill* icon if it's not already highlighted (top, **Figure 7.70**), then click the palette's color tab if that tab's content is not visible (bottom, **Figure 7.70**).

4. Choose a new color by clicking any square in the palette (**Figure 7.71**). The color is applied to the background (**Figure 7.72**).

Figure 7.68 To change background colors and patterns, make sure the Accents Palette is visible.

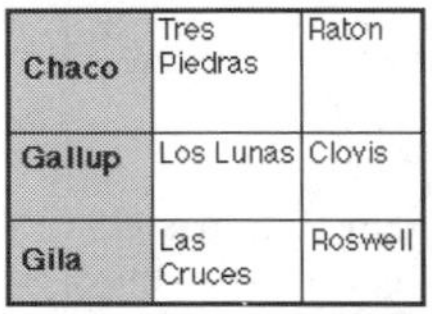

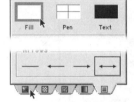

Figure 7.69 Select the cells whose background you want to change.

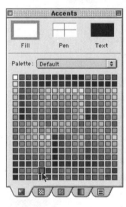

Figure 7.70 Click the Accents Palette's *Fill* icon (top) and color tab (bottom) if they are not already selected.

Figure 7.71 Choose a new color by clicking any square in the Accents Palette color panel.

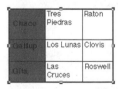

Figure 7.72 The new color is applied to the selected cells.

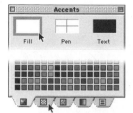

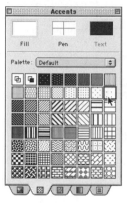

Figure 7.73 Click the Accents Palette's *Fill* icon (top) and pattern tab (bottom) if they are not already selected.

Figure 7.74 Choose a new color by clicking any square in the Accents Palette pattern panel.

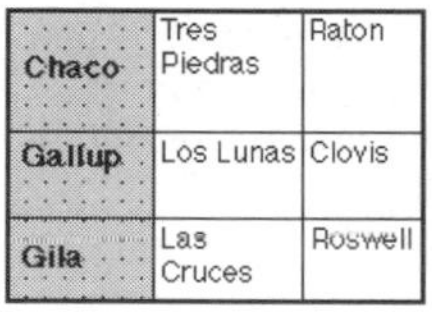

Chaco	Tres Piedras	Raton
Gallup	Los Lunas	Clovis
Gila	Las Cruces	Roswell

Figure 7.75 The new pattern is applied to the selected cells.

To change background patterns:

1. Make sure the Accents Palette is visible by choosing Window > Show Accents (⌘K) (**Figure 7.68**).

2. Select the cell, cells, or entire table whose background you want to change (**Figure 7.69**).

3. Click the Accents Palette's *Fill* icon if it's not already highlighted (top, **Figure 7.73**), then click the palette's pattern tab if that tab's content is not visible (bottom, **Figure 7.73**).

4. Choose a new pattern by clicking any square in the palette (**Figure 7.74**). The pattern is immediately applied to the table's background (**Figure 7.75**).

Changing Borders

You are limited to changing only the line style (solid, dashed, double, etc.) for the border of individual cells. However, AppleWorks will let you change the entire table's border width and color.

To change individual cell border style:

1. Select the border of the cell or cells you want to change.

2. Choose Table > Line Styles and select a choice from the submenu (**Figure 7.76**). The new style will be applied to the selected border.

To change the table's border width:

1. Make sure the Accents Palette is visible by choosing Window > Show Accents (⌘K).

2. Select the entire table (**Figure 7.77**).

3. Click the Accents Palette's *Pen* icon if it's not already highlighted (top, **Figure 7.78**), then click the palette's line style tab if that tab's content is not visible (bottom, **Figure 7.78**).

4. Within the *Line Width* panel, click a new line width (**Figure 7.79**). If you click *Other*, a dialog box will appear where you can enter a number for a custom width (**Figure 7.80**). The new width will be applied to the table's border (**Figure 7.81**).

Figure 7.76 To change the border of an individual cell, choose Table > Line Styles and select a choice from the submenu.

Figure 7.77 To change the border for a table, first select it by clicking anywhere outside the border.

Figure 7.78 Click the Accents Palette's *Pen* icon (top) and line style tab (bottom) if they are not already selected.

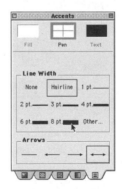

Figure 7.79 Click a new line width within the Accents Palette's *Line Width* panel.

Figure 7.80 If you click *Other* in the *Line Width* panel, the Line Width dialog box will let you enter a custom width.

Figure 7.81 The new border width is applied to the entire table.

Accents
Fill
Pen
Text
Arrows

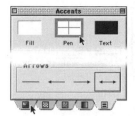

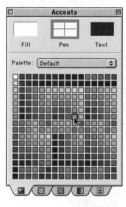

Figure 7.82 Click the Accents Palette's *Pen* icon (top) and color tab (bottom) if they are not already selected.

Accents
Fill
Pen
Text
Palette: Default

Figure 7.83 Choose a new color by clicking any square in the Accents Palette color panel.

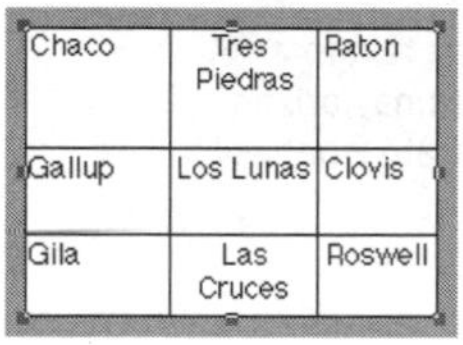

Chaco
Tres Piedras
Raton
Gallup
Los Lunas
Clovis
Gila
Las Cruces
Roswell

Figure 7.84 The new color is applied to the table's border.

To change the table's border color:

1. Make sure the Accents Palette is visible by choosing Window > Show Accents (⌘K).
2. Select the entire table by clicking anywhere outside its border.
3. Click the Accents Palette's *Pen* icon if it's not already highlighted (top, **Figure 7.82**), then click the palette's color tab if that tab's content is not visible (bottom, **Figure 7.82**).
4. Choose a new color by clicking any square in the palette (**Figure 7.83**). The color is immediately applied to the table's border (**Figure 7.84**), which makes it easy to try several colors until you find one to your liking.

Converting Tables and Text

As long as you follow the few guidelines mentioned below, it is easy to convert AppleWorks tables to text—and vice versa. That way you can use the format best suited to your document or, if you're exporting the text, the destination application. You also can save AppleWorks tables as HTML (HyperText Markup Language), the coding used to create Web pages. For more information, see *Saving Documents for the Web* on page 419.

To convert tables to text:

1. Select the table you want to convert (**Figure 7.85**).

2. Choose Table > Convert To Text (**Figure 7.86**). The table will be converted to text with tabs separating the former columns and line returns marking the former rows (**Figure 7.87**).

To convert text to a table:

1. Make sure tabs separate the text items horizontally and that line returns separate what will become the rows (**Figure 7.88**).

2. Choose Table > Convert To Table (**Figure 7.89**). The text will be reformatted into a table (**Figure 7.90**).

✔ Tip

■ It will be much easier to spot your tabs and line returns if you turn on normally invisible characters. Choose Edit > Preferences > General and check the *Show Invisibles* box within the *Options* panel.

To move left	Press command + left arrow
To move right	Press command + right arrow
To move up	Press command + up arrow
To move down	Press command + down arrow

Figure 7.85 Select the table you want to convert to text.

Table
Insert Table... ⌘Y
Convert To Text
Select Current Cell
Insert Cells

Figure 7.86 To convert the table, choose Table > Convert To Text.

To move left　Press command + left arrow
To move right　Press command + right arrow
To move up　Press command + up arrow
To move down　Press command + down arrow

Figure 7.87 Once converted to text, tabs separate the former columns and line returns mark the former rows.

Davis→　A+→　English↵
Heft→　A+→　Art↵
Van Ness→　A+→　Geometry↵
Glossbrenner→　A+→　English↵

Figure 7.88 Before converting text to a table, use tabs to separate items horizontally and line returns to separate what will become rows.

Table
Insert Table... ⌘Y
Convert To Table
Select Current Cell
Insert Cells

Figure 7.89 To convert the text, choose Table > Convert To Table.

Davis	A+	English
Heft	A+	Art
Van Ness	A+	Geometry
Glossbrenner	A+	English

Figure 7.90 The former plain text formatted as a table.

8

TEXT EXTRAS

This chapter highlights some of the extra tricks and procedures tucked away in AppleWorks's text capabilities. Style sheets enable you to quickly apply custom text treatments to any text. Outlines make it much easier to organize longer documents. The spelling checker and thesaurus give you an edge in producing quality documents. Finally, the ability to wrap text around objects and frames, plus the option of linking text frames, enable you to create sharp looking layouts once you are done writing.

Using and Changing Styles

By creating and applying styles you can change multiple aspects of the selected text, for example its font, size, and indentation, in a single action. Styles can be a tremendous time saver when you are creating documents—especially since changes you make to a style are automatically applied to the current document.

Styles also can be created for spreadsheets, drawn objects, presentations, and frames. In fact, AppleWorks includes a wonderful variety of pre-configured spreadsheet and table styles. For more information, see the *Tip* for *To create a style* on page 175.

To apply styling:

1. Make sure the Styles window is visible by choosing Format > Show Styles ((Shift)(⌘)(W)) (**Figure 8.1**).

2. Select the text you want styled (**Figure 8.2**).

3. Click in the Styles window on the style you want to use and click *Apply* (**Figure 8.3**). The style will be applied to the selection (**Figure 8.4**).

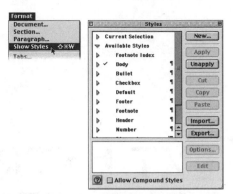

Figure 8.1 Choose Format > Show Styles ((Shift)(⌘)(W)) to make the Styles window visible.

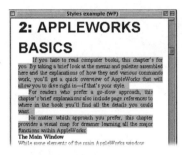

Figure 8.2 Select the text you want styled.

Figure 8.3 Click on the style you want to use, then click *Apply*.

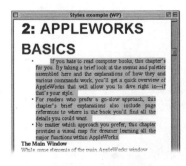

Figure 8.4 The selected text after the bullet style has been applied.

✔ Tips

- If you plan on applying a style to an entire paragraph, just click anywhere in the paragraph. Certain styles, bullets for example, cannot be applied to any selection smaller than an entire paragraph.

- The Styles window will only display styles that make sense for what you have selected. For example, drawing styles will not appear if you have selected text.

- The Styles window includes an *Allow Compound Styles* checkbox. Check it if you want to apply more than one style to an item—assuming the styles don't conflict. For example, text can be bold and italic but you cannot apply a header and footer style to the same text.

USING AND CHANGING STYLES

To remove styling:

1. Make sure the Styles window is visible by choosing Format > Show Styles (Shift ⌘ W).

2. Select the text whose style you want removed (**Figure 8.5**).

3. In the Styles window, click on the current style, which is checked, and click *Unapply* (**Figure 8.6**). The style will be removed (**Figure 8.7**).

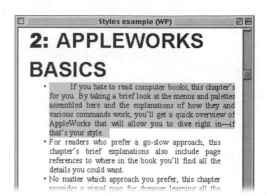

Figure 8.5 Select the text whose style you want removed.

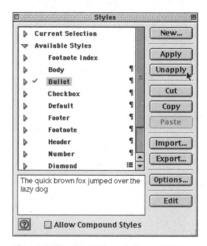

Figure 8.6 In the Styles window, click on the current style and then click *Unapply*.

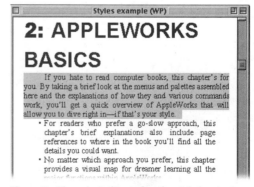

Figure 8.7 The selected text after the style has been removed.

Figure 8.8
To change a style, select it in the Styles window and click *Edit*.

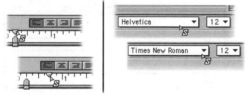

Figure 8.9 As you use the text ruler, menus, or the Accents Palette to make changes, your cursor will appear as a small S.

Figure 8.10.
Once you have made all your changes, which are listed in the Styles window, click *Done*.

Figure 8.11
To delete a style attribute, highlight it (top). Press Delete and it will be removed (bottom).

To edit a style:

1. Make sure the Styles window is visible by choosing Format > Show Styles (Shift ⌘ W).

2. Click in the Styles window on the style you want to change and click *Edit* (**Figure 8.8**).

3. Use the text ruler, menus, or the Accents Palette to make the changes you want. Your cursor will appear as a small S to denote that you are in edit mode (**Figure 8.9**). Do not click inside the document itself or you will cancel edit mode and have to start again.

4. As you change the style, the new settings will be listed in the Styles window. Once you have made all the changes you want, click *Done* (**Figure 8.10**). The style is changed and AppleWorks switches out of style editing mode.

✔ Tips

■ Remember: When you edit a style, the changes are applied to any part of the document that uses that style.

■ What if you make a mistake or change your mind while editing a style? If you need to delete a particular style attribute, highlight it in the Styles window (top, **Figure 8.11**). Press Delete and when the warning dialog box appears, click *OK*. The attribute will be deleted from the Styles window (bottom, **Figure 8.11**).

USING AND CHANGING STYLES

Creating a new style

When creating a new style, you do not have to start from scratch and, in fact, seldom will. Instead, AppleWorks lets you base your new style on an existing style or even inherit the characteristics of any selected text.

To create a style:

1. Make sure the Styles window is visible by choosing Format > Show Styles ((Shift)(⌘)(W)).

2. If you want your new style to share the aspects of text already in the document, select that text now.

3. In the Styles window, click *New* (**Figure 8.12**).

4. When the New Style dialog box appears, check *Inherit document selection format* if you selected text in step 2 (**Figure 8.13**). You also can choose a *Style Type* and use the drop-down menu if the new style will be *Based on* an existing style (**Figure 8.14**). Once you have made your choices, give the style a name and click *OK* (**Figure 8.15**).

Figure 8.12 To create a style, click *New* in the Styles window.

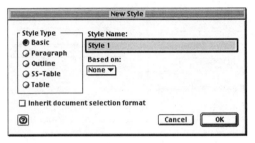

Figure 8.13 When the New Style dialog box appears, first choose a *Style Type*.

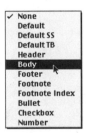

Figure 8.14 Use the drop-down menu if the new style will be based on an existing style.

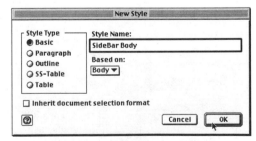

Figure 8.15 Once you have made your choices, give the style a name and click *OK*.

Figure 8.16 The new style name will be highlighted in the Styles window, but will not yet have any *Text Attributes*.

Figure 8.17 After editing the new style, its *Text Attributes* appear in the Styles window.

Figure 8.18 If you choose the *SS-Table* or *Table Style Type* in step 4, you can then use the Styles window's preview area to browse AppleWorks's pre-configured choices.

5. The new style name will be highlighted in the Styles window (**Figure 8.16**). It will be based on your selection in step 4 but will not yet have any *Text Attributes*.

6. Change your new style as explained in step 3 of *To edit a style* on page 173. As you change the new style, its *Text Attributes* will be listed in the Styles window. Once you have made all your changes, click *Done* (**Figure 8.17**). AppleWorks switches out of style editing mode.

✔ Tip

■ To use AppleWorks's pre-configured spreadsheet and table styles, choose the *SS-Table* or *Table Style Type* in step 4 (see **Figure 8.13**). Then in step 5, you will be able to browse through these Table styles using the preview area in the Styles window (**Figure 8.18**).

To delete a style:

1. Make sure the style you want to delete is not already being used in the document, then open the Styles window by choosing Format > Show Styles ([Shift][⌘][W]).

2. Click in the Styles window on the style you want to delete, then click *Cut* (**Figure 8.19**). Unless the style is being used in your document, the style listing will be deleted from the window.

✔ Tip

■ If AppleWorks displays an alert dialog box when you try to delete the style, then you are using it in the active document (**Figure 8.20**). If you are sure you want to delete the style, change the document style to something else and you will then be able to delete the first style.

Figure 8.19 To delete a style, select it in the Styles window and click *Cut*.

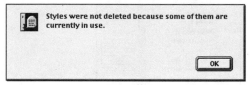

Figure 8.20 If an alert dialog box appears when you try to delete a style, the style is being used in the active document.

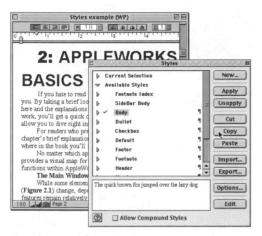

Figure 8.21 To copy a style, first select it in your source document and click *Copy*.

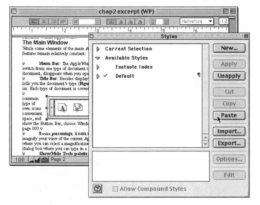

Figure 8.22 Now click in your destination document and click *Paste* in the Styles window.

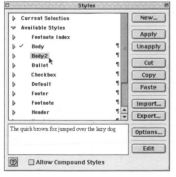

Figure 8.23 The style will be copied from the first document into the Styles window of the second document.

To copy a style to another document:

1. Open the document whose style you want to copy (the *source*) and the document where you want to paste the style (the *destination*). Make sure the Styles window is visible by choosing Format > Show Styles ([Shift][⌘][W]).

2. Click in your source document, and its Styles window will be visible. Click on the style listing you want to duplicate and click *Copy* (**Figure 8.21**).

3. Now click in your destination document and the Styles window will display that document's styles. Click *Paste* in the Styles window (**Figure 8.22**). The style will be copied and listed in the window (**Figure 8.23**).

✔ Tip

■ If you try to paste a style into a document that already has a style with the same name, a warning dialog box will appear. Type in a new name for the style you want to paste and click *Rename* (**Figure 8.24**).

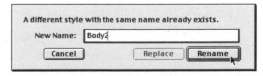

Figure 8.24 If you try to paste in a style with the same name as an existing style, a warning dialog box will ask you to first rename the style you want to paste.

Creating and Using Outlines

The main advantage of using an outline is that it lets you reorganize a document based on the topics within it. If you change your mind about where a topic belongs, you simply rearrange the topic order and the document instantly reflects the changes. The longer the document, the more valuable outlines become. Selectively collapsing or expanding your outline, for example, can make it easier to see the overall organization.

In AppleWorks, outlines are organized at the paragraph level with each paragraph representing a "topic" or "subtopic." Subtopics are simply paragraphs nested beneath a higher level paragraph or topic. Using AppleWorks's outline commands, these topics and subtopics can be promoted, demoted, and reordered as needed.

To create an outline:

1. Type in the text of your first topic and, if you are building an outline from scratch press (Return).

   or

   Click in a paragraph if you are turning an existing document into an outline.

2. Choose Outline > Label Style and pick a style from the submenu (**Figure 8.25**).

3. Release the cursor and the style will be applied to the current topic (paragraph) (**Figure 8.26**). For more information on the styles, see **Table 8.1** on page 179.

4. To add another topic *at the same level* in the outline, choose Outline > New Topic ((Return)) (**Figure 8.27**). The cursor will move to the next line (top, **Figure 8.28**). You can then type in your next topic (bottom, **Figure 8.28**).

   or

Figure 8.25 To create an outline, choose Outline > Label Style and pick a style from the submenu.

Figure 8.26 Release the cursor and the style will be applied to the current topic.

Figure 8.27 To add another topic *at the same level* in the outline, choose Outline > New Topic.

Figure 8.28 Once you create a new topic, the cursor moves to the next line (top), where a label will appear once you type in the topic (bottom).

Figure 8.29 To add a subtopic, which will be *indented to the right*, choose Outline > New Topic Right.

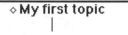

Figure 8.30 After you type in a new subtopic, the topic label changes from hollow (top) to filled (bottom). The new subtopic label is hollow since it has no subtopics of its own.

Figure 8.31 To add a topic that will be *indented to the left*, choose Outline > New Topic Left.

Figure 8.32 Once you choose New Topic Left, the cursor bumps left on to the next line (top). A label appears once you type in the topic (bottom).

Table 8.1

Outline Label Styles	
STYLE	**APPEARANCE**
Diamond	◆ ◇
Checkbox	❏
Harvard	I, II, III; A, B, C; 1, 2, 3; a, b, c
Leader	+, −*
Legal	1, 2, 3; 1.1, 2.1, 3.1; 1.1.1...
Letter Caps	A, B, C *
Letter	a, b, c *
Numeric	1, 2, 3 *
Roman Caps	I, II, III *
Roman	i, ii, iii *

*No further subdivisions

To add a subtopic, which will be *indented to the right*, choose Outline > New Topic Right (⌘R) (**Figure 8.29**). The cursor will move to the next line and automatically indent to the right (top, **Figure 8.30**). You can then type in your next topic (bottom, **Figure 8.30**).

or

To add a topic that will be *indented to the left*, choose Outline > New Topic Left (⌘L) (**Figure 8.31**). The cursor will move to the next line and automatically indent to the left (top, **Figure 8.32**). You can then type in your next topic (bottom, **Figure 8.32**).

5. Repeat the variations in step 4 until you've added the desired topics and their rough organization. To fine-tune your outline, see *Promoting and demoting topics* on page 181 and *Reordering outline topics* on page 183.

✔ Tips

■ The New Topic Left command will only work if the current topic has been moved right (indented or demoted) at least once. Otherwise, there will be no room to create a topic on the left.

■ As you can see in **Figure 8.30**, the topic labels change from hollow to filled to reflect whether a topic has any subtopics.

■ If you want to change a label's style, choose Outline > Label Style and pick a new style from the submenu. For more information on the styles, see **Table 8.1**.

Selecting outline topics

Selecting outline topics involves clicking the topic's "label," which sits immediately to the left of any topic.

To select an outline topic:

1. When you click in the outline text, or to the right of the text, the cursor will appear as an I-beam (top, **Figure 8.33**).

2. Move the cursor to the beginning of the outline topic and the cursor will become an arrow (middle, **Figure 8.33**).

3. Click again and the outline topic will be selected—plus all its subtopics (bottom, **Figure 8.33**).

✔ Tips

- If you choose "None" in *To create an outline* as your label style, the label will not be visible—but it is still there for selecting (middle right, **Figure 8.33**). Once you click on the label, the outline topic and all its subtopics will be highlighted (bottom right, **Figure 8.33**).

- If you do not want to select all of a topic's subtopics, click the cursor just to the *right* of the last subtopic that you want selected and drag the cursor to highlight it and the main topic (**Figure 8.34**).

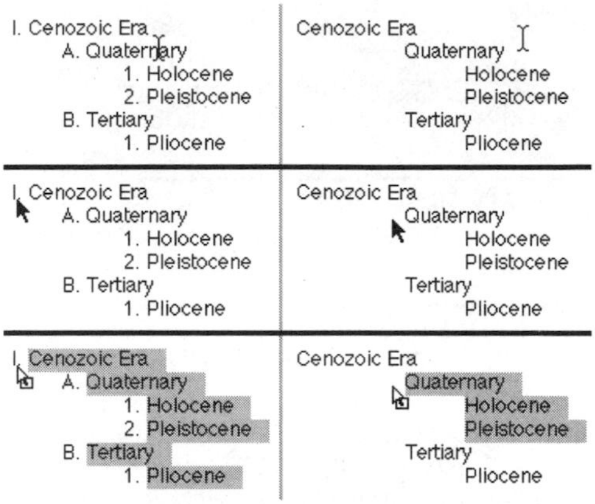

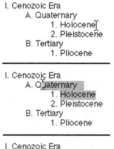

Figure 8.33 If you click in the text, the cursor appears as an I-beam (top), but becomes an arrow as you move to the label, even if it's invisible (middle). Once you click the label, the topic and its subtopics are selected (bottom).

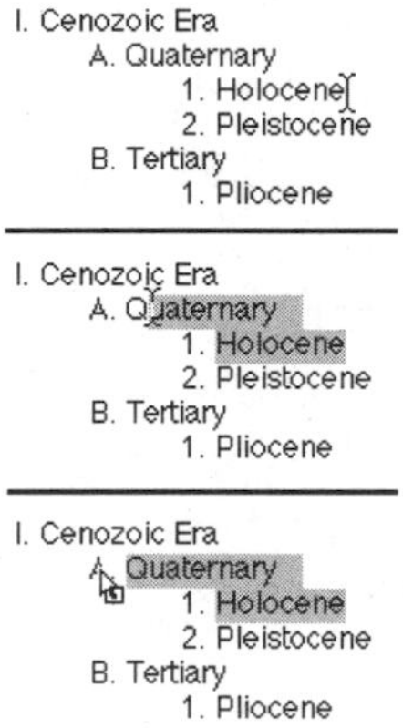

Figure 8.34 If you do not want to select *all* of a topic's subtopics, click to the *right* of the last subtopic that you want selected and drag the cursor up and to the left.

```
I. Cenozoic Era
    A. Quaternary
        1. Holocene
        2. Pleistocene
    B. Tertiary
        1. Pliocene
            a) Earliest human artifacts (Lucy)
        2. Miocene
        3. Oligocene
        4. Paleocene
II. Mesozoic Era
```

Figure 8.35 Click on the *label* of a topic you want to promote.

Figure 8.36 Choose Outline > Move Left > With Subtopics.

```
I. Cenozoic Era
    A. Quaternary
        1. Holocene
        2. Pleistocene
II. Tertiary
    A. Pliocene
        1. Earliest human artifacts (Lucy)
    B. Miocene
    C. Oligocene
    D. Paleocene
III. Mesozoic Era
```

Figure 8.37 ...The topic and *all its subtopics* will be promoted.

Figure 8.38 Choose Outline > Move Left > Without Subtopics.

```
I. Cenozoic Era
    A. Quaternary
        1. Holocene
        2. Pleistocene
II. Tertiary
    A. Pliocene
        1. Earliest human artifacts (Lucy)
        2. Miocene
        3. Oligocene
        4. Paleocene
III. Mesozoic Era
```

Figure 8.39 Only the topic and the *selected* subtopics will be promoted. Note the change from Figure 8.35: *Miocene* and *Pliocene* are no longer on the same level.

Promoting and demoting topics

Promoting and demoting change a topic's level within the outline. If, for example, a topic labeled IB is promoted by one level, its label will become II.

To promote a topic:

1. Click on the label of a topic you want to promote (**Figure 8.35**).

2. Choose Outline > Move Left > With Subtopics ([Shift][⌘][L]) (**Figure 8.36**). The topic and *all its subtopics* will be promoted (**Figure 8.37**).

   or

   Choose Outline > Move Left > Without Subtopics (**Figure 8.38**) and only the topic and the *selected* subtopics will be promoted (**Figure 8.39**). (Note how *Miocene* is no longer on the same level as *Pliocene*.)

✔ Tips

- If you want to promote the topic and its subtopics, you also can click the Promote button in the Button Bar (**Figure 8.40**).

- Raising a topic (**Figure 8.41**) does the same thing as promoting a topic with its subtopics.

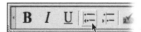

Figure 8.40 To promote a topic and its subtopics, you also can click the Promote button in the Button Bar.

Figure 8.41 Raising a topic does the same thing as promoting a topic with its subtopics.

CREATING AND USING OUTLINES

181

To demote a topic:

1. Click on the label of a topic you want to demote (**Figure 8.42**).

2. Choose Outline > Move Right > With Subtopics ((Shift)(⌘)(R)) (**Figure 8.43**). The topic and *all its subtopics* will be demoted (**Figure 8.44**).

   or

   Choose Outline > Move Right > Without Subtopics (**Figure 8.45**) and only the topic and the *selected* subtopics will be demoted (**Figure 8.46**). (Note how *Tertiary* is no longer on the same level as *Pleistocene*.)

✔ Tip

■ If you want to demote the topic and its subtopics, you also can click the Demote button in the Button Bar (**Figure 8.47**).

Figure 8.47 To demote the topic and its subtopics, you also can click the Demote button in the Button Bar.

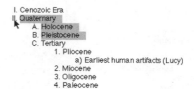

Figure 8.42 Click on the label of a topic you want to demote.

Figure 8.43 Choose Outline > Move Right > With Subtopics.

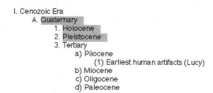

Figure 8.44 The topic and *all its subtopics* are demoted.

Figure 8.45 Choose Outline > Move Right > Without Subtopics.

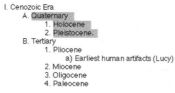

Figure 8.46 Only the topic and the *selected* subtopics are demoted. Note the change from Figure 8.42: *Tertiary* and *Pleistocene* are no longer on the same level.

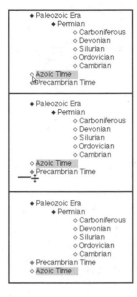

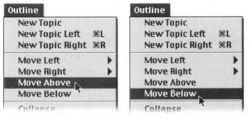

Figure 8.48 To reorder an outline topic, click on its label and drag it to its new position.

Figure 8.49 To reorder a topic by *one level only*, you also can choose Outline > Move Above or Outline > Move Below.

Reordering outline topics

Reordering, or rearranging, topics works a bit differently than promoting and demoting. As their menu commands suggest, promoting and demoting move topics left and right but do not change their relative order in an outline. In contrast, reordering affects *only* the order. If, for example, a topic is nested two levels in from the left before reordering, it will still be two levels in from the left even in its new position.

To reorder outline topics:

1. Click on the label of a topic you want to move higher or lower in the outline (top, **Figure 8.48**).

2. Drag the label to its new position, which will be marked by a dark horizontal bar (middle, **Figure 8.48**).

3. Release the cursor and the topic (and all its subtopics) will move to the new position (bottom, **Figure 8.48**).

✔ Tip

■ If you want to reorder a topic by *one level only*, you also can choose Outline > Move Above or Outline > Move Below (**Figure 8.49**).

CREATING AND USING OUTLINES

Expanding and collapsing outlines

By selectively expanding and collapsing the outline, you can focus on the section you are currently working on.

To expand an outline:

1. Click on the label of the topic you want to expand (**Figure 8.50**).

2. Choose Outline > Expand (**Figure 8.51**). The topic will expand to reveal the *next level* of topics below it (**Figure 8.52**).

   or

   Choose Outline > Expand All (**Figure 8.53**). The topic will expand to reveal *all* the topics below it (**Figure 8.54**).

   or

   Choose Outline > Expand To (**Figure 8.55**). When the Expand To dialog box appears, enter a number for how many levels you want to reveal and click *OK* (**Figure 8.56**). The topic will expand to reveal the specified number of levels.

✔ Tips

- To quickly reveal only the next level below the selected topic, double-click its label.

- By default, the number that initially appears in the Expand To dialog box is the maximum number of levels below the selected topic.

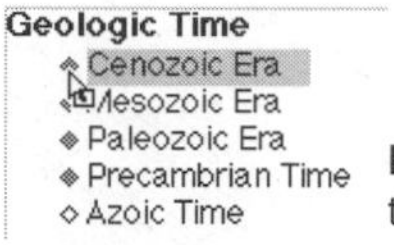

Figure 8.50 Click on the label of the topic you want to expand.

Figure 8.51 Choose Outline > Expand.

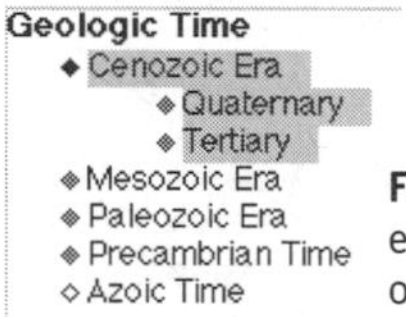

Figure 8.52 The topic will expand to reveal the *next level* of topics below.

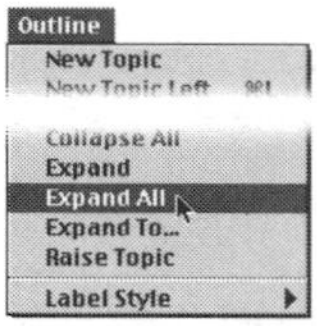

Figure 8.53 Choose Outline > Expand All.

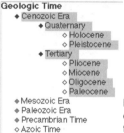

Figure 8.54 The topic will expand to reveal *all* the topics below it.

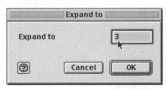

Figure 8.55 Choose Outline > Expand To.

Figure 8.56 Enter a number for how many levels you want to reveal.

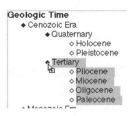

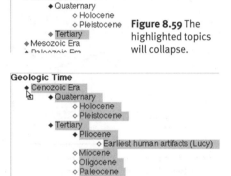

Figure 8.57 Click on the label of the topic you want to collapse.

Figure 8.58 Choose Outline > Collapse.

Geologic Time
- ◆ Cenozoic Era
  - ◆ Quaternary
    - ◇ Holocene
    - ◇ Pleistocene
  - ◆ Tertiary
- ◆ Mesozoic Era
- ◆ Paleozoic Era

Figure 8.59 The highlighted topics will collapse.

Geologic Time
- ◆ Cenozoic Era
  - ◆ Quaternary
    - ◇ Holocene
    - ◇ Pleistocene
  - ◆ Tertiary
    - ◆ Pliocene
      - ◇ Earliest human artifacts (Lucy)
    - ◇ Miocene
    - ◇ Oligocene
    - ◇ Paleocene

Figure 8.60 To collapse the entire outline, click on the label of the topmost topic.

Outline
New Topic
New Topic Left   ⌘L
New Topic Right   ⌘R
Move Left   ▶
Move Right   ▶
Move Above
Move Below
Collapse
Collapse All
Expand

Figure 8.61 Choose Outline > Collapse All.

Geologic Time
- ◆ Cenozoic Era
- ◆ Mesozoic Era
- ◆ Paleozoic Era
- ◆ Precambrian Time
- ◇ Azoic Time

Figure 8.62 All the highlighted topics will be collapsed beneath the topmost topic.

To collapse an outline topic:

1. Click on the label of the topic you want to collapse (**Figure 8.57**).

2. Choose Outline > Collapse (**Figure 8.58**). The highlighted topics will collapse (**Figure 8.59**).

✔ Tip

- You also can double-click the label of any topic to collapse everything below it.

To collapse the entire outline:

1. Click on the label of the topmost topic in the outline (**Figure 8.60**).

2. Choose Outline > Collapse All (**Figure 8.61**). All the highlighted topics will be collapsed beneath the topmost topic (**Figure 8.62**).

Using the Spelling Checker and Thesaurus

AppleWorks's spelling checker gives you the option of checking an entire document or only the portion that you select. If your writing frequently uses special terms, you can create what AppleWorks calls a user dictionary where you can add terms and edit them later as needed. AppleWorks will then check words against the user dictionary, as well as its built-in main dictionary. If you have already built a special terms dictionary in another program or an older version of AppleWorks, you can import it into version 6 of AppleWorks and save yourself a lot of work.

To check spelling:

1. With the document open, you can check the spelling in the entire document by choosing Edit > Writing Tools > Check Document Spelling (⌘=) (top, **Figure 8.63**).

    or

    Check a word or a portion of a document by selecting it and choosing Edit > Writing Tools > Check Selection Spelling (Shift⌘Y) (bottom, **Figure 8.63**).

2. When the Spelling dialog box appears, the first word of questionable spelling will be highlighted in the *Word* window with suggested replacement words listed in the bottom window (**Figure 8.64**).

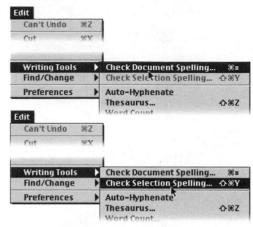

Figure 8.63 You can check spelling for the entire document (top) or just a selected portion of it (bottom).

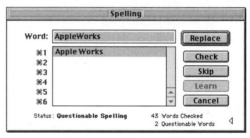

Figure 8.64 Ironic isn't it: AppleWorks's own spelling checker wants to replace AppleWorks (top highlight) with Apple Works (bottom highlight).

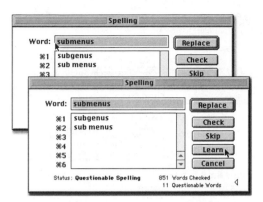

Figure 8.65 To add a word to the dictionary, highlight your special term in the *Word* window (top) and click *Learn* (bottom).

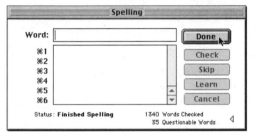

Figure 8.66 When you finish checking the spelling of the document or selection, click *Done*.

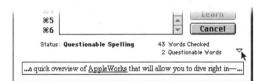

Figure 8.67 Click the bottom-right arrow in the Spelling dialog box to see a questionable word in context.

3. If the word highlighted in the bottom window is correct, click *Replace* and the spelling checker will move on to the next questionable word. You also can fix the word manually by typing a new spelling in the *Word* window and clicking *Replace*.

or

If you are sure the word is spelled correctly, click *Skip* and the spelling checker will move on to the next questionably spelled word.

or

If you have already created a user dictionary, you can add special terms to it and the spelling checker won't stop on that word in future checks. Highlight your special term in the *Word* window and click *Learn* to add the word to your dictionary (**Figure 8.65**). For more information, see *To create a user dictionary* on page 188.

4. When you finish checking the spelling of the document or selection, click *Done* (**Figure 8.66**). The Spelling dialog box will close and you'll be returned to your document.

✔ Tips

- If you want to see the questionable word in context, click the bottom-right arrow in the Spelling dialog box. The line in the document where the questionable word appears will be displayed (**Figure 8.67**).

- You can quickly choose a suggested word by using the command key sequence listed next to it (⌘① for the first word listed, ⌘② for the second word listed, and so on).

To create a user dictionary:

1. Choose Edit > Writing Tools > Select Dictionaries (**Figure 8.68**).

2. When the Select Dictionaries dialog box appears, select *User Dictionary* in the *Dictionaries* panel, and click *New* (**Figure 8.69**).

3. When the New User Dictionary Name dialog box appears, navigate to where you want to store the new dictionary, give it a name, and click *Save* (**Figure 8.70**). The new dictionary will be created, which you must then select to actually use. For more information, see *To select a dictionary* on the next page.

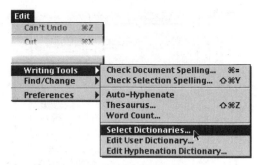

Figure 8.68 To pick a dictionary, choose Edit > Writing Tools > Select Dictionaries.

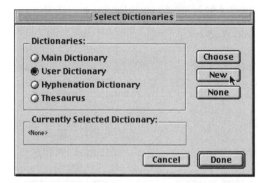

Figure 8.69 Select *User Dictionary* in the *Dictionaries* panel and click *New*.

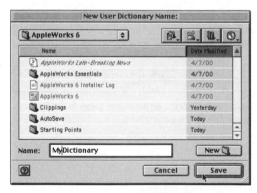

Figure 8.70 When the New User Dictionary Name dialog box appears, navigate to where you want to store the new dictionary, give it a name, and click *Save*.

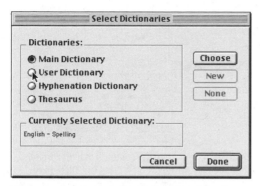

Figure 8.71 When the Select Dictionaries dialog box appears, the *Main Dictionary* button will be selected and its specific name displayed in the *Currently Selected Dictionary* panel.

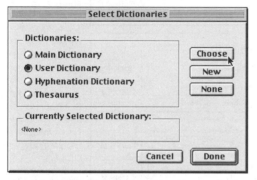

Figure 8.72 To select a user dictionary, click *User Dictionary* in the *Dictionaries* panel and click *Choose*.

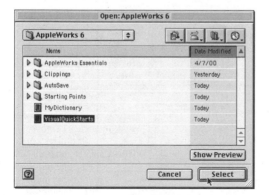

Figure 8.73 When the Open dialog box appears, navigate to the dictionary you want to use, click it, and then click *Select*.

To select a dictionary:

1. Choose Edit > Writing Tools > Select Dictionaries (**Figure 8.68**).

2. When the Select Dictionaries dialog box appears, the *Main Dictionary* button will be selected and its specific name displayed in the *Currently Selected Dictionary* panel (**Figure 8.71**). Select *User Dictionary* in the *Dictionaries* panel, and click *Choose* (**Figure 8.72**).

3. When the Open dialog box appears, navigate to the dictionary you want to use, click it and then click *Select* (**Figure 8.73**). The Select Dictionaries dialog box reappears with the dictionary you just picked listed in the *Currently Selected Dictionary* panel (**Figure 8.74**). If you are satisfied with your choice, click *Done* and that dictionary will be made active, along with the main dictionary. To choose another user dictionary, repeat these steps, though only two dictionaries will be active at any one time: the main dictionary and the selected user dictionary.

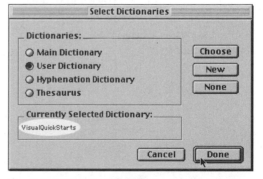

Figure 8.74 When the Select Dictionaries dialog box reappears, the dictionary you just picked is listed in the *Currently Selected Dictionary* panel.

To edit a dictionary:

1. Choose Edit > Writing Tools > Edit User Dictionary (**Figure 8.75**).

2. When the dialog box for the currently selected dictionary appears, it will display all the terms already added to the dictionary (top, **Figure 8.76**).

3. To add a word, type it into the *Entry* window and click *Add* (middle, **Figure 8.76**). The word will be added to the dictionary's list (bottom, **Figure 8.76**).

4. To remove or correct a word, select it in the list and click *Remove* (top, **Figure 8.77**). The word will be removed from the list, but remain in the *Entry* window (middle, **Figure 8.77**). Type in the correction in the *Entry* window and click *Add* (bottom, **Figure 8.77**). The corrected word will be added to the dictionary.

5. Once you have added, removed, and corrected words, click *OK* and the list will close.

✔ Tip

■ AppleWorks includes a hyphenation dictionary that it uses when breaking words across lines. You can add to it like any other dictionary by choosing Edit > Writing Tools > Edit Hyphenation Dictionary.

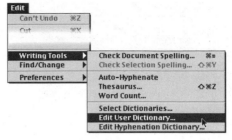

Figure 8.75 To change the contents of a dictionary, choose Edit > Writing Tools > Edit User Dictionary.

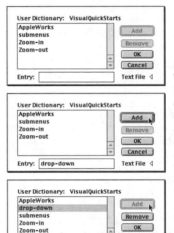

Figure 8.76 When the dialog box for the current user dictionary appears, it lists all the terms already added to it (top). To add a word, type it into the *Entry* window, click *Add* (middle) and it is added to the list (bottom).

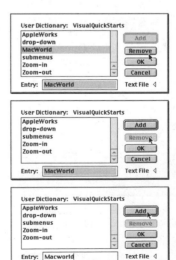

Figure 8.77 To correct a word in a user dictionary, highlight it and click *Remove* (top). The word is removed from the list, but remains in the *Entry* window (middle), where you can type in a correction and click *Add* (bottom).

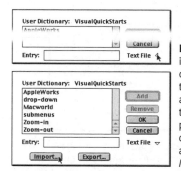

Figure 8.78 To import a dictionary, click the *Text File* arrow and when the lower portion of the dialog box appears, click *Import*.

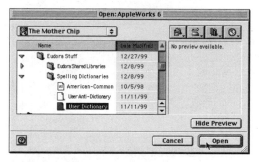

Figure 8.79 When the Open dialog box appears, navigate to the dictionary whose contents you want to add and click *Open*.

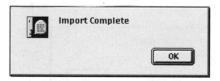

Figure 8.80 Once the dictionary is imported, an alert dialog box will appear. Click *OK*.

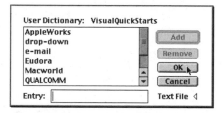

Figure 8.81 After the import is finished, the AppleWorks dictionary lists the words added from the other dictionary.

To import another dictionary:

1. Choose Edit > Writing Tools > Edit User Dictionary (**Figure 8.75**).

2. When the dialog box for the currently selected dictionary appears, click the *Text File* arrow and when the lower portion of the dialog box appears, click *Import* (**Figure 8.78**).

3. When the Open dialog box appears, navigate to the dictionary whose contents you want to add and click *Open* (**Figure 8.79**).

4. After a moment, the import will be complete. Click *OK* in the alert dialog box (**Figure 8.80**). The AppleWorks dictionary list will reappear with words added from the other dictionary (**Figure 8.81**). Click *OK* and the list will close.

To export an AppleWorks dictionary:

1. Choose Edit > Writing Tools > Edit User Dictionary (**Figure 8.75**).

2. When the dialog box for the currently selected dictionary appears, click the *Text File* arrow and when the lower portion of the dialog box appears, click *Export* (**Figure 8.82**).

3. When the Save the User Dictionary as dialog box appears, navigate to where you want to store the dictionary, give it a name, and click *Save* (**Figure 8.83**).

4. A dialog box will appear once the export is complete (**Figure 8.84**). Click *OK* and when the dictionary list reappears, click *OK* again.

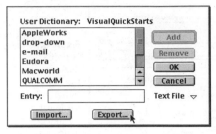

Figure 8.82 To export a dictionary, click the *Text File* arrow and when the lower portion of the dialog box appears, click *Export*.

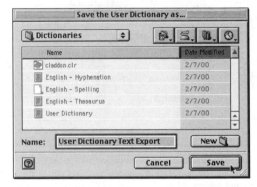

Figure 8.83 Navigate to where you want to store the exported dictionary, give it a name, and click *Save*.

Figure 8.84 Once the dictionary is exported, an alert dialog box will appear. Click *OK*.

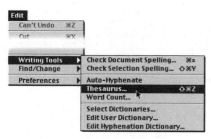

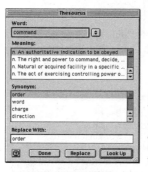

Figure 8.85 To find a synonym, choose Edit > Writing Tools > Thesaurus (Shift ⌘ Z).

Figure 8.86 When the Thesaurus dialog box appears, check the *Meaning* window to make sure the correct term is being used.

Figure 8.87 Scroll through the *Meaning* list until you find a more appropriate meaning, click the meaning, and the *Synonym* list of words will be updated.

Figure 8.88 Once you find a synonym to your liking, click it in the *Synonym* list and click *Replace*.

To find a synonym:

1. Select the word in the document for which you want to find a synonym.

2. Choose Edit > Writing Tools > Thesaurus (Shift ⌘ Z) (**Figure 8.85**).

3. When the Thesaurus dialog box appears, inspect the *Meaning* window to make sure the correct term is being used (**Figure 8.86**). If not, scroll through the *Meaning* list until you find a more appropriate meaning, click that meaning, and the *Synonym* list of words will be updated (**Figure 8.87**).

4. Once you find a synonym to your liking, click it in the *Synonym* list and click *Replace* (**Figure 8.88**). Click *Done* and the thesaurus will close.

✔ Tip

- You also can look for a synonym by choosing Edit > Writing Tools > Thesaurus, typing into the *Word* window, and clicking *Look Up* (**Figure 8.89**). A list of possible synonyms will appear.

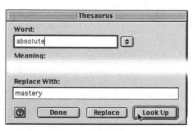

Figure 8.89 You also can look for a synonym by typing into the *Word* window and clicking *Look Up*.

Wrapping Text Around Frames and Objects

AppleWorks gives you two ways to wrap text. The first involves wrapping the main word-processing document's text around a floating frame. The second is a variation: Wrapping the text *inside a frame* around an object also floating within that frame. It's a bit of a mirror-inside-a-mirror trick, as you will see in the example. For more information on creating and inserting floating frames, see *Using Frames* on page 61. Linking frames is explained in the next section on page 197.

To wrap text around a frame:

1. Select the floating frame by clicking it (**Figure 8.90**).

2. Choose Options > Text Wrap (**Figure 8.91**) or Ctrl-click the frame and choose *Text Wrap* from the drop-down menu (**Figure 8.92**).

3. When the Text Wrap dialog box appears, click *Regular* or *Irregular*, depending on how you want the text wrapped (**Figure 8.93**).

4. Use the *Gutter* window to set how much white space (in pixels) you want separating the frame and the surrounding text. Click *OK* and the wrap will be applied (**Figure 8.94**). To make the wrap look its best, you may need to slightly reposition the frame using the arrow keys.

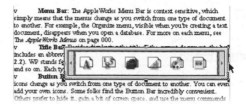

Figure 8.90 First select the floating frame by clicking it.

Figure 8.91 To wrap text around a frame, choose Options > Text Wrap.

Figure 8.92 You also can Ctrl-click the frame and choose *Text Wrap* from the drop-down menu.

Figure 8.93 When the Text Wrap dialog box appears, click *Regular* or *Irregular*, depending on how you want the text wrapped and set the *Gutter* width.

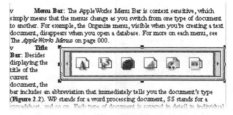

Figure 8.94 After the wrap is applied, the text flows around the frame.

Figure 8.95 You also can click the Text Wrap button to make the document's previous content flow around the new frame.

✔ Tips

- In step 2 you also can click the Text Wrap icon in the Button Bar (**Figure 8.95**) and the settings in the Text Wrap dialog box will be automatically applied to the frame.

- You can adjust the gutter or type of wrap at any time after you first apply it.

- If the Text Wrap command is grayed out in step 2, your frame may be inline instead of floating. For more information, see *Changing frame types* on page 65.

To cancel text wrapping:

1. Click to select the frame the text is wrapped around.

2. Choose Options > Text Wrap (**Figure 8.91**) or [Ctrl]-click the frame and choose *Text Wrap* from the drop-down menu (**Figure 8.92**).

3. When the Text Wrap dialog box appears, click *None* and *OK*. The text wrapping will be cancelled.

To wrap text around objects in a text frame:

1. Click to select the text frame that has been placed within the main word-processing document (**Figure 8.96**).

2. Choose Options > Frame Links (⌘L) (**Figure 8.97**). The text frame will become linked, as indicated by small boxes at the top and bottom of the text frame (**Figure 8.98**).

3. Click and drag or paste the object inside the text frame, where it will float atop the text (**Figure 8.99**).

4. Choose Options > Text Wrap (**Figure 8.91**) or Ctrl-click the frame and choose *Text Wrap* from the drop-down menu (**Figure 8.92**).

5. When the Text Wrap dialog box appears, click *Regular* or *Irregular*, depending on how you want the text wrapped (**Figure 8.93**), set the *Gutter* width and click *OK*. The text in the frame will wrap around the object (**Figure 8.100**).

✔ Tip

■ Step 2 is crucial. If you do not link the frame, the object will float on top of the text no matter what you choose in the Text Wrap dialog box in the last step.

Figure 8.96 Select the text frame placed within the main word-processing document.

Figure 8.97 The crucial step: Choose Options > Frame Links.

Figure 8.98 Once the text frame is linked, a small box appears at the top and bottom of the frame.

Figure 8.99 When the object first appears in the text frame, it floats on top of the text.

Figure 8.100 After applying the text wrap, the frame's text flows around the object.

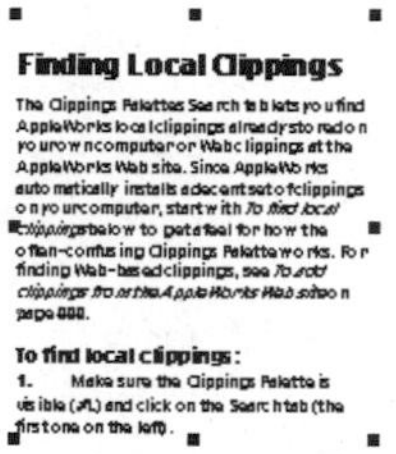

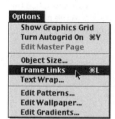

Figure 8.101 First select the text frame by clicking it with the Arrow Tool.

Figure 8.102 To add a link to an existing text frame, choose Options > Frame Links.

Figure 8.103 Click the link icon at the bottom of the text frame...

Figure 8.104 ...and press [Option] as you drag the cursor to create a new text frame.

Linking Text Frames

Linked text frames are particularly useful when creating layouts for newsletters or other multiple-page documents. By linking the text frames, you can connect columns or blocks of text so that any overflow (or cuts) in the first block is reflected in the other blocks. Such links, for example, would enable you to start text on page 1 of a document and have it jump to page 4 so that you can put another story on pages 2 and 3.

To add a link to an existing text frame:

1. Open your document and make sure the Frame tab of the Tools Palette is visible. Use the Arrow Tool to select the existing text frame, to which you want to link (add) a new frame (**Figure 8.101**).

2. Choose Options > Frame Links ([⌘][L]) (**Figure 8.102**).

3. Click the bottom link icon, which now appears on the text frame (**Figure 8.103**).

4. Press [Option] as you drag the cursor, which becomes an I-beam with a bar across it, to create a new text frame (**Figure 8.104**).

(continued)

5. Release the cursor and the new text frame will appear (**Figure 8.105**). A chain icon on the top of the new frame indicates that it is linked to the first text frame. Repeat steps 3–5 to add as many new text frames as you need. You can then add text to the first frame and any overflow will automatically spill into the new linked frame (**Figure 8.106**).

✔ Tip

- In step 4 in most cases, you'll be adding the text frame to a *word-processing* document, which is why you must press `Option` as you drag the cursor. If you are adding the text frame to another type of document, just click and drag the cursor.

Finding Local Clippings

The Clippings Palettes Search tab lets you find AppleWorks local clippings already stored on your own computer or Web clippings at the AppleWorks Web site. Since AppleWorks automatically installs a decent set of clippings on your computer, start with *To find local clippings* below to get a feel for how the often-confusing Clippings Palette works. For finding Web-based clippings, see *To add clippings from the AppleWorks Web site* on page 000.

To find local clippings:
1. Make sure the Clippings Palette is visible (⌘L) and click on the Search tab (the first one on the left).

Figure 8.105 Release the cursor and the new text frame appears.

Finding Local Clippings

The Clippings Palettes Search tab lets you find AppleWorks local clippings already stored on your own computer or Web clippings at the AppleWorks Web site. Since AppleWorks automatically installs a decent set of clippings on your computer, start with *To find local clippings* below to get a feel for how the often-confusing Clippings Palette works. For finding Web-based clippings, see *To add clippings from the AppleWorks Web site* on page 000.

To find local clippings:
1. Make sure the Clippings Palette is visible (⌘L) and click on the Search tab (the first one on the left). As you add type to the

first text frame, it spills into the linked frame that you have added. This gives you a lot of flexibility in laying out a newsletter or any other multiple page text document.

Figure 8.106 Once the frames are linked, any text overflow automatically spills into the new frame.

Figure 8.107 Before drawing a new text frame, click the Text Frame tool.

Figure 8.108 Press (Option) as you drag the cursor to create a new text frame in the document.

Figure 8.109 Click the Arrow Tool in the Frame tab before trying to select the new text frame.

Figure 8.110 Now click the frame's bottom link icon...

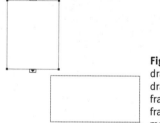

Figure 8.111 ...and drag the cursor to draw the second frame. (The first frame would not normally be visible.)

To create and link new text frames:

1. Open your document and make sure the Frame tab of the Tools Palette is visible.

2. Choose Options > Frame Links (⌘L) (**Figure 8.102**).

3. Click the Text Frame tool in the Frame tab. Now press (Option) as you drag the cursor, which becomes an I-beam with a bar across it, to create a new text frame in the document (**Figures 8.107** and **Figure 8.108**).

4. Click the Arrow Tool in the Frame tab, click the new text frame to select it, and when it appears click the frame's bottom link icon (**Figures 8.109** and **8.110**).

5. Click where you want the next text frame to begin and drag the cursor to draw the second frame (**Figure 8.111**).

6. Repeat steps 4 and 5 to add as many text frames as you need (**Figure 8.112**).

(continued)

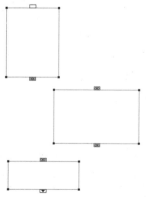

Figure 8.112 You can add as many new text frames as needed.

LINKING TEXT FRAMES

7. To add text to the linked frames, click inside the first frame so that the cursor becomes an I-beam. Begin typing in the first frame or paste text copied from another document; any overflow text will spill from one frame to the next (**Figure 8.113**). You then can move and resize the frames and add adjacent illustrations as desired to complete the layout (**Figure 8.114**).

✔ Tips

- You cannot link two *existing* text frames. You can only add a *new* text frame to an existing one.

- In laying out text frames across multiple pages, you may find it easier to arrange your pages side by side. Choose Format > Document and select *Mirror Facing Pages* and *Facing Pages Side-by-Side* in the Document dialog box (**Figure 8.115**).

- If you want to add *unlinked* frames to a document that already contains linked frames, you need to turn off the linking first. Choose Options > Frame Links (⌘L). If you later want to add some more *linked* frames, just choose Frame Links again.

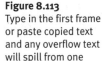

Figure 8.113
Type in the first frame or paste copied text and any overflow text will spill from one frame to the next.

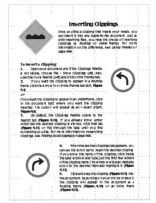

Figure 8.114
Once you have added text, you can move and resize the frames and add adjacent illustrations.

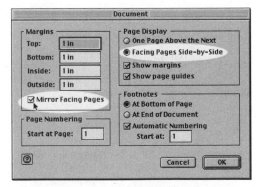

Figure 8.115 To make it easier to create text frames across multiple pages, select *Mirror Facing Pages* and *Facing Pages Side-by-Side* in the Document dialog box.

PART III

USING SPREADSHEETS

CREATING SPREADSHEETS

9

Way back in the 1980s, it was the spreadsheet that kick-started the desktop computer revolution. Thanks to the program Lotus 1-2-3, business folks suddenly had the power to build their own budgets and create a thousand what-if scenarios right on their personal computers. Today, spreadsheets remain no less amazing. If you need to track constantly changing numbers, dates, and how they affect each other, the spreadsheet is your best bet.

A spreadsheet is simply a grid of cells arranged in rows and columns (**Figure 9.1**). Each cell can contain numbers, formulas, dates, or text—all of which can be updated automatically when a change is made in any one cell. Spreadsheet data also can be used to generate charts to help you spot trends and relationships that might otherwise remain buried, as the following chapter explains. AppleWorks's Button Bar, by the way, automatically displays spreadsheet-related icons whenever you are working in a spreadsheet document or spreadsheet frame (**Figure 9.2**).

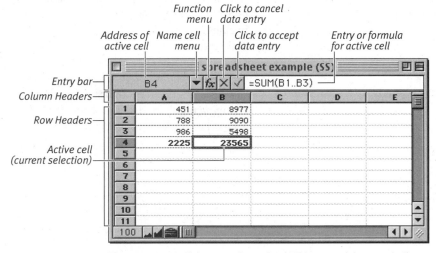

Figure 9.1 Many of the controls used to build a spreadsheet are built right into the document window.

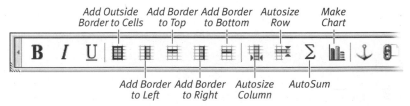

Figure 9.2 The Button Bar automatically displays spreadsheet-related icons when you work in a spreadsheet document or spreadsheet frame.

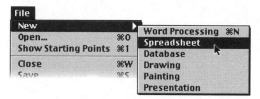

Figure 9.3 To create a spreadsheet document, choose File > New > Spreadsheet.

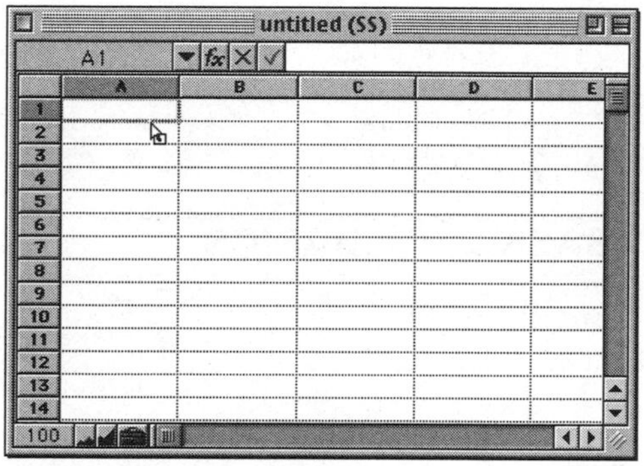

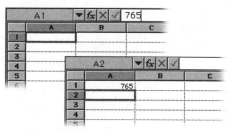

Figure 9.4 The A1 cell is automatically selected when a new spreadsheet is created.

Figure 9.5 Click the cell and when you begin typing, your entry appears in the entry bar (top). Press [Return] or [Enter] or click the Accept button and the data appears in the cell (bottom).

Starting a Spreadsheet

This section is intended to give you a jump on creating a spreadsheet. The details of working with spreadsheets—and there are plenty—are covered in the rest of the chapter.

To start a spreadsheet:

1. Choose File > New > Spreadsheet (**Figure 9.3**). A new untitled spreadsheet will open (**Figure 9.4**).

2. Choose File > Save As ([Shift][⌘][S]) and when the Save dialog box appears, navigate to where you want to store the file, give it a name, and click *Save*. The spreadsheet will be saved under its new name.

3. Click on the cell where you want the data to appear and begin typing your number, formula, or text. Your entry will appear in the entry bar (top, **Figure 9.5**).

4. Press [Return] or [Enter] or click the Accept button (the green check just left of the entry bar). The data will appear in the selected cell (bottom, **Figure 9.5**). Repeat to enter the other data you need. For information on using formulas, see *Entering and Editing Formulas* on page 229.

✔ Tips

- You can create a spreadsheet *frame* in an already open document by clicking the Spreadsheet Tool in the Frames tab, then dragging your cursor in the document (**Figures 9.6** and **9.7**). For more information on creating spreadsheet frames, see *Using Frames* on page 61.

- In step 4, if you press ⟨Return⟩ the cursor automatically moves to the next cell. If you click the green check, the cursor remains in the current cell. Depending on which cell you want to move to after making your entry, you have several other choices. See **Table 9.1** for more information. You even can change the settings for these keys if you like. See *To change spreadsheet preferences* on the next page.

Figure 9.6 Create a spreadsheet *frame* by clicking the Spreadsheet Tool in the Frames tab...

Figure 9.7 ...and drag the cursor to add a spreadsheet to an open document.

Table 9.1

Moving around in a spreadsheet*

To move to	Press
Below active cell	⟨Return⟩ or ⟨↓⟩
Above active cell	⟨Shift⟩⟨Return⟩ or ⟨↑⟩
Right of active cell	⟨Tab⟩ or ⟨→⟩
Left of active cell	⟨Shift⟩⟨Tab⟩ or ⟨←⟩
Specific cell	⟨⌘⟩⟨G⟩, enter address (e.g. A3)

*Default values; see *To change spreadsheet preferences* on the next page.

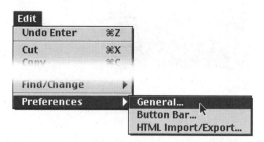

Figure 9.8 To change how the cursor moves from cell to cell, choose Edit > Preferences > General.

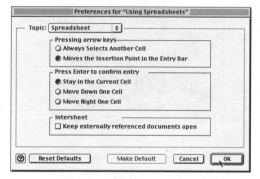

Figure 9.9 When the Preferences dialog box appears, set the behavior of the arrow and command keys.

To change spreadsheet preferences:

1. Choose Edit > Preferences > General (**Figure 9.8**).

2. When the Preferences dialog box appears (**Figure 9.9**), make your choices to control how the arrow keys and Enter (and the Return key) behave. Click *OK* and the changes are applied immediately.

Making Selections

Selecting cells, rows, or columns is usually the first step whenever you need to edit, rearrange, format, or sort a spreadsheet.

To select a cell:

- Click inside the cell and a border will indicate that it is selected or active (top, **Figure 9.5**)

To select adjacent cells:

- Click in the first cell, then drag your cursor to the last cell (**Figure 9.10**).

or

- Click in the first cell, then press Shift and the appropriate arrow key to move in any direction and select the adjacent cells.

To select all cells with data:

- Press Option while clicking in the top-left corner of the spreadsheet (**Figure 9.11**).

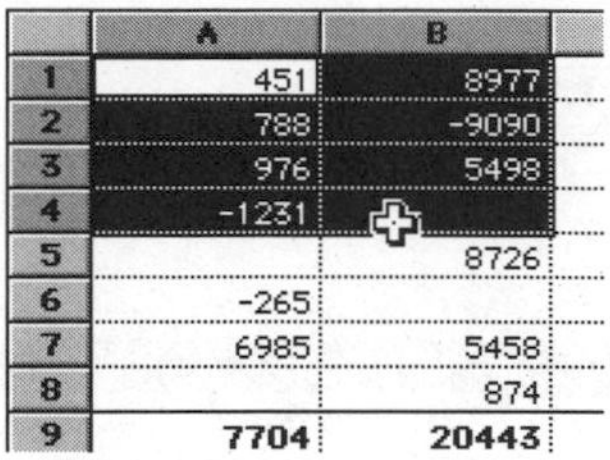

	A	B
1	451	8977
2	788	-9090
3	976	5498
4	-1231	
5		8726
6	-265	
7	6985	5458
8		874
9	7704	20443

Figure 9.10 To select adjacent cells, click in the first cell and drag your cursor to the last cell.

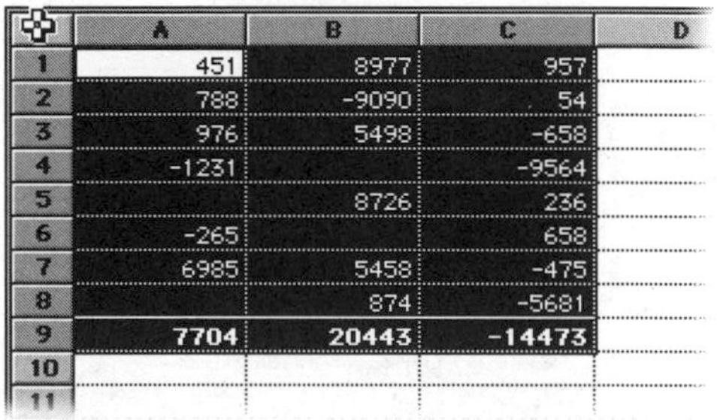

	A	B	C	D
1	451	8977	957	
2	788	-9090	54	
3	976	5498	-658	
4	-1231		-9564	
5		8726	236	
6	-265		658	
7	6985	5458	-475	
8		874	-5681	
9	7704	20443	-14473	
10				
11				

Figure 9.11 To select all cells containing data, press Option while clicking in the top-left corner of the spreadsheet.

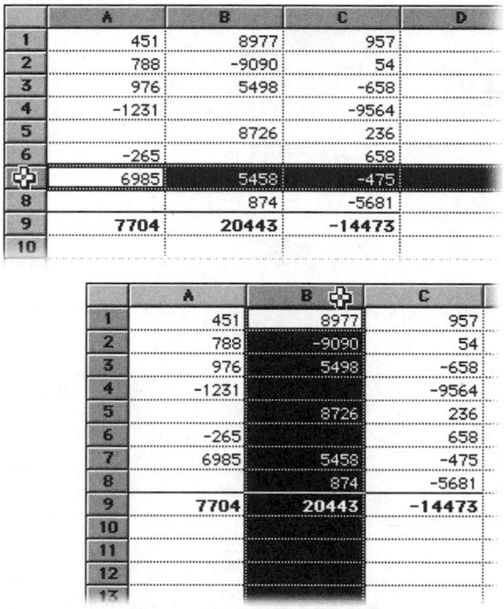

Figure 9.12 To select a row or column, click the Row Header (top) or Column Header (bottom).

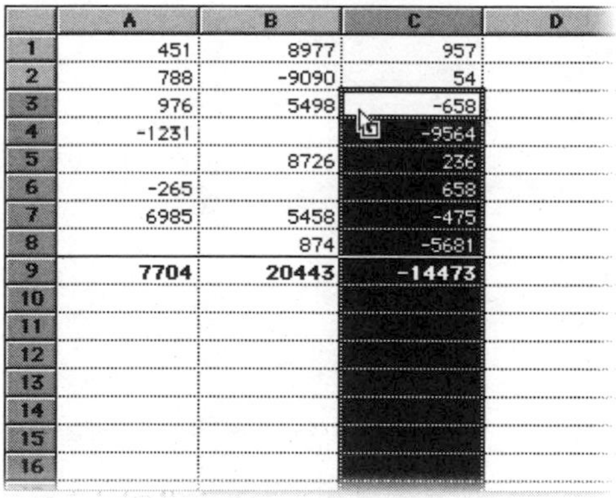

Figure 9.13 To select to the end of a row or column, click the first cell and press Shift ⌘ with the appropriate arrow key.

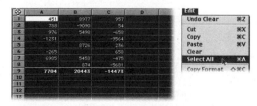

Figure 9.14 To select the *entire* spreadsheet, click the spreadsheet's top-left corner (left) or choose Edit > Select All (right).

To select a row or column:

◆ Click the Row Header or Column Header (**Figure 9.12**).

To select to the end of a row or column:

◆ Click in the first cell you want, then press Shift ⌘ and the appropriate arrow key (**Figure 9.13**).

To select an entire spreadsheet:

◆ Click in the top-left corner of the spreadsheet, or choose Edit > Select All (⌘A) (**Figure 9.14**).

Editing, Copying, and Moving Cells

One of the main advantages of spreadsheets over pencil and paper is that you can change your mind without generating more work for yourself. By editing, copying, or moving the contents of cells, you can quickly change a cell entry, even one based on a formula, with a minimum of fuss. For information on formulas, see *Entering and Editing Formulas* on page 229. For information on setting the alignment, appearance, or format of an entry, see *Formatting Spreadsheets* on page 223.

To edit cells without formulas:

1. Click in the cell you want to change (top, **Figure 9.15**).

2. Type in a new entry, which will appear in the entry bar at the top of the spreadsheet (middle, **Figure 9.15**).

3. Press (Return) or (Enter) or click the green Accept check. The cell entry will be updated to reflect your new entry (bottom, **Figure 9.15**).

✔ Tip

- If you make a mistake or change your mind in the middle of making an entry, press (Esc) or click the Cancel button (the red X). The original entry will reappear in the entry bar.

To edit cells with formulas:

1. Click in the cell you want to change (top, **Figure 9.16**).

2. In the entry bar, select the part of the formula that needs changing and type in the correction (middle, **Figure 9.16**).

3. Press (Return) or (Enter) or click the green Accept check. The formula will be updated and reflected in the cell originally selected (bottom, **Figure 9.16**).

Figure 9.15 To edit a cell, click it (top), type in a new entry (middle), and press (Return) or (Enter) or click the green Accept check.

Figure 9.16 To edit a formula, click the *cell* containing it (top). Select the formula *in the entry bar* and change it (middle). Press (Return) or (Enter) or click the green Accept check, and the change is applied (bottom).

Figure 9.17 Select the cell or cells whose *content* you want to delete.

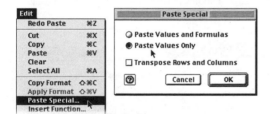

Figure 9.18 Press [Delete] and the content will be deleted, leaving an empty cell or cells ready for new content.

Edit	
Redo Paste	⌘Z
Cut	⌘X
Copy	⌘C
Paste	⌘V
Clear	
Select All	⌘A
Copy Format	⇧⌘C
Apply Format	⇧⌘V
Paste Special...	
Insert Function...	

Paste Special

○ Paste Values and Formulas
● Paste Values Only
□ Transpose Rows and Columns

[Cancel]　[OK]

Figure 9.19 If a cell contains a formula but you want to copy just the number, choose Edit > Paste Special (left) and choose *Paste Values Only* (right).

786	-9564		
8726	236		
8734	658		
5458	-475		
874	-5681		

786	-9564		
8726	236		
8734	658		
5458	-475		
874	-5681		

786	-9564		
8726	236	786	-9564
8734	658	8726	236
5458	-475	8734	658
874	-5681		

Figure 9.20 To *copy* multiple cells, click in the top-left cell and drag your cursor to select all the cells (top). Then press [Option] while dragging the cells to the top-left cell of the *new* range (middle). Release the cursor and all the cells are copied (bottom).

To delete cells:

1. Select the cell or cells whose *content* you want to delete (**Figure 9.17**).

2. Press [Delete] and the content will be deleted, leaving an empty cell or cells ready for new content (**Figure 9.18**).

To copy cells:

1. Click in the cell whose contents you want to copy.

2. Choose Edit > Copy (⌘C).

3. Click in the cell where you want the copied data to appear.

4. Choose Edit > Paste (⌘V). The data will be pasted into the cell.

✔ Tips

- If the selected cell contains a formula but you want to copy just the number, in step 4 choose Edit > Paste Special. When the Paste Special dialog box appears, choose *Paste Values Only* and click *OK* (**Figure 9.19**). The number, but not the formula that generated the number, will be pasted into the cell.

- To copy a range of cells, click in the top-left cell of the range and drag your cursor to select all the cells. Then press [Option] while dragging the cells to the top-left cell of the new range, and release the cursor. The original range will be copied to the destination cells (**Figure 9.20**).

- When copying and moving cells containing formulas, you need to keep in mind how the change will affect cell references used in the formula. For more information, see *Entering and Editing Formulas* on page 229.

To move cells:

1. Click in the cell or cells whose contents you want to move.

2. Choose Edit > Cut ($\mathcal{H}$$X$).

3. Click in the cell to which you will be moving the data (or the top-left cell of what will be the new range of cells).

4. Choose Edit > Paste ($\mathcal{H}$$V$). The data will be moved to the new cell or range of cells.

✔ Tips

- You can move a range of cells without messing with menu commands: Select the range, drag the cursor to the top-left cell of what will be the new range of cells, and release the cursor (**Figure 9.21**). The cells will be moved.

- Here's a way to move cells that is especially useful when working in large spreadsheets where you cannot see the selected cells and destination cells at the same time. Select the cells and choose Calculate > Move. When the Move dialog box appears, enter the column-and-row address for what will be the top-left cell in the destination range, and click *OK*. The cells will be moved (**Figure 9.22**).

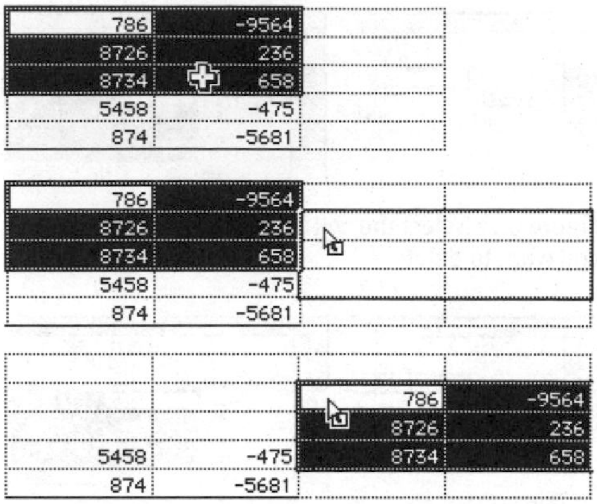

Figure 9.21 To *move* multiple cells, click in the top-left cell and drag your cursor to select all the cells (top). Then drag the cells to the top-left cell of the *new* range (middle). Release the cursor and all the cells are moved (bottom).

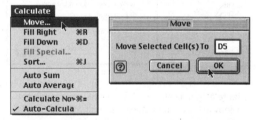

Figure 9.22 To move cells to parts of the spreadsheet that you cannot see, select the cells and choose Calculate > Move (left). Enter the address for what will be the top-left cell in the new range and click *OK* (right).

Figure 9.23 Click the cell whose content you want repeated and drag your cursor to select the other cell(s) where you want the data to appear.

Figure 9.24 To automatically fill the cells, choose Calculate > Fill Right for rows or Fill Down for columns.

Figure 9.25 The selected cells will be filled automatically.

Filling and Locking Cells

AppleWorks spreadsheets include an automatic cell filling feature that can reduce the tedium of building a spreadsheet cell by cell. While you can use this feature for numbers, it also can be used for filling in dates or text. The Fill Special command even lets you automatically repeat a pattern over multiple cells.

If you want to make sure that the contents of particular cells are not changed, you can lock them. This is not the same thing as locking rows or columns, which simply keeps their titles from scrolling out of sight. For more information on locking rows or columns, see page 242.

To automatically fill cells with data:

1. Click on the cell you want to repeat and drag your cursor to select the other cell(s) where you want the data repeated (**Figure 9.23**).

2. Choose Calculate > Fill Right (⌘R) for rows or Calculate > Fill Down (⌘D) for columns (**Figure 9.24**). The selected cells will be filled (**Figure 9.25**).

To fill cells with repeating numbers, times, or dates:

1. Select the cells that you want to fill with a series of numbers, times, or dates (**Figure 9.26**).

2. Choose Calculate > Fill Special (**Figure 9.27**).

3. When the Fill Special dialog box appears, choose *Number*, *Time*, or another of the seven radio buttons down the left side (**Figure 9.28**). Use the text window and drop-down menus to choose where the series should *Start*, the *Increment*, and (if available) whether to *Abbreviate* the entry. Click *OK*. The selected cells will be filled in based on your choice (**Figure 9.29**).

✔ Tip

■ With its main choices, drop-down menus, and text windows, the Fill Special dialog box can generate an amazing variety of combinations. Experiment to discover the combinations that work best for your needs.

Figure 9.26 Select the cells you want to fill with a series of numbers, times, or dates.

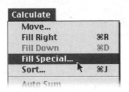

Figure 9.27 Choose Calculate > Fill Special.

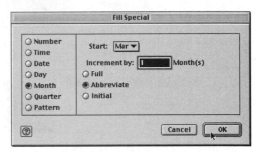

Figure 9.28 Choose one of the seven radio buttons, where the series should *Start*, the *Increment*, and whether to *Abbreviate* the entry.

Figure 9.29 The selected cells are filled in based on your choices in Figure 9.28.

Figure 9.30 Select the cells with the data *and* the cells where you want it repeated.

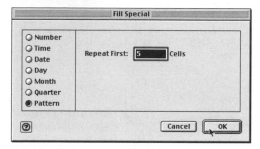

Figure 9.31 Use the Fill Special dialog box to choose the *Pattern* and the number of cells with data automatically appears in the *Repeat First* window.

Figure 9.32 The pattern is repeated in all the cells selected in Figure 9.30.

Figure 9.33 Select the cells you do not want changed and choose Options > Lock Cells.

Figure 9.34 A padlock appears in the Address window of locked cells.

To fill cells with a repeating pattern:

1. Type into a series of adjacent cells the data or text you want to repeat.

2. Select the cells with the data *and* the cells where you want it repeated (**Figure 9.30**).

3. Choose Calculate > Fill Special (**Figure 9.27**).

4. When the Fill Special dialog box appears, choose *Pattern* and the number of cells with data will automatically appear in the *Repeat First* window (**Figure 9.31**). Click *OK* and the pattern will be repeated in all the cells selected in step 1 (**Figure 9.32**).

To lock cells:

1. Select the cells you want to lock.

2. Choose Options > Lock Cells (⌘H) (**Figure 9.33**).

3. The selected cells will be locked, as denoted by the lock icon in the address of the active cell (**Figure 9.34**).

✔ Tip

■ To unlock cells, select them and choose Options > Unlock Cells (Shift⌘H) and the lock icon will not longer appear in the address of the selected cells.

FILLING AND LOCKING CELLS

Working with Rows or Columns

By inserting, deleting, resizing, and transposing rows or columns, you can reshape your spreadsheet on a larger scale than cell by cell.

To insert a blank row:

1. Select the row just below where you want the blank row inserted (**Figure 9.35**).

2. Choose Format > Insert Cells ([Shift][⌘][I]) (**Figure 9.36**). A blank row will be inserted (**Figure 9.37**).

✔ Tip

■ If you want to increase the *overall* size of the spreadsheet, choose Format > Document and when the Document dialog box appears, use the *Size* panel to increase the *Columns Across* or *Rows Down* (**Figure 9.38**).

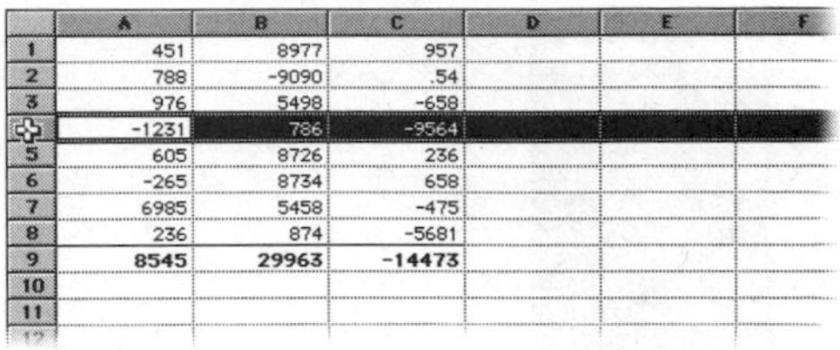

Figure 9.35 Select the row just *below* where you want the blank row inserted.

Figure 9.36 To insert a row or column, choose Format > Insert Cells.

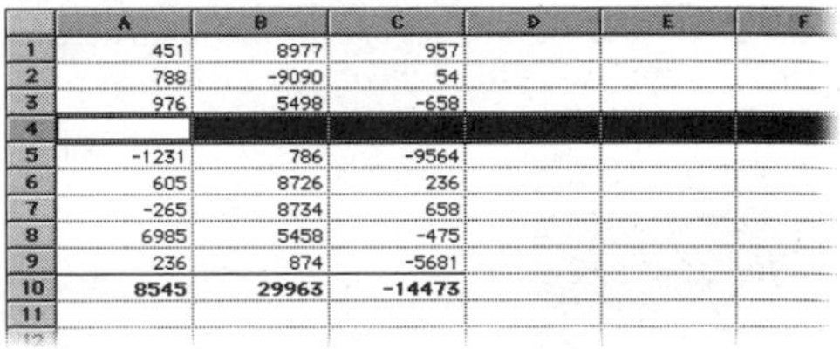

Figure 9.37 A new blank row is inserted.

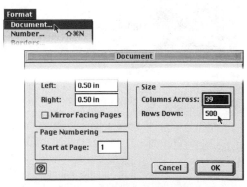

Figure 9.38 To increase the *overall* size of the spreadsheet, choose Format > Document (top) and use the *Size* panel to increase the *Columns Across* or *Rows Down* (bottom).

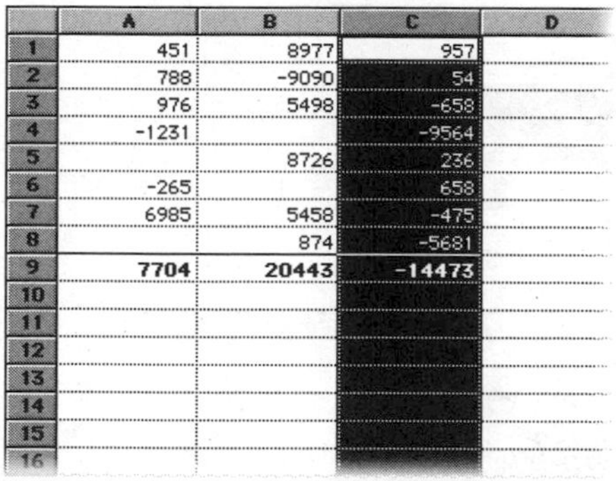

	A	B	C	D
1	451	8977	957	
2	788	-9090	54	
3	976	5498	-658	
4	-1231		-9564	
5		8726	236	
6	-265		658	
7	6985	5458	-475	
8		874	-5681	
9	7704	20443	-14473	
10				
11				
12				
13				
14				
15				
16				

Figure 9.39 Select the column to the *right* of where you want a blank column inserted.

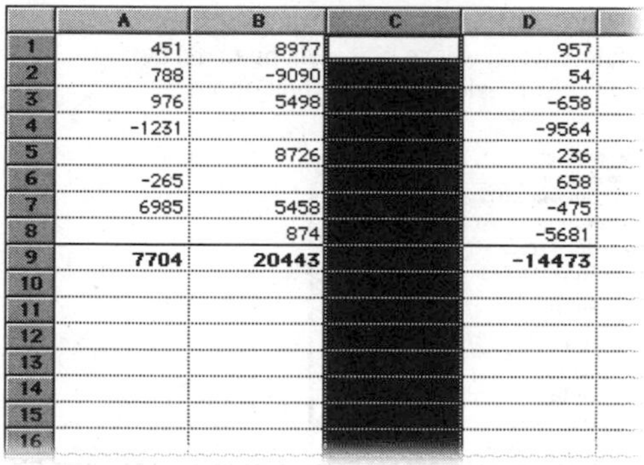

	A	B	C	D
1	451	8977		957
2	788	-9090		54
3	976	5498		-658
4	-1231			-9564
5		8726		236
6	-265			658
7	6985	5458		-475
8		874		-5681
9	7704	20443		-14473
10				
11				
12				
13				
14				
15				
16				

Figure 9.40 A new blank column is inserted.

To insert a blank column:

1. Select the column to the *right* of where you want to insert a blank column (**Figure 9.39**).

2. Choose Format > Insert Cells (Shift ⌘ I) (**Figure 9.36**). A blank column will be inserted (**Figure 9.40**).

To delete a cell or range of cells:

1. Select the cell or range of cells you want to delete (top, **Figure 9.41**).

2. Choose Format > Delete Cells (Shift ⌘ K) (**Figure 9.42**).

3. When the Delete Cells dialog box appears, choose whether you want the remaining cells to move *Up* or *Left* and click *OK* (**Figure 9.43**). The cells will be deleted and the remaining cells will shift up or left based on your choice (bottom, **Figure 9.41**).

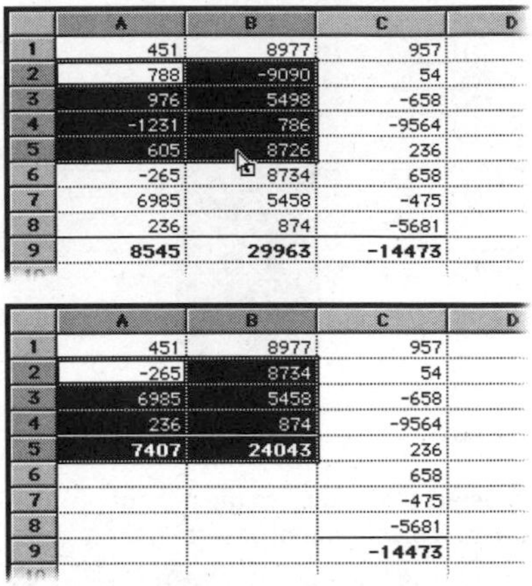

Figure 9.41 Select a cell or range of cells to delete (top), whose place will be taken by the cells previously below them (bottom).

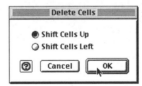

Figure 9.42 To delete the cells, choose Format > Delete Cells.

Figure 9.43 When the Delete Cells dialog box appears, choose whether you want the remaining cells to move *Up* or *Left*.

	A	B	C	D	E	F
1	451	8977	957			
2	788	-9090	54			
3	976	5498	-658			
4	-1231	786	-9564			
5	605	8726	236			
6	-265	8734	658			
7	6985	5458	-475			
8	236	874	-5681			
9	8545	29963	-14473			
10						

Figure 9.44 Select the row you want to delete.

	A	B	C	D	E	F
1	451	8977	957			
2	788	-9090	54			
3	976	5498	-658			
4	605	8726	236			
5	-265	8734	658			
6	6985	5458	-475			
7	236	874	-5681			
8	9776	29177	-4909			
9						
10						

Figure 9.45 After a row is deleted, the row below it shifts upward.

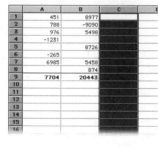

	A	B	C	D
1	451	8977	957	
2	788	-9090	54	
3	976	5498	-658	
4	-1231		-9564	
5		8726	236	
6	-265		658	
7	6985	5458	-475	
8		874	-5681	
9	7704	20443	-14473	
10				
11				
12				
13				
14				
15				
16				

Figure 9.46 Select the column you want to delete.

	A	B	C	D
1	451	8977		
2	788	-9090		
3	976	5498		
4	-1231			
5		8726		
6	-265			
7	6985	5458		
8		874		
9	7704	20443		
10				
11				
12				
13				
14				
15				
16				

Figure 9.47 After the column is deleted, the column to the right, which is blank in this case, will fill the space.

To delete a row:

1. Select the row or rows you want to delete (**Figure 9.44**).

2. Choose Format > Delete Cells ([Shift][⌘][K]) (**Figure 9.42**). The row or rows will be deleted (**Figure 9.45**).

To delete a column:

1. Select the column or columns you want to delete (**Figure 9.46**).

2. Choose Format > Delete Cells ([Shift][⌘][K]) (**Figure 9.42**). The column or columns will be deleted (**Figure 9.47**).

WORKING WITH ROWS OR COLUMNS

To resize rows or columns:

1. Select the rows or columns you want to resize (**Figure 9.48**).

2. Choose Format > Row Height or Format > Column Width (**Figure 9.49**).

3. When the Row Height or Column Width dialog box appears, the current size will be highlighted (top, **Figure 9.50**). Type in what you want the new size to be and click *OK* (bottom, **Figure 9.50**). The rows or columns will be resized based on your choice (**Figure 9.51**).

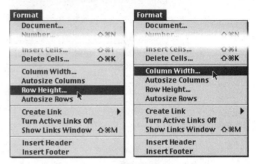

Figure 9.48
Select the rows or columns you want to resize.

Figure 9.49 To resize rows, choose Format > Row Height (left). To resize columns, choose Format > Column Width (right).

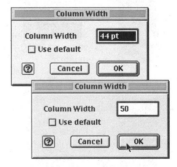

Figure 9.50 When either the Row Height or Column Width dialog box first appears, the *current* size will be highlighted (top). Type in what you want the *new* size to be and click *OK* (bottom).

Figure 9.51 The rows or columns are resized based on your choice in Figure 9.50.

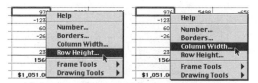

Figure 9.52 You also can change the selected cells by Ctrl-clicking them and choosing *Row Height* or *Column Width* from the drop-down menu.

Figure 9.53 You also can resize a row or column by clicking and dragging in the header area.

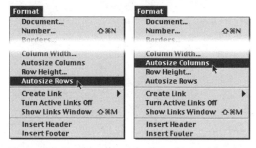

Figure 9.54 You can automatically resize a selected row or column by choosing Format > Autosize Rows or Format > Autosize Columns.

Figure 9.55 You can "hide" a column by reducing its size to 0 in the Column Width dialog box.

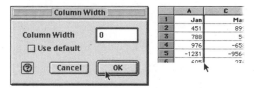

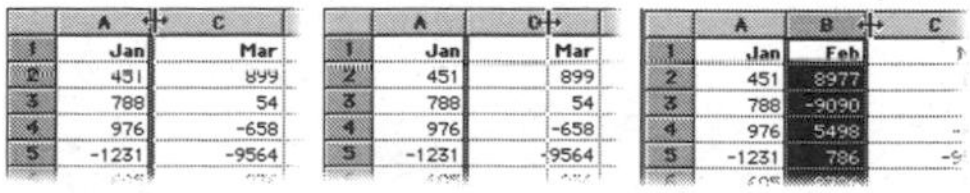

Figure 9.56 To restore a hidden row or column, click in the header and use the double-arrow cursor to drag it back into sight.

✔ Tips

■ You also can change the selected cells by Ctrl-clicking them and choosing *Row Height* or *Column Width* from the drop-down menu (**Figure 9.52**).

■ If a row or column doesn't need to be an exact size, select it and then click in the heading area and drag the double-arrow cursor. Release the cursor when the row or column is resized to your liking (**Figure 9.53**). If you use this trick with multiple rows or columns, they will become the same height or width—even if they were not the same size beforehand.

■ You can automatically resize a row or column to accommodate the longest element, by selecting it and choosing Format > Autosize Rows or Format > Autosize Columns (**Figure 9.54**). Or use the Autosize buttons in the Button Bar (**Figure 9.2** on page 204.).

■ In step 3, you can "hide" a row or column by reducing its size to 0 (**Figure 9.55**). The content will not be visible onscreen or in a printout, though it will be obvious that a row or column is tucked out of sight. But it can be useful when you want to highlight portions of a spreadsheet. To show a hidden row or column, click in the header and use the double-arrow cursor to drag it back into sight (**Figure 9.56**).

To transpose rows and columns:

1. Select the cells you want to transpose by making the rows into columns and the columns into rows (**Figure 9.57**).
2. Choose Edit > Cut (⌘X) or Edit > Copy (⌘C).
3. Click in the cell that will become the upper-left cell of the range of cells and choose Edit > Paste Special.
4. When the Paste Special dialog box appears, check Transpose Rows and Columns (**Figure 9.58**). If the cells you selected contained formulas, also choose Paste Values and Formulas. Click *OK*. The rows and columns will be transposed (**Figure 9.59**).

✔ Tip

- Transposing rows and columns is not simply a slick trick: In some cases, a transposition can make the data easier to understand or read.

	A	B	C
1	Jan	Feb	Mar
2	451	8977	899
3	788	-9090	54
4	976	5498	-658
5	-1231	786	-9564
6	605	8726	236
7	-265	8734	658
8	6985	5458	-475
9	236	874	-5681
10	8545	29963	-14826

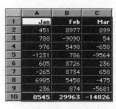

Figure 9.57 Select the cells you want to transpose by making the rows into columns and the columns into rows.

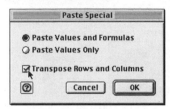

Figure 9.58 When the Paste Special dialog box appears, check *Transpose Rows and Columns*.

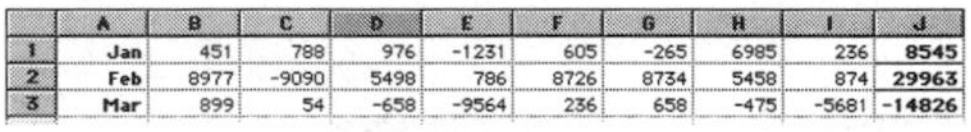

	A	B	C	D	E	F	G	H	I	J
1	Jan	451	788	976	-1231	605	-265	6985	236	8545
2	Feb	8977	-9090	5498	786	8726	8734	5458	874	29963
3	Mar	899	54	-658	-9564	236	658	-475	-5681	-14826

Figure 9.59 The results after the cells in Figure 9.57 are transposed.

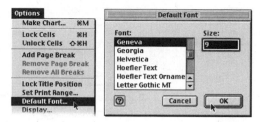

Figure 9.60 Choose Options > Default Font and use the dialog box to set a *Font* and *Size* for the current spreadsheet.

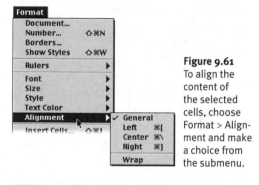

Figure 9.61 To align the content of the selected cells, choose Format > Alignment and make a choice from the submenu.

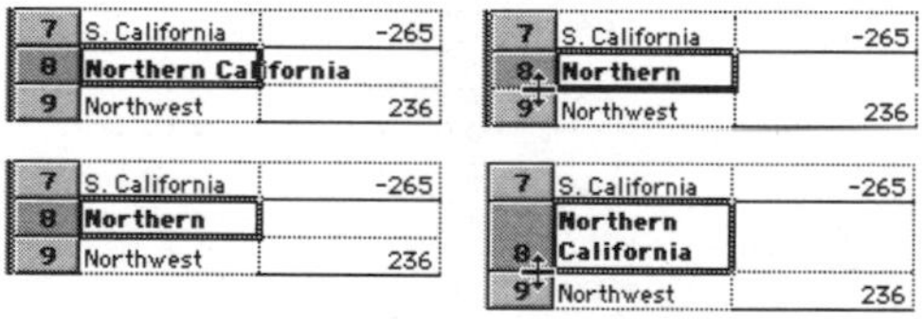

Figure 9.62 After choosing Wrap in Figure 9.61, text spilling into the adjacent cell rewraps (on the left, top and bottom). You can then resize the row to reveal the second line (on the right, top and bottom).

Formatting Spreadsheets

Spreadsheets don't have to look dull. In fact, spreadsheets can be formatted using many of the same options AppleWorks offers for text such as changing text styles, adding page numbers, or creating headers and footers. For more information, see *Formatting Text* on page 117.

Setting a default spreadsheet font

AppleWorks lets you pick a default font for your active spreadsheet, which is set independently of whatever fonts you may be using in word-processing documents. It is applied to every cell of the active spreadsheet. If you wish, you can set different default fonts for different spreadsheets.

To set a default font for the current spreadsheet:

1. Open the spreadsheet whose font you want to set.

2. Choose Options > Default Font and when the Default Font dialog box appears, choose a *Font* and *Size* (**Figure 9.60**). Click *OK* and the font will be applied to the entire spreadsheet.

To align the content of cells:

1. Select the cells whose content you want to align.

2. Choose Format > Alignment and make a choice from the submenu that appears (**Figure 9.61**). The content will be realigned based on your choice.

✔ Tip

■ In step 2, choose *Wrap* in the submenu if you have cells where the text spills into the adjacent empty cell (**Figure 9.62**). The content will wrap to a second line, which may force you to adjust the row height as well.

FORMATTING SPREADSHEETS

To format cell borders:

1. Select the cells whose borders you want to format.

2. Choose Format > Borders (left, **Figure 9.63**).

3. When the Borders dialog box appears, check your choice or choices and click *OK* (right, **Figure 9.63**). The borders will be applied to the selected cells.

✔ Tips

- If the Button Bar is visible, it's sometimes faster to select your cells and then click one of the five border buttons (**Figure 9.64**).

- You also can change the selected cells by [Ctrl]-clicking them and choosing *Borders* from the drop-down menu (**Figure 9.65**).

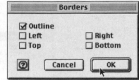

Figure 9.63 To format cell borders, choose Format > Borders and check your choices in the Borders dialog box.

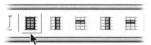

Figure 9.64 If the Button Bar is visible, you can use any of the five border buttons.

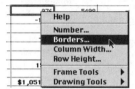

Figure 9.65 You also can change the selected cells by [Ctrl]-clicking them and choosing *Borders* from the drop-down menu.

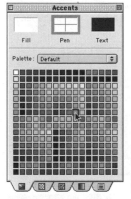

Figure 9.66 Click the Accents Palette's *Pen* icon (top) and color tab (bottom) if they are not already selected.

Figure 9.67 Choose a new color by clicking any square in the Accents Palette color panel.

To change the cell border color:

1. Make sure the Accents Palette is visible by choosing Window > Show Accents (⌘K).

2. Select the cells whose border color you want to change.

3. Click the Accents Palette's *Pen* icon if it's not already highlighted (top, **Figure 9.66**), then click the palette's color tab if that tab's content is not visible (bottom, **Figure 9.66**).

4. Choose a new color by clicking any square in the palette (**Figure 9.67**). The color is immediately applied to the cell borders, making it easy to try several colors until you find one to your liking.

✔ Tip

- You also can change the fill color or pattern of spreadsheet cells. See *Changing background colors or patterns* on page 164.

FORMATTING SPREADSHEETS

To format numbers, dates, or times:

1. Select the cells where you want to format the numbers, dates, or times (left, **Figure 9.68**).

2. Choose Format > Number ((Shift)(⌘)(N)) (**Figure 9.69**).

3. When the Format Number, Date, and Time dialog box appears, choose *Number*, *Date*, or *Time* (**Figure 9.70**).

4. Use the appropriate drop-down menu to fine-tune the formatting (**Figure 9.71**). If you are formatting numbers, also decide if you want to select either of the two checkboxes and, if appropriate, enter a number in the *Decimal Precision* window.

5. Click *Apply* to see how your choices look in the cells. If you want to tweak your choices do so, otherwise click *OK* and the cells will be formatted (right, **Figure 9.68**).

✔ Tips

- If you are formatting a single cell, double-click it to open the Format Number, Date, and Time dialog box directly.

- You also can change the selected cells by (Ctrl)-clicking them and choosing *Number* from the drop-down menu (**Figure 9.72**).

- Some of your basic time and date formatting choices are dictated by your Mac's settings. To check them, open the Date & Time control panel (**Figure 9.73**).

FORMATTING SPREADSHEETS

Figure 9.68 Numbers before being formatted (left) and afterward with currency, commas, and decimals applied (right).

Figure 9.69 To format numbers, dates, or times, choose Format > Number.

Figure 9.70 When the dialog box appears, choose *Number*, *Date*, or *Time* depending on what you are formatting.

Figure 9.71 Use the drop-down menus to fine-tune the formatting for numbers, dates, and times (from left).

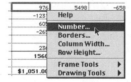

Figure 9.72 You also can format the selected cells by (Ctrl)-clicking them and choosing *Number* from the drop-down menu.

Figure 9.73 Use the Apple menu to reach the Date & Time control panel, which dictates basic time and date formatting.

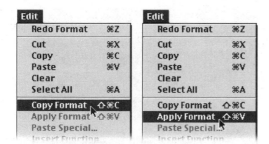

Figure 9.74 Select the cells whose formatting you want to copy and choose Edit > Copy Format (left). Then select the cells you want formatted and choose Edit > Apply Format (right).

To copy a cell format to another cell:

1. Select the cell or cells whose formatting you want to copy.

2. Choose Edit > Copy Format (Shift ⌘ C) (left, **Figure 9.74**).

3. Now, select the cells to which you want the formatting applied.

4. Choose Edit > Apply Format (Shift ⌘ V) (right, **Figure 9.74**). The formatting will be applied to the cells, saving you a lot of time.

To delete cell data but preserve formatting:

◆ Select the cells whose content you want to delete. Press Delete . The contents will be deleted but the formatting remains and will be applied to any contents added later.

To delete cell data and the formatting:

◆ Select the cells where you want to empty the content *and* the formatting applied to it. Choose Edit > Cut (⌘ X) or Edit > Clear. The cells will be emptied and any formatting removed.

To apply styles to spreadsheets:

1. Open a spreadsheet and select the entire spreadsheet (⌘A) or just the cells you want to style (**Figure 9.75**).

2. Choose Format > Show Styles (Shift⌘W) (**Figure 9.76**).

3. When the Styles window appears, click on any of the *Available Styles* to see how it appears in the preview window (**Figure 9.77**). Once you've made your choice, click *Apply* and the style will be applied to the spreadsheet (**Figure 9.78**). When you're done, close the Styles window.

✔ Tip

- For more information on applying styles, customizing style attributes, and editing styles see *Using and Changing Styles* on page 170.

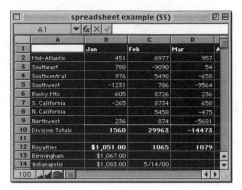

Figure 9.75 Select the cells to which you want to apply a style.

Figure 9.76 To open the Styles window, choose Format > Show Styles.

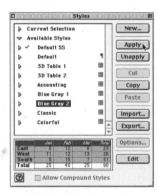

Figure 9.77 Click any of the *Available Styles* and use the preview window to see how it looks. Once you make a choice, click *Apply*.

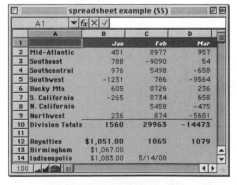

Figure 9.78 The cells in Figure 9.75 after having a pre-configured style applied.

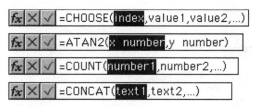

Figure 9.79 Each function includes *arguments*, which are placeholders for the values you need to add to complete the formula.

Entering and Editing Formulas

Beneath a sometimes confusing mix of terms and definitions, formulas are simple. Using a specific set of instructions, formulas take data from one or more cells, calculate or compare or summarize it, then display the results. That's it. The twist comes in that word specific: Formulas must be constructed in a set order, or syntax. Mess up the syntax and the formula won't work properly, if at all.

To build a formula, it helps to understand a few terms first. *Cell references*, such as A2 or C9, direct a formula to use the value in the cell or cells. *Constants* or *values* are fixed numbers used in a formula. Dates, times, or numbers are examples of constants or values. *Operators* such as +, –, /, enable a formula to compare the contents of two or more cells. For example, the addition sign, +, is simply an operator that combines the value appearing before it with the value appearing after it: Subtotal + Tax. *Functions* are predefined formulas with a set name, such as SUM. Functions perform a particular calculation and return a single value. AppleWorks includes more than 100 functions, which can be reached easily from a drop-down menu in every spreadsheet. Each function includes what are called *arguments*—placeholders for the values you need to add to complete the formula (**Figure 9.79**).

To enter a simple formula:

1. Click in the cell that will contain the formula and type an = sign, which will appear in the entry bar (top, **Figure 9.80**).

2. Click in the first cell whose value you want used in the formula and its address will be added in the entry bar (middle, **Figure 9.80**).

3. If you need to use an arithmetic operator, such as +, type it into the entry bar (bottom, **Figure 9.80**).

4. Enter any other cell references, arithmetic operators, or values needed to build your formula.

5. Once you have finished building your formula, press [Return] or [Enter] or click the Accept button next to the entry bar (top, **Figure 9.81**). The calculation will appear in the cell selected in step 1 (bottom, **Figure 9.81**).

✔ Tip

■ If you try to create what's called a circular reference, AppleWorks will display an alert dialog box and place bullets in the problem cells (**Figure 9.82**). A circular reference occurs if your formula refers to a cell that refers back to the cell where you are building the formula. Don't you get dizzy just reading about it?

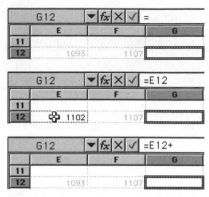

Figure 9.80 Click the cell that will contain the formula and type an = sign, which appears in the entry bar (top). Click the first cell whose value you want used in the formula and its address is added in the entry bar (middle). Type arithmetic operators directly into the entry bar (bottom).

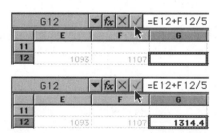

Figure 9.81 After building the formula, click the Accept button (top) and the calculation appears in the cell selected in Figure 9.80 (bottom).

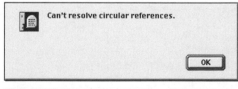

Figure 9.82 An alert appears if you mistakenly create a circular reference, which occurs when two cells (G12 and G13) contain formulas referencing the other cell.

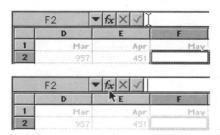

Figure 9.83 Select the cell where you want to use a formula, click in the entry bar (top), and then click the Function menu (bottom).

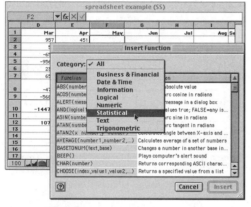

Figure 9.84 Use the *Category* drop-down menu to narrow your search for the correct function.

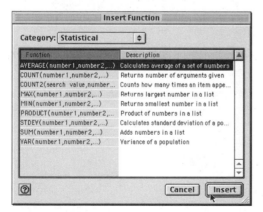

Figure 9.85 Once you find the function you want, select it and click *Insert*.

To use a function in a formula:

1. Select the cell where you want to use a formula and then click in the entry bar (top, **Figure 9.83**).

2. Click the Function menu (bottom, **Figure 9.83**).

3. When the Insert Function dialog box appears, use the *Category* drop-down menu to narrow your search for the correct function (**Figure 9.84**).

4. Use the Insert Function dialog box's scroll bar to find the function you need in the shorter list that now appears. Once you find the function, select it and click *Insert* (**Figure 9.85**). The formula will appear in the entry bar with the first argument you need to replace highlighted (top, **Figure 9.86**).

5. Replace the first highlighted argument with the needed cell reference, value, or constant (middle, **Figure 9.86**).

(continued)

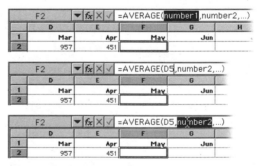

Figure 9.86 The formula appears in the entry bar with the first argument you need to replace highlighted (top). After clicking a cell, its reference replaces the argument (middle). Double-click the next argument to replace it (bottom) and so on until you are done.

6. Double-click the next argument to select it so that you can replace it (bottom, **Figure 9.86**). Enter the needed cell reference, value, or constant. Continue until you are done replacing the arguments.

7. Once you have finished building your formula, press ⌐Return⌐ or ⌐Enter⌐ or click the Accept button next to the entry bar. The results will appear in the cell selected in step 1 (**Figure 9.87**).

✔ Tips

■ In step 7, an alert dialog box may appear if you make a mistake in building the formula (**Figure 9.88**). Make sure you didn't leave any arguments blank, which will appear as an ellipsis (**Figure 9.89**).

■ If you click the *Description* header in the Insert Function dialog box, the function list will be reordered based on the purpose of the functions. That can be a big help if you know what you want to do, but don't know its actual name.

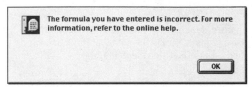

Figure 9.87 Once you have finished building your formula, click the Accept button and the results will appear in the cell first selected in Figure 9.83.

> ⚠ The formula you have entered is incorrect. For more information, refer to the online help.
>
> OK

Figure 9.88 An alert dialog box appears if you make a mistake in building the formula.

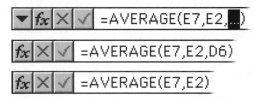

Figure 9.89 A common problem and two fixes: A placeholder ellipsis remains in the function (top). Replace it with a reference (middle) or delete it (bottom).

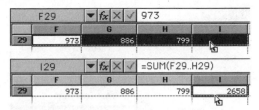

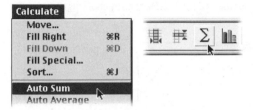

Figure 9.90 To use Auto Sum, select the cells to be added plus an extra *blank* cell (top). The results appear in the previously blank cell and the Auto Sum formula in the entry bar (bottom).

Figure 9.91 Choose Calculate > Auto Sum or click the Auto Sum button in the Button Bar.

Figure 9.92
To automatically average selected cells, choose Calculate > Auto Average.

Using Auto Sum and Auto Average

Auto Sum does just what it sounds like: automatically adds up a selected range of cells. Auto Average takes a range of cells and automatically averages their values. These two simple functions will save you lots of time as you build spreadsheets.

To use Auto Sum:

1. Select the range of cells you want to add plus an extra *blank* cell for the result to be displayed (top, **Figure 9.90**).

2. Choose Calculate > Auto Sum or click the Auto Sum button in the Button Bar (**Figure 9.91**).

3. The sum of the selected cells will be displayed in the previously blank cell with the formula in the entry bar (bottom, **Figure 9.90**).

To use Auto Average:

1. Select the range of cells you want to average plus an extra *blank* cell for the result to be displayed.

2. Choose Calculate > Auto Average (**Figure 9.92**).

3. The average of the selected cells will be displayed in the previously blank cell and the formula in the entry bar.

ENTERING AND EDITING FORMULAS

Controlling Auto Calculate

By default, AppleWorks automatically calcu-
lates results whenever you enter or change
a formula. In a large, complex spreadsheet,
however, this can slow down the whole program, especially for older Macs. For such
times, AppleWorks has a feature that lets you
turn Auto Calculate off.

To turn off Auto Calculate:

◆ With your spreadsheet open, choose
Calculate > Auto-Calculate (left, **Figure
9.93**). Automatic calculation will be
turned off, but you can trigger it manually by choosing Calculate > Calculate
Now ([Shift][⌘][=]) (right, **Figure 9.93**).

To turn Auto Calculate back on:

◆ With your spreadsheet open, choose
Calculate > Auto-Calculate again
(**Figure 9.94**). Automatic calculation
will be turned back on.

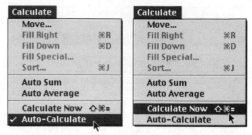

Figure 9.93 If a large, formula-packed spreadsheet
slows down your Mac, choose Calculate > Auto-
Calculate to turn the checkmark off (left). You can
manually trigger calculations by choosing Calculate >
Calculate Now (right).

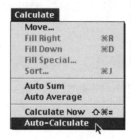

Figure 9.94 Choose Auto-
Calculate again to make
the checkmark reappear.

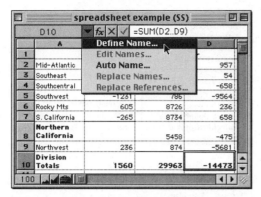

Figure 9.95 To name a cell reference, choose *Define Name* from the drop-down menu next to the Address window.

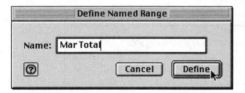

Figure 9.96 Give the cell or range of cells a descriptive name you'll remember and click *Define*.

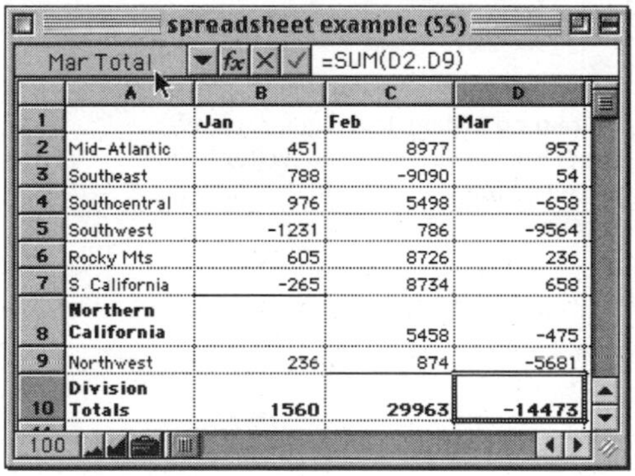

Figure 9.97 Cell D10 now displays the *Mar Total* name in the Address window.

Naming cell references

If you tire of trying to remember whether that key cell is K47 or G47, AppleWorks offers the option of giving such cell references descriptive names instead. The name does not appear in the cell but instead acts as an alias to the letter-number address. These cell names are stored in a handy drop-down menu at the top of the spreadsheet, which you can edit any time. The cell names can be used in formulas instead of the cell number. You also can switch a name reference in a formula to a cell number, or vice versa, at any time.

To name a cell reference:

1. Select the cell or range of cells you want to name.

2. Choose *Define Name* from the drop-down menu next to the Address window (**Figure 9.95**).

3. When the Define Named Range dialog box appears, give the cell or range of cells a name you'll remember and click *Define* (**Figure 9.96**). The cell selected in step 1, D10, now displays a name in the Address window instead of the letter-number (**Figure 9.97**). Continue defining names as you need them and they will be added to the drop-down menu.

✔ Tips

- In step 3, if you enter an unacceptable character in the *Name* window (for example, a +, which could be mistaken for an arithmetic operator), the *Define* button will dim until you remove the character.

- If you name a *range* of cells, the name applies to the full range, not the individual cells in that range.

To jump to a named cell reference:

◆ Click the Name cell menu and choose the name you need from the drop-down menu (**Figure 9.98**). That cell will appear in the spreadsheet.

✔ Tip

■ You also can jump to a particular cell address by clicking in the Address window, typing the address into the Go To Cell dialog box when it appears, and clicking *OK* (**Figure 9.99**). It does not matter whether you capitalize the letter in a cell address (middle, **Figure 9.99**).

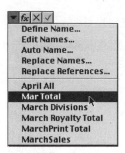

Figure 9.98 To jump to a named cell reference, choose the name from the drop-down menu.

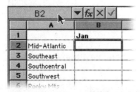

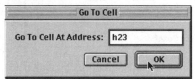

Figure 9.99 To jump to a regular cell reference, click the Address window (top), type the cell address in the Go To Cell dialog box, and click *OK*.

ENTERING AND EDITING FORMULAS

Figure 9.100 To change a cell reference name or its address, choose *Edit Names* from the drop-down menu.

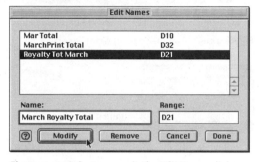

Figure 9.101 Select a name in the Edit Names dialog box's list to change its *Name* or *Range*.

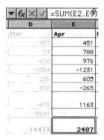

Figure 9.102 To switch cell references and cell names in formulas, first select the cell *containing the formula*.

Figure 9.103 To replace the formula's cell references (e.g., E2) with named references, choose *Replace References*.

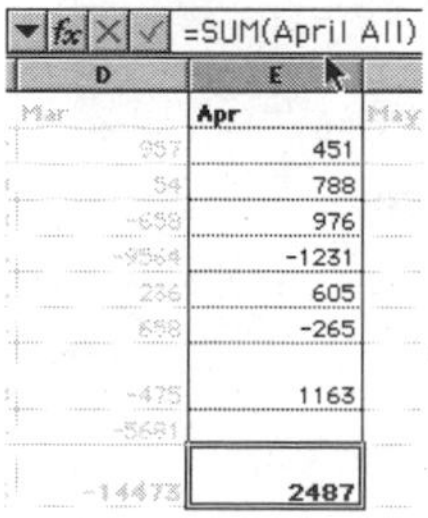

Figure 9.104 After making the switch, the formula displays cell names instead of letter-number references.

To edit a cell reference name:

1. Choose *Edit Names* from the drop-down menu next to the Address window (**Figure 9.100**).

2. When the Edit Names dialog box appears, click a name in the list (**Figure 9.101**). You can then:

   Use the *Name* or *Range* text windows to change the name or its cell reference. Click *Modify* when you are done.

   or

   Click *Remove* if you want to delete a name from the list.

3. Once you are happy with the changes, click *Done* and the changes will be applied to the drop-down menu.

To switch cell references and cell names in formulas:

1. Select the cell *containing the formula* (not the cells referenced in the formula) (**Figure 9.102**).

2. To replace the formula's cell references (e.g., E2) with named references, choose *Replace References* from the drop-down menu (**Figure 9.103**). The names will replace the letter-number references (**Figure 9.104**).

   or

   To replace a formula's named references with cell references, choose *Replace Names* from the drop-down menu. The letter-number references will replace the named references.

ENTERING AND EDITING FORMULAS

Sorting Spreadsheets

By sorting parts or all of a spreadsheet, you can analyze data, spot trends, and generally make sense of what can otherwise become information overload.

To sort a spreadsheet:

1. Select the cells, rows, or columns you want to sort (**Figure 9.105**).

2. Choose Calculate > Sort (⌘J) (**Figure 9.106**).

3. When the Sort dialog box appears, use the *1st Order Key* and its related radio buttons to set the basis of the first sort: *Ascending* or *Descending*, and *Vertical* or *Horizontal* (**Figure 9.107**). See the *Tip* on how to set *2nd* and *3rd* sorts.

4. Click *OK* and the sort will be applied to the selected cells (**Figure 9.108**).

	A	B	C	D
1		Jan	Feb	Mar
2	Mid-Atlantic	1111	8977	-9564
3	N. California	429	5458	957
4	Northwest	236	874	-5681
5	Rocky Mts	567	8726	236
6	S. California	2169	8734	658
7	Southcentral	1181	5498	-475
8	Southeast	1255	-9090	-658
9	Southwest	964	786	54
10	Division Totals	7912	29963	-14473

Figure 9.105 Select the cells you want to sort.

Figure 9.106 To sort the selected cells, choose Calculate > Sort.

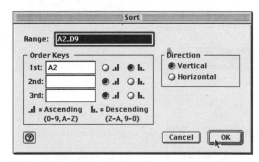

Figure 9.107 Use the *1st Order Key* and its related radio buttons to set the basis of the first sort: *Ascending* or *Descending*, and *Vertical* or *Horizontal*.

	A	B	C	D
1		Jan	Feb	Mar
2	Southwest	964	786	54
3	Southeast	1255	-9090	-658
4	Southcentral	1181	5498	-475
5	S. California	2169	8734	658
6	Rocky Mts	567	8726	236
7	Northwest	236	874	-5681
8	N. California	429	5458	957
9	Mid-Atlantic	1111	8977	-9564
10	Division Totals	7912	29963	-14473

Figure 9.108 After sorting, the *A* column cells are displayed in descending alphabetical order.

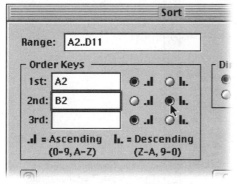

	A	B	C	D
1		Jan	Feb	Mar
2	Atlanta	978	887	-475
3	Atlanta	964	786	54
4	Atlanta	705	3420	-475
5	Boston	1181	5498	-475
6	Chicago	1255	-9090	-658
7	Denver	567	8726	236
8	Los Angeles	2169	8734	658
9	Phoenix	1111	8977	-9564
10	San Jose	429	5458	957
11	Seattle	236	874	-5681
12	Division Totals	9595	34270	-15423

Figure 9.109 You only need to use the second and third *Order Key* windows if the selection contains duplicates, such as the three instances of *Atlanta* sorted in this selection.

Figure 9.110 To sort the duplicates in the Figure 9.109 selection, a second *Descending* sort order was applied using the second column (*B2*).

✔ Tip

■ You only need to use the second and third *Order Key* windows if the first sort selection contains duplicate values. For example, **Figure 9.109** contains three instances of *Atlanta*, so a second *Descending* sort order was applied using the second column (*B2*) (**Figure 9.110**).

Viewing Spreadsheets

Spreadsheets can quickly become unwieldy to work with, especially onscreen. AppleWorks offers several ways to control your view of the spreadsheet and make it easier to see what you need. Among the options are splitting the spreadsheet into panes, zooming in and out, viewing multiple windows, and locking row or column labels in place.

Splitting the spreadsheet into panes

Splitting a spreadsheet into panes enables you to see and compare different parts of it simultaneously. It's indispensable when working with larger spreadsheets. AppleWorks allows you to create up to nine panes: three across and three down.

To split a spreadsheet:

1. Move your cursor to the far left of the spreadsheet's horizontal scroll bar, between the toolbox and the small arrow, and it will become a double arrow (left, **Figure 9.111**).

   or

   Move your cursor to the top of the spreadsheet's vertical scroll bar, just above the small arrow, and it will become a double arrow (right, **Figure 9.111**).

2. Now drag the double-arrow to divide the spreadsheet into two panes (**Figure 9.112**). Repeat the steps to create up to nine panes (three across, three down). Each pane will have its own scroll bars.

To remove panes:

◆ Move your cursor over the pane divider until it becomes a double arrow, then click and drag the divider to the side and off the spreadsheet. The pane will disappear.

Figure 9.111 Split a spreadsheet into panes using the double-arrow by the toolbox icon or in the upper-right corner above the vertical scroll bar.

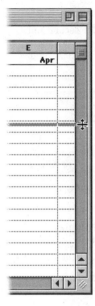

Figure 9.112 Drag the double-arrow to divide the spreadsheet into two panes.

Figure 9.113 To view an already open spreadsheet in multiple windows, choose Window > New View.

To zoom in or out:

◆ Depending on whether you need a close-up look or an overall view, click the zoom-in or zoom-out icons in the spreadsheet's lower-right corner. The view will change accordingly.

or

◆ If you want to set your view at a particular magnification, click the zoom percentage box and make a choice from the pop-up menu. Release the cursor and the view will be reset to that percentage.

To view the spreadsheet in multiple windows:

◆ With the spreadsheet already open, choose Window > New View (**Figure 9.113**). A second window displaying the spreadsheet will open, which can be scrolled and sized independently of the first. Repeat to open as many windows as you need.

✔ Tip

■ To keep multiple windows from getting out of hand, choose Window > Tile Windows or Window > Stack Windows. The first command will arrange the open windows in a grid on your screen; the second will overlap the windows with the top edge of each visible.

Locking row or column titles

If you lock the position of a row or column title, it will remain onscreen no matter where you scroll in the spreadsheet. This is useful in large spreadsheets where it can be hard to connect individual cells with the rows and columns. While locking the titles prevents them from being changed, this is not the same as locking cells to protect their contents. For information on locking cells see page 215.

To lock row or column titles:

1. Select the rows or columns you want to lock.

2. Choose Options > Lock Title Position (**Figure 9.114**). The selected rows or columns will remain visible no matter where you scroll in the spreadsheet (**Figure 9.115**).

✔ Tips

- To unlock a title, select the rows or columns and choose Options > Lock Title Position again.

- If you need to do any substantial restructuring of the spreadsheet, you will need to unlock the titles first.

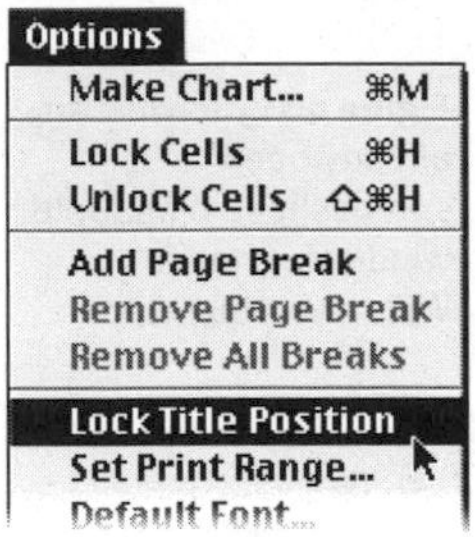

Figure 9.114
To lock a selected row or column title so that it is always onscreen, choose Options > Lock Title Position.

	A	B	C	D
1		Jan	Feb	Mar
2	Mid-Atlantic	451	8977	957
3	Southeast	788	-9090	54
4	Southcentral	976	5498	-658
5	Southwest	-1231	786	-9564
6	Rocky Mts	605	8726	236
7	S. California	-265	8734	658
8	N. California	6985	5458	-475
9	Northwest	236	874	-5681
10	Division Totals	8545	29963	-14473

	A	B	C	D
1		Jan	Feb	Mar
252		4843	856	802
253		4859	904	819
254		4875	952	836
255		4891	1000	853
256		4907	1048	870
257		4923	1096	887

Figure 9.115 With the row titles locked, they remain visible no matter how far down you scroll.

VIEWING SPREADSHEETS

10

MAKING CHARTS

AppleWorks's chart making feature is wonderfully straightforward. Using the default settings, you can literally create a chart from your spreadsheet in seconds. Or, by using all the chart-formatting options available, you could take a bit longer and spin out a customized chart fit for a board of directors meeting. *To create a chart* on page 244 gets you building charts quickly while the sections following it walk you through the details of adding labels and titles, building data series, and changing more general aspects of the chart. It is easy, by the way, to go back later and modify even the simplest of charts.

It is also easy to add extra text or supporting graphics by adding text or paint frames to the chart. For more information, see *Using Frames* on page 61. To change the colors, fills, and patterns used by the various chart types use the Accents Palette. For more information, see *Using the Accents Palette* on page 340. With so many choices, feel free to experiment until you find the combination that makes your chart look its best.

Creating a Chart

AppleWorks gives you 13 basic chart types from which to choose. Add in the various formatting choices that come with each type and you'll find what you need for any occasion.

To create a chart:

1. Select the spreadsheet cells you want to use in the chart (**Figure 10.1**).

2. Choose Options > Make Chart (⌘M) (**Figure 10.2**).

3. When the Chart Options dialog box appears, use the *Gallery* panel to choose which type of chart you want to use. If you wish, check any of the optional choices, such as *Color*, *Shadow*, or *Horizontal* (**Figure 10.3**).

4. If you do not want to use the default settings for that chart type, click any of the buttons in the *Modify* panel (*Axes*, *Series*, *Labels*, and *General*). The details for each are covered in separate sections.

5. Once you have made your choices, click *OK* and the chart will appear in its own frame floating on top of your spreadsheet (**Figure 10.4**).

✔ Tip

- As long as you leave the chart within the spreadsheet, any changes in the data will be reflected in the chart automatically. If you copy the chart elsewhere, however, the data will no longer be updated and instead the chart becomes a fixed graphic. For more information, see *Copying, Pasting, and Resizing Charts* on page 253.

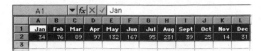

Figure 10.1 Select the spreadsheet cells you want to use in the chart.

Figure 10.2 Choose Options > Make Chart (⌘M).

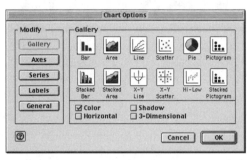

Figure 10.3 Use the *Gallery* panel to choose which of 13 chart types you want to use.

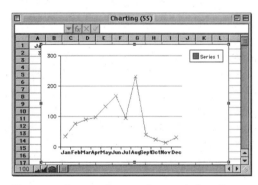

Figure 10.4 Once you have made your choices, the new chart will appear in its own frame floating on top of your spreadsheet.

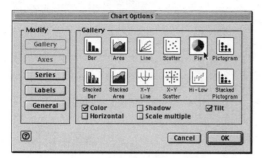

Figure 10.5 To change a chart, double-click it and make a new choice from the *Gallery*.

Modifying the Chart Type

It's not uncommon to realize after you begin working with one type of chart that another type would be better suited for your purposes. AppleWorks lets you change the type of chart you are using at any time.

To modify the chart type:

1. Double-click the chart you want to modify.

2. When the Chart Options dialog box appears, look through your choices in the *Gallery* panel and click the one you want to use (**Figure 10.5**).

3. In the unlabeled panel just below the *Gallery*, the available options change based on the chart type you choose. Check any options you want to use. You may also need to modify your *Axes*, *Series*, *Labels*, and *General* choices once you change the chart type.

4. Click another button in the *Modify* panel if you want to make further changes to the chart.

or

Once you have made your choices, click *OK* and the chart type will change.

✔ Tip

■ Some of the buttons in the Chart Options dialog box will dim, depending on what chart type you choose. For example, if you choose *Pie*, the *Axes* button is dimmed since pie charts do not have axes (**Figure 10.5**)

Modifying the Axes

This part of the Chart Options dialog box lets you control the appearance, label, and divisions for the chart's horizontal (*x*) and vertical (*y*) axes.

To modify the chart axes:

1. Double-click the chart you want to modify and when the Chart Options dialog box appears, click the *Axes* button.

   or

   Double-click directly on the axis you want to change.

2. When the dialog box's *Axis* panel appears, depending on your choice in step 1, the *X axis* or *Y axis* button will already be selected (**Figure 10.6**). Each axis is modified independently of the other; click the button for the other axis if you want to change it instead.

3. Type a name for the axis into the *Axis Label* text window.

4. Use the *Tick Marks* pop-up menu to set their appearance and position. If you want subdivisions added to the tick marks, enter the number in the *Minor* text window (e.g., *4* will create four subdivisions).

5. If you want a background grid to appear in the chart, check *Grid Lines*.

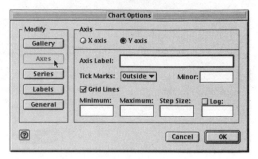

Figure 10.6 Use the *Axis* panel of the Chart Options dialog box to set and label the axes, plus control how tick marks are displayed.

6. If you want to show only a portion of the data for the selected axis, type values based on that axis into the *Minimum* and *Maximum* text windows.

7. Use the *Step Size* text window to set the increment points for the axis. If, for example, you enter *15*, then major tick marks will appear at 15, 30, 45, and so on.

8. If you want to display the axis values logarithmically, check *Log* and enter a base number in the text window.

9. If you want to modify the other axis, click its radio button now and repeat the steps.

or

Click another button in the *Modify* panel if you want to make further changes to the chart.

or

If you are done making your choices, click *OK* and the *Axes* modifications will be applied to the chart.

✔ Tip

■ You also can use the data in the first row or column of your selection as a label. For more information, see *Making General Changes* on page 252.

Modifying Data Series

Each set of values in a chart represents a data series, often simply called a series. For example, each row selected in the source spreadsheet becomes a single data series. Select two rows and a chart generates two data series (**Figure 10.7**). This portion of the Chart Options dialog box lets you control the appearance and positioning of each data series.

To modify the chart's data series:

1. Double-click the chart you want to modify and when the Chart Options dialog box appears, click the *Series* button.

2. When the dialog box's *Series* panel appears (**Figure 10.8**), use the *Edit series* pop-up menu to control whether you will be modifying *All* the series at once or each series individually (**Figure 10.9**).

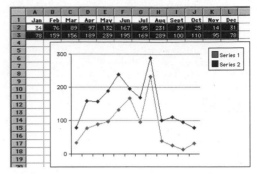

Figure 10.7 Selecting multiple rows or columns in the spreadsheet (top) generated multiple sets of data, also called data series (bottom).

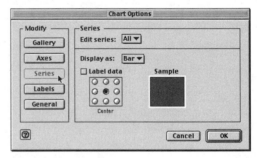

Figure 10.8 Use the *Series* panel of the Chart Options dialog box to control the appearance and positioning of each data series.

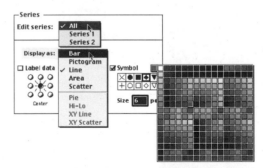

Figure 10.9 The various menus in the *Series* panel give you wide control over how the data series looks.

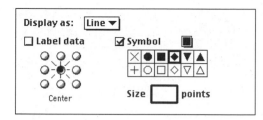

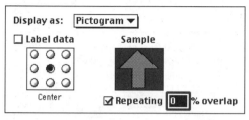

Figure 10.10 Your choices will vary widely depending on what you select with the *Display as* menu.

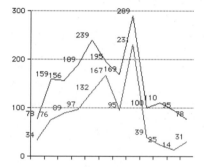

Figure 10.11 Selecting the *Label data* checkbox will trigger the display of your data points inside the chart.

3. Use the *Display as* pop-up menu to set how the data series will be displayed. Your choices in the rest of the panel will vary based on your *Display as* choice (**Figure 10.10**).

4. Depending on your *Display as* choice, a color drop-down menu may also be available (**Figure 10.9**).

5. Check *Label data* if you want the values for each data point to appear on the chart. The nine-circle graphic controls where the label appears relative to the data point (**Figure 10.11**).

6. If you want to modify another data series, use the *Edit series* menu to choose it and repeat the above steps.

or

Click another button in the *Modify* panel if you want to make further changes to the chart.

or

If you are done making your choices, click *OK* and the *Series* modifications will be applied to the chart.

Modifying the Labels

You can easily add a title and legend box to any chart. AppleWorks includes several options to dress them up with drop shadows and other effects.

To modify the chart labels:

1. Double-click the chart you want to modify and when the Chart Options dialog box appears, click the *Labels* button.

   or

   If the chart already has a title or a legend box, you can double-click it to jump straight to the *Labels* panel.

2. When the dialog box's *Labels* panel appears (**Figure 10.12**), use the *Title* text window if you want to create a label for the whole chart. Check *Horizontal* or *Shadow* to apply those effects to the label. By default, the title will be centered at the top of the chart, but you can move it relative to the chart by clicking any of the eight positioning circles (**Figure 10.13**).

3. Check *Legend* if you want a key to your data series to appear in the chart. Check any of the effects you like to apply, and move it relative to the chart by clicking any of the eight positioning circles (**Figure 10.14**).

4. Click another button in the *Modify* panel if you want to make further changes to the chart.

   or

   If you are done making your choices, click *OK* and the modifications to *Labels* will be applied to the chart.

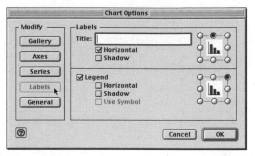

Figure 10.12 Use the *Labels* panel of the Chart Options dialog box to add a title and legend box.

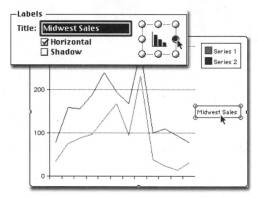

Figure 10.13 Use the eight positioning circles in the *Labels* panel to control where the title appears relative to the data.

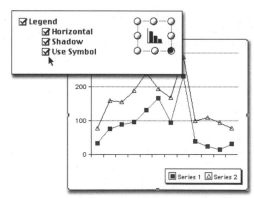

Figure 10.14 The *Legend* panel not only positions the legend box but sets its layout and appearance.

✔ Tips

- In step 3, the *Legend* choice, *Use Symbol*, only works if you also use the dialog box's *Series* panel to choose symbols for your data series. For more information, see *Modifying Data Series* on page 248.

- Contrary to what you might expect, you do not use the Chart Options dialog box to change the text attributes of the title or legend. Instead, you use the Format menu. Click once on the title or legend, choose Format and then choose *Font*, *Size*, *Style*, or *Text Color* from the submenu.

Making General Changes

Use the Chart Options dialog box's General button to change some overall items that affect the chart's construction: the chart's range, whether it builds the data series based on rows or columns, and whether to use the data in the first row or column for labels.

To make general changes:

1. Double-click the chart you want to modify and when the Chart Options dialog box appears, click the *General* button.

2. When the dialog box's *General* panel appears (**Figure 10.15**), you can use the *Chart range* window to shrink or expand the number of spreadsheet cells the chart uses (**Figure 10.16**).

3. Use the *Series in* choices to control how the chart builds its data series. By default, the data series is based on the spreadsheet's *rows* (e.g., A1–H10). Click *Columns* if you want the series built from the columns (i.e., A1–A10). Any change will be reflected in the list of *Series names*.

4. The two *Use numbers as labels in* choices let you use the data in the *First row* or *First column* data to help label the chart.

5. Click any other button in the *Modify* panel if you still want to make further changes to the chart.

   or

   Once you have made your choices, click *OK* and the changes to the chart's general construction will be applied.

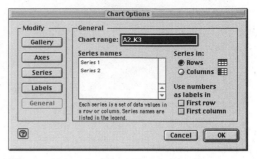

Figure 10.15 Use the *General* panel of the Chart Options dialog box to set the chart's data range and how it builds data series.

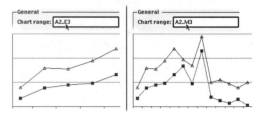

Figure 10.16 By changing the cell addresses used in the *Chart range*, you can shrink (left) or expand (right) the number of data points.

Copying, Pasting, and Resizing Charts

You can copy, paste, and resize a chart as easily as you can any other AppleWorks graphic. For example, you can easily select and copy a chart to another frame in the same document or to another AppleWorks document. Be aware, however, that it will sever the "live" link between the chart and the source spreadsheet data and the chart will no longer be updated automatically whenever the spreadsheet changes.

To copy and paste a chart:

1. Click on the chart to select it.

2. Choose Edit > Copy (⌘C).

3. Move to another place in the same document or open another AppleWorks document and click where you want the chart to appear.

4. Choose Edit > Paste (⌘V) and the chart will be pasted into the new location as a freestanding graphic.

✔ Tip

■ You can paste the chart as an inline frame or a floating frame, depending on your needs. For more information, see *Using Frames* on page 61.

To resize a chart:

◆ Click any of the eight black handles that mark the chart's edge and drag your cursor until the chart reaches the size you need. A dotted outline of the chart will guide your progress as you resize it.

PART IV

WORKING
WITH DATABASES

11

Using Databases

This chapter begins by explaining some of the basic concepts behind databases, starting with how they work and how to plan building your own database. It then walks you through the process of creating fields to hold your data. It also explains how to import data from another database, which can be a big time-saver when you first begin building your database.

The following chapter, *Creating Database Layouts* on page 273, explains how to arrange and format your database so that users find it easy to use and understand. The last chapter in this section, *Working with Records* on page 299, shows you how to navigate through the records, and the tricks of using the find and sort functions to zero in on the data you are seeking.

Anatomy of a Database

Databases are everywhere: address books, cookbooks, television program listings, and to-do lists scribbled on envelopes. None of those involves a computer, but each illustrates a fundamental concept: databases *organize* information. An address book organizes information alphabetically. A cookbook organizes information by ingredient or by course. Television listings organize information by time and channel. To-do lists organize information by task and time. Each lets you find what you need precisely because of how the information is organized. A computer database is not so different except for one major advantage: it can quickly organize the *same* information in *multiple* ways.

Understanding this notion of content vs. form is the key to tapping the real power of any database. Do not confuse what a database contains (the content) with how it looks (the form). As important as data may be, it's not what gives a database its power. Instead, the power is in the program's ability to organize—and instantly reorganize—the display of that data (**Figure 11.1**). Tapping the power behind any database boils down to understanding and effectively using just a few items: fields, records, and layouts.

The power of fields, records, and layouts

Databases often contain huge amounts of information, yet can fetch tiny pieces of that data almost instantly. That's because everything is organized into categories, or *fields* (**Figure 11.2**). Fields let a database keep track of what information goes where. Each field contains data but also carries a

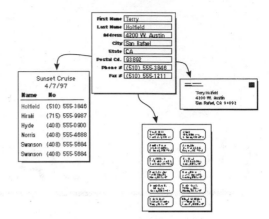

Figure 11.1 A database's real power comes from being able to display a single record's data in multiple ways.

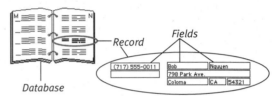

Figure 11.2 Every database organizes its information into individual records, which then contain fields for each bit of data.

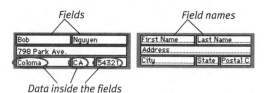

Fields — Field names

Data inside the fields

Figure 11.3 Each field contains data, but also carries a description, called a field name, which makes it possible to quickly manipulate even a large database.

description, called a *field name*. The field name helps the database sort, sift, and manipulate without necessarily needing to deal directly with the data itself. It can be a bit confusing, but remember: fields, field names, and the data inside the fields are three different things (**Figure 11.3**). More importantly, remember this as well: The more specific the fields you create within a database, the more powerful the database.

Put a bunch of fields together and you have a *record*. A single record contains related information about a single topic, person, or activity. In an address book, for example, the equivalent of a record would be the entry for one person. That entry or record would contain several related items—the person's name, address, and telephone number—which are equivalent to database fields. Combine a bunch of records on a single topic and you have a database.

A *layout*, sometimes called a *view*, is simply a way to control how the information in a database is displayed. When you first begin building AppleWorks databases, you may find yourself occasionally confusing records with layouts. Again, the difference boils down to content vs. form: One record (content) can have many different layouts (forms).

At its most basic, a record is *all* of the information for a single entry, while a layout shows a view of only the portion you need at the moment. If you need mailing labels, you can take address records and create layouts that only show the address. This notion of showing only what you need becomes especially important when you're working with a database containing dozens, or hundreds, of records and fields.

Planning and Building Databases

Start planning your database by listing the fields you'll need for all the information you'll want to track. If you're building a customer database, for example, you'll want the obvious fields for names, addresses, and phone numbers. You may also want a field or two or three for things like a customer's email address, pager number, and weekend message service. Don't forget that you're not limited to just fields for text and numbers. How about a picture field in the product catalog?

Next, list the possible layouts you'll need. Assign a separate layout to each task: mailing labels get their own layout, so do grading reports, lesson plans, etc. You should also consider creating a different layout for each type of user. Students, for example, may need to see different data than the teacher.

Figure 11.4 By default, a database opens in Browse mode but you can switch to it any time by choosing Layout > Browse ((Shift)(⌘)(B)).

Figure 11.5 To switch to List mode, choose Layout > List ((Shift)(⌘)(I)).

Figure 11.6 To switch to Find mode, choose Layout > Find ((Shift)(⌘)(F)).

Figure 11.7 To switch to Layout mode, choose Layout > Layout ((Shift)(⌘)(L)).

Switching Database Modes

When working with an AppleWorks database, you will always be in one of four different modes, sometimes called views. By default, a database opens in Browse mode, which helps you see more detail within a particular record. Using the List mode makes it easier to compare one record to another. The Find mode is used when you are searching for records or sorting them. The Layout mode is where you arrange the fields, their labels, and generally fine-tune the appearance of your database.

To switch to Browse mode:

◆ To view one record at a time, choose Layout > Browse ((Shift)(⌘)(B)) (**Figure 11.4**). AppleWorks will switch to Browse mode.

To switch to List mode:

◆ To view as many records as your screen can accommodate, choose Layout > List ((Shift)(⌘)(I)) (**Figure 11.5**). AppleWorks will display the records as a list.

To switch to Find mode:

◆ To search for records within the database, choose Layout > Find ((Shift)(⌘)(F)) (**Figure 11.6**). AppleWorks will switch to Find mode and display a blank record in which you can build a find request. For more information, see *Finding and Sorting Records* on page 306.

To switch to Layout mode:

◆ To view one record at a time, choose Layout > Layout ((Shift)(⌘)(L)) (**Figure 11.7**). AppleWorks will switch to Layout mode and automatically display the Tools Palette. For more information, see *Creating Database Layouts* on page 273.

Defining Fields

Creating records in AppleWorks is a two-step process of defining fields and setting entry options for those fields. As you create fields for your database, you'll need to assign names and field types (for example, text or number), then choose how they will be displayed.

Controlling the *appearance* of your database and its records is covered separately in *Creating Database Layouts* on page 273. Working directly with individual records—viewing them, adding and deleting records—is covered in *Working with Records* on page 299.

Choosing a field type

AppleWorks offers you the choice of 14 different types of fields, which are assigned via the *Field Type* drop-down menu within the Define Database Fields dialog box (**Figure 11.8**). For step-by-step instructions on using this dialog box, see *To define a field* on page 264. But first, here's a quick rundown on the best uses for each field type:

◆ **Text:** A text field can contain letters, symbols, and numbers as text. Even items that at first blush might not seem to be text sometimes should be placed in text fields. For example, telephone numbers usually contain non-numeric hyphens or slashes, and, so, are best placed in text fields.

◆ **Number:** A number field can contain up to 255 characters. Number fields can be sorted (1–100 or 100–1) and used in formulas for calculations and summary fields.

◆ **Date:** Date fields must contain at least the day and month of a date. To avoid Y2K problems, be sure to use four-digit years.

◆ **Time:** Time fields can only contain the hours, minutes, and seconds of a time. Time fields can be sorted (earliest–latest or latest–earliest) and used in formulas for calculations and summary fields.

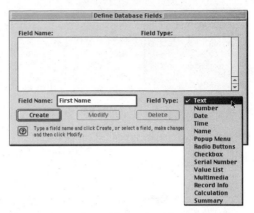

Figure 11.8 Use the *Field Type* drop-down menu to assign one of 14 types of fields.

Figure 11.9 Use a popup menu field to present a cursor-triggered list of preset choices.

Figure 11.10 A radio button field forces the user to pick *one* of several preset choices.

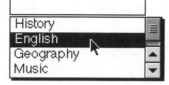

Figure 11.11 A value list field presents a scrolling list of preset choices.

◆ **Name:** While you can sort using just a portion of a single name field, it is more effective and less confusing to create a first name and a last name field. This is especially important when using mail merge to generate labels.

◆ **Popup Menu:** A popup menu presents a cursor-triggered list of preset choices (**Figure 11.9**).

◆ **Radio Buttons:** A radio button field forces the user to pick just *one* of several preset choices (**Figure 11.10**).

◆ **Checkbox:** The default for a checkbox field can be set to be checked or unchecked. You also can create a group of checkboxes for multiple items.

◆ **Serial Number:** A serial number field automatically generates a number whenever a new record is created. You can set the increment used by the field.

◆ **Value List:** A value list field presents a scrolling list of preset choices (**Figure 11.11**).

◆ **Multimedia:** These fields hold pictures or movies, including QuickTime movies.

◆ **Record Info:** A record info field automatically generates a time, date, or user name whenever a new record is created.

◆ **Calculation:** Calculation fields display the results of calculations made using other fields and, so, cannot have values typed directly into them. The result can be text, a number, date, time, or container. Calculation fields operate on data *within single records*.

◆ **Summary:** Like calculation fields, summary fields cannot have values entered directly into them. Instead, they display summary values based on other fields in the database. In general, summary fields operate on data *from a group of records*.

To define a field:

1. Create a new database by choosing File > New > Database (left, **Figure 11.12**) or open an existing database and choose Layout > Define Fields (⬆️⌘D) (right, **Figure 11.12**).

2. When the Define Database Fields dialog box appears, type the name of your first field in the *Field Name* text box, and use the *Field Type* pop-up menu to assign an appropriate type to the field (**Figure 11.13**). For more on deciding which field type best suits your needs, see *Choosing a field type* on page 262. Click the *Create* button and the name of your new field will appear in the center window of the Define Database Fields dialog box.

3. You can further define some fields by highlighting the name in the center window of the Define Database Fields dialog box and then clicking the *Options* button. Or double-click the field in the list. For more information, see *Setting field entry options* on page 266.

4. Repeat steps 2–3 to create more fields.

5. When you've finished creating fields (you can always add more fields later), click *Done* (**Figure 11.14**). AppleWorks will then display the created fields in Browse mode (**Figure 11.15**). To dress up a field's appearance and layout, see *Creating Database Layouts* on page 273.

✔ Tip

- In naming the fields, you should avoid using any of the symbols or words needed to calculate functions:
, (comma), +, -, *, /, ^, &, =, >, <, (,), ", ;, :, AND, OR, XOR, NOT.

Figure 11.12 To define a field, either create a *new* database by choosing File > New > Database (left), or open an existing database and choose Layout > Define Fields (right).

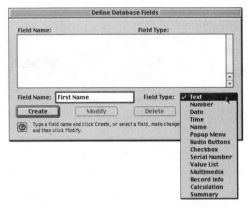

Figure 11.13 When the Define Database Fields dialog box appears, type the name of your first field in the *Field Name* text box, and use the *Field Type* pop-up menu to assign an appropriate type to the field.

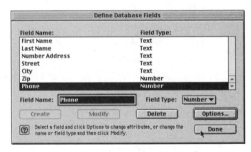

Figure 11.14 Once you finish creating and defining fields, click *Done*.

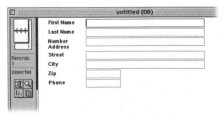

Figure 11.15 After you define the fields, AppleWorks displays them in a no-frills *standard* layout.

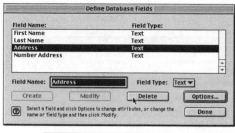

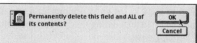

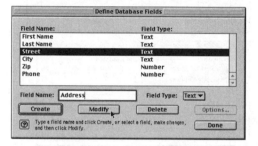

Figure 11.16 To *permanently* remove a field, select it and click *Delete* (top) and—if you are sure—click *OK* in the alert dialog box (bottom).

Figure 11.17 After changing the *Field Name* or *Field Type*, click *Modify* to save the changes.

To delete a field:

1. Choose Layout > Define Fields (Shift ⌘ D) (right, **Figure 11.12**).

2. When the Define Database Fields dialog box appears, select a field name, and click *Delete* (top, **Figure 11.16**).

3. When the alert dialog box appears, if you are sure you want to delete the field, click *OK* (bottom, **Figure 11.16**). The field will be *permanently* deleted from the database, so be sure.

4. Click *Done* to close the Define Database Fields dialog box.

To change a field's name or type:

1. Choose Layout > Define Fields (Shift ⌘ D) (right, **Figure 11.12**).

2. When the Define Database Fields dialog box appears, select a field name and enter a new *Field Name*.

3. Use the pop-up menu to choose another *Field Type*.

4. When you are done making the changes, click *Modify* (**Figure 11.17**). The field name and/or type will be changed.

5. You can then change another field or, if you are done making changes, click *Done* and the Define Database Fields dialog box will close.

Setting field entry options

The *Options* button in the Define Database Fields dialog box can help reduce keyboard mistakes and problem-generating format variations. The options can be set while you're defining fields—or added later.

While the Options dialog boxes vary with the field type, many share the same options to ensure that the field is not left empty, is a unique value, falls within a set range of values, or is automatically filled with a pre-set value.

To set field entry options:

1. Whether you want to set entry options for a new field or add them to an existing field, the steps are the same: Choose Layout > Define Fields ([Shift][⌘][D]).

2. When the Define Database Fields dialog box appears, select a field in the center window, and click the *Options* button (**Figure 11.18**). Or double-click the field name or field type in the center window on the field you want.

3. The Options dialog box that appears will vary depending on the field type (**Figure 11.19**). Once you have made your choices, click *OK*.

4. When the Define Database Fields dialog box reappears, you can set entry options for other fields. Once you're ready, click *Done*.

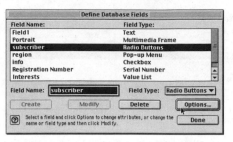

Figure 11.18 To set entry options for a new field or add them to an existing field, select the field and click *Options*.

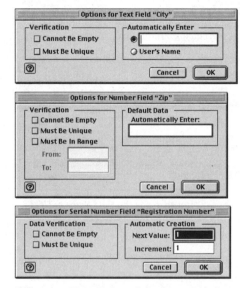

Figure 11.19 Most Options dialog boxes include *Verification* items (to make sure a field is filled, unique, or meets a range of values) and a way to *Automatically Enter* pre-set values.

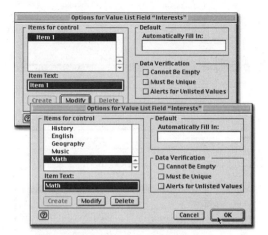

Figure 11.20 The Options dialog boxes for pop-up menus, radio buttons, and value lists all work similarly: The *Items for control* window lets you build a pre-set list of values or choices.

✔ Tip

■ The Options dialog boxes for pop-up menus, radio buttons, and value lists all work similarly. The generically named *Item 1*, *Item 2*, etc., representing the menu, button, or value list choices appear in the *Items for control* window (top, **Figure 11.20**). Click in the *Item Text* window, give the item a new name, and click *Modify*. The name will be added to the *Items for control* window. Repeat until you have created and named the needed items (bottom, **Figure 11.20**). Use the right-side *Default* and *Data Verification* panels to set which item appears automatically and what values will be accepted. Click *OK* to close the dialog box and return to step 4 on the previous page.

Using calculation and summary fields

You cannot enter anything directly into a calculation or summary field. Instead, the fields store and display the results of calculations and formulas. While creating a calculation field is fairly straightforward, summary fields involve a two-step process. First you define the field, then you create what's called a summary part in the layout. That's because summary fields gather information from across several records, so they cannot appear within the body of a *single* record. For more information, see *To insert a summary part* on page 286. For more information on using calculations and formulas, see *Entering and Editing Formulas* on page 229.

To define a calculation or summary field:

1. Choose Layout > Define Fields (Shift ⌘ D).

2. When the Define Database Fields dialog box appears, give the new field a *Field Name*, choose *Calculation* or *Summary* in the *Field Type* pop-up menu, and click *Create* (**Figure 11.21**).

3. When the Enter Formula dialog box appears, click the first of the *Fields* you want to use. Use the *Operators* or *Functions* list to choose what will be done with the value in the first field. Continue clicking in each window to add the *Fields*, *Operators*, or *Functions* needed to complete your calculation or summary (**Figure 11.22**). When you finish building the calculation, click *OK*.

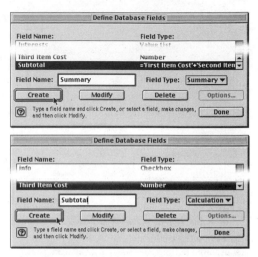

Figure 11.21 Use the *Field Type* pop-up menu to define a *Summary* (top) or *Calculation* (bottom) field.

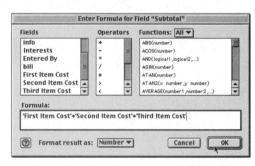

Figure 11.22 Use the *Fields*, *Operators*, and *Functions* lists to build formulas for summary or calculation fields.

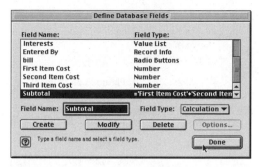

Figure 11.23 Once you build a calculation or summary field, its formula will appear in the Define Database Fields dialog box.

4. The Define Database Fields dialog box will reappear with the calculation or summary field listed, along with its formula (**Figure 11.23**). If you want to create other calculation or summary fields, repeat steps 2 and 3.

5. When you are finished, click *Done* and the Define Database Fields dialog box will close. If you are creating calculation fields, that's it. If you are creating summary fields, however, you also will need to add a summary part to your layout. See *To insert a summary part* on page 286 for more information.

✔ Tips

- For more information on using formulas and functions, see *Entering and Editing Formulas* on page 229.

- If you ever need to edit a calculation field's formula, choose Layout > Define Fields ([Shift][⌘][D]) and double-click the field. The Enter Formula dialog box will appear and you can change the formula as necessary.

USING CALCULATION, SUMMARY FIELDS

Importing Data into a New Database

Records from other database programs (and spreadsheets programs such as Excel) can be imported into an AppleWorks database. The process takes a few extra steps, but works much like importing text into AppleWorks from Microsoft Word (see page 48). The trick is using a format common to virtually all databases and spreadsheets: comma-separated text or tab-separated text. You will lose whatever fancy formatting you may have had in the other program but that sure beats re-entering the data.

While you cannot directly export AppleWorks database records, you can insert them into spreadsheet and word-processing documents using a process called mail merge. For more information, see *Creating Form Letter Layouts with Mail Merge* on page 280.

To import records:

1. Using the other database program, save the records as comma-separated text or tab-separated text.

2. Switch back to AppleWorks and create a new database and define fields to handle the data you'll be importing from the comma-separated text or tab-separated file.

3. With the AppleWorks new database open, choose File > Insert (**Figure 11.24**).

4. When the Open dialog box appears, select *All Available* from the *File Format* drop-down menu, navigate to where you have saved the comma- or tab-separated version of the other database, select it, and click *Insert* (**Figure 11.25**).

Figure 11.24 To import records from another database or spreadsheet program, choose File > Insert.

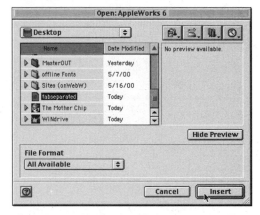

Figure 11.25 Make sure the *File Format* is set to *All Available*, then navigate to the comma- or tab-separated version of the other database or spreadsheet, and click *Insert*.

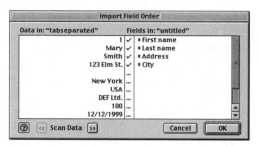

Figure 11.26 When the Import Field Order dialog box first appears, values from the comma-separated text or tab-separated file (left) may not match up with your database's fields (right).

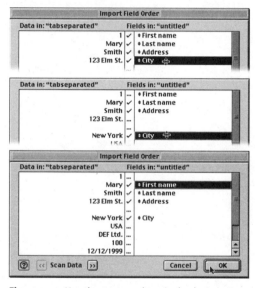

Figure 11.27 Use the center column's checks to set which values are imported, and use your cursor to rearrange the right-side fields to match up with the left-side values.

Figure 11.28 The time-saver: AppleWorks cleanly imports 30 records from another database program.

5. When the Import Field Order dialog box appears, the left side will list the values from the comma-separated text or tab-separated file (**Figure 11.26**).

6. Use the checks in the center column to control which values will be imported (checked ones will be, unchecked won't be). Use your cursor, which will become a double-arrow to rearrange the right-side fields to match up with the left-side values (**Figure 11.27**). When you're done, click *OK*. The comma- or tab-separated data will be imported into the AppleWorks database as new records (**Figure 11.28**).

✔ Tip

■ To double-check the data-field matchups in step 6, click the *Scan Data* arrows in the lower-left of the dialog box. When you do, the left side will display the next data entry. Most times the matchups will be fine. Occasionally, you will spot a value on the left side for which you forgot to create a field in step 2. If that happens, click *Cancel* and go back to define an additional field in the AppleWorks database.

IMPORTING DATA INTO A NEW DATABASE

CREATING DATABASE LAYOUTS

12

AppleWorks's layouts allow you to vary the *appearance* of your data without changing the data itself. This gives you the freedom to create layouts tailored to specific tasks and users. A layout does not need to display every field in the database. In fact, the more you can pare down a layout to just the essential information, the easier it will be to use.

Choosing a Layout Type

When you first define fields in a database, AppleWorks by default generates a *standard* layout—a plain-vanilla layout with equally sized fields arranged top-to-bottom (**Figure 12.1**). You're free to modify that default layout anyway you like. Or you may save yourself some trouble by choosing one of the other layout types built into AppleWorks. Here's a quick comparison of each type:

Standard: This layout displays all the database's fields in the order they were created. The field labels for each field appear just *left* of the fields (**Figure 12.1**). It includes a blank header and footer. Most of the time, a standard layout will serve as the starting point for your own custom layouts.

Duplicate: Use this layout to exactly duplicate whatever layout is active.

Blank: This layout is entirely blank—nothing appears in the header, body, or footer. Since the standard layout automatically inserts *every* field in the database, sometimes it can be easier to start with a clean slate and only add fields as you're ready.

Columnar: This layout places the database's fields in a row across a single page. The labels for the fields appear in the header *above* the body of the record (**Figure 12.2**). You determine the order of the fields when creating the layout or you can go back and rearrange them any time.

Labels: Use this layout only for mailing labels: you can't enter data into it directly. AppleWorks lets you choose from dozens of pre-set Avery label styles. For more information, see *Creating Label Layouts* on page 278.

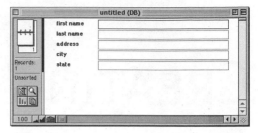

Figure 12.1 AppleWorks by default generates a plain-vanilla *standard* layout with equally sized fields arranged top-to-bottom.

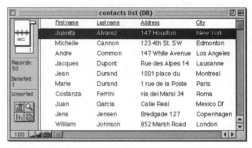

Figure 12.2 The columnar layout places the database fields in a row across the page.

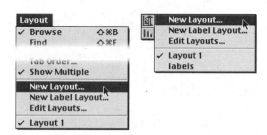

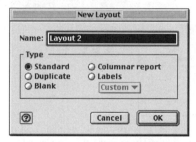

Figure 12.3 To create a new layout, choose Layout > New Layout (left) or click the layout icon's pop-up menu and choose *New Layout* (right).

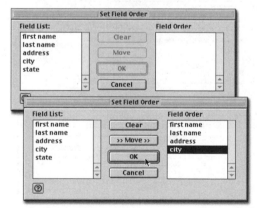

Figure 12.4 Use the New Layout dialog box to give the layout a descriptive *Name* and choose the *Type* of layout you need.

Figure 12.5 When creating a columnar layout, you need to set the *Field Order* by using the *Field List* and the *Move* button.

Creating Layouts

By default, AppleWorks automatically generates a standard layout when you first create a database, which you can then customize as needed. If you want to use another type of layout, or just start fresh, you will need to create a new layout. Creating label layouts is covered separately on page 278.

To create a new layout:

1. Choose Layout > New Layout or click the layout icon's pop-up menu and choose *New Layout* (**Figure 12.3**).

2. When the New Layout dialog box appears, give the layout a descriptive *Name* and choose the *Type* of layout you need (**Figure 12.4**).

3. Click *OK* and a new layout will appear based on your choice in step 2. You can then insert or remove, resize, and rearrange the fields as needed. For more information, see *Working with Fields in Layouts* on page 289 and *Formatting Layout Fields* on page 295.

✔ Tip

- If you choose *Columnar* in step 2, the Set Field Order dialog box will appear. In the *Field List*, select the field you want to appear as the first column and click *Move* (top, **Figure 12.5**). Continue adding fields to the *Field Order* until you are done, then click *OK* (bottom, **Figure 12.5**).

To duplicate a layout:

1. Use the Layout menu or the layout icon's pop-up menu to select the layout you want to copy (**Figure 12.6**).

2. Choose Layout > New Layout (**Figure 12.3**).

3. When the New Layout dialog box appears, give the layout a descriptive *Name*, choose *Duplicate* in the *Type* panel, and click *OK*. The layout selected in step 1 will be copied.

To change a layout name:

1. Choose Layout > Edit Layouts or click the layout icon and chose *Edit Layouts* from the pop-up menu (**Figure 12.7**).

2. When the Edit Layouts dialog box appears, select the layout you want to change in the *Current Layouts* list and click *Modify* (top, **Figure 12.8**).

3. When the Layout Info dialog box appears, type in a new layout name (bottom, **Figure 12.8**). Once you have made your choices, click *OK*.

4. When the Edit Layouts dialog box reappears, you can select another layout to edit in the *Current Layouts* list or click *OK* if you are done. The changes will be applied to the selected layout.

✔ Tip

■ The Layout Info dialog box (bottom, **Figure 12.8**) also controls how records are printed. See *To adjust the label layout* on page 279.

Figure 12.6 Use the Layout menu (left) or the layout icon's pop-up menu (right) to select the layout you want to change.

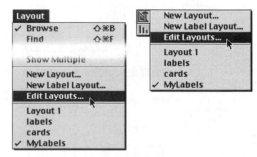

Figure 12.7 To change a layout's name, choose Layout > Edit Layouts (left) or click the layout icon and chose *Edit Layouts* (right).

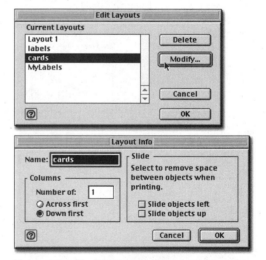

Figure 12.8 In the Edit Layouts dialog box, select the layout you want to modify (top), and change its name in the Layout Info dialog box (bottom).

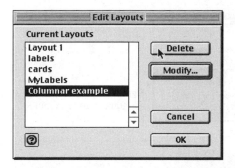

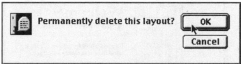

Figure 12.9 In the Edit Layouts dialog box, select the layout you want to delete (top), and click *OK* when the alert dialog box appears (bottom).

To delete a layout:

1. Choose Layout > Edit Layouts or click the layout icon and chose *Edit Layouts* from the pop-up menu (**Figure 12.7**).

2. When the Edit Layouts dialog box appears, select the layout you want removed from the *Current Layouts* list and click *Delete* (top, **Figure 12.9**).

3. When the alert dialog box appears, click *OK* (bottom, **Figure 12.9**). The layout will be deleted from the *Current Layouts* list. Click *OK* and the Edit Layouts dialog box will close.

DELETING LAYOUTS

Creating Label Layouts

Few computer tasks are as consistently frustrating as trying to create labels. Fortunately, AppleWorks includes a labels assistant that makes it a snap. For those who want a more customized approach, AppleWorks also lets you create labels more directly. But it's hard to beat the labels assistant.

To use the labels assistant:

1. Choose Layout > New Label Layout (**Figure 12.10**).

2. When the AppleWorks Assistant appears, just follow the step-by-step instructions and click *Next* to move to the next screen (**Figure 12.11**). At the end, you'll have labels with less head scratching.

To create a labels layout:

1. Choose Layout > New Layout or click the layout icon's pop-up menu and choose *New Layout* (**Figure 12.12**).

2. When the New Layout dialog box appears, give the layout a descriptive *Name* and choose *Labels* in the Type panel. Use the pop-up menu to choose the appropriate Avery size, based on the labels you're using (**Figure 12.13**). Click *OK*.

Figure 12.10 To use the labels assistant, choose Layout > New Label Layout.

Figure 12.11 When the AppleWorks Assistant appears, follow the step-by-step instructions and click *Next* to move to the next screen.

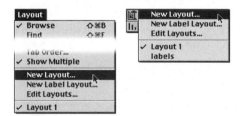

Figure 12.12 To create labels without an assistant, choose Layout > New Layout (left) or click the pop-up menu and choose *New Layout* (right).

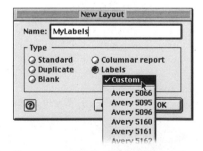

Figure 12.13 Give the layout a descriptive *Name*, choose *Labels* in the Type panel, and pick the appropriate Avery-based size from the pop-up menu.

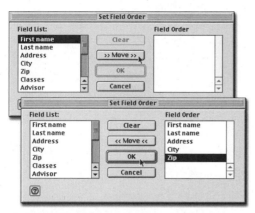

Figure 12.14 Select the field you want at the top of the *Field Order* and click *Move* (top). Once you set the *Field Order*, click *OK* (bottom).

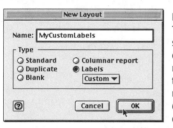

Figure 12.15 To create a label size *not* based on an Avery number, leave the pop-up menu set to *Custom* and click *OK*.

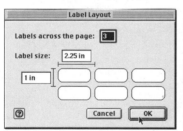

Figure 12.16 Set how many labels you want arranged across the page and the *Label size* dimensions.

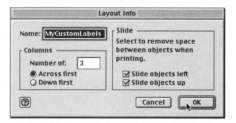

Figure 12.17 Set how many labels will run across the page and whether they will print out *Across* or *Down* the page first. Check both boxes in the *Slide* panel.

3. When the Set Field Order dialog box appears, select in the *Field List* the field you want at the top of the *Field Order* and click *Move* (top, **Figure 12.14**).

4. Continue adding fields to the *Field Order* until you are done, then click *OK* (bottom, **Figure 12.14**). The order will be applied to the layout.

✔ Tips

■ Even non-Avery label packages usually list an Avery-equivalent stock number.

■ If you want to create the label size directly, leave the pop-up menu set to *Custom* in step 2 and click *OK* (**Figure 12.15**). When the Label Layout dialog box appears, enter how many labels you want arranged across the page and the *Label size* dimensions (**Figure 12.16**). Click *OK* and the custom dimensions will be applied to the layout.

To adjust the label layout:

1. Choose Layout > Edit Layouts or click the layout icon and chose *Edit Layouts* from the pop-up menu.

2. When the Edit Layouts dialog box appears, select the layout you want to change in the *Current Layouts* list and click *Modify*.

3. When the Layout Info dialog box appears, use the *Columns* panel to set the *Number of* labels that will be arranged across the page and whether the labels will print out *Across* the page first or *Down* the page first (**Figure 12.17**). Check both boxes in the *Slide* panel and click *OK*. The labels printing arrangement will be adjusted.

CREATING LABEL LAYOUTS

Creating Form Letter Layouts with Mail Merge

Form letters—standard letters containing bits of customized information—are easy to create using AppleWorks's mail merge feature. By creating a layout that's mostly text with a few judiciously placed merge fields, you can create a customized letter:

Dear Mr. Jones,

Here's an opportunity better than any IPO! Like most of us, you probably have big dreams and a tiny checkbook. We can help. Because of your outstanding credit, stellar social skills, and stunning wardrobe, you and your dog Binx are eligible for an appearance on our hit show *Doesn't Everyone Want to Be a Gadzillionaire?*

Call us today and we can turn your nightmares into a gadzillion dreams!

Sincerely,

James Smith

In AppleWorks, which uses << and >> to mark merge fields, the letter looks like this before the mail merge is performed:

Dear <<Courtesy Title>> <<Last Name>>,

Here's an opportunity better than any IPO! Like most of us, you probably have big dreams and a tiny checkbook. We can help. Because of your outstanding credit, stellar social skills, and stunning wardrobe, you and your <<significant other>> <<significant other's name>> are eligible for an appearance on our hit show *Doesn't Everyone Want to Be a Gadzillionaire?*

Call us today and we can turn your nightmares into a gadzillion dreams!

Sincerely,

<<user name>>

Form letters with merge fields can be a powerful tool and tremendous time-saver.

Figure 12.18 Click the cursor where you want the first merge field to appear.

Figure 12.19 To insert the first field, choose File > Mail Merge.

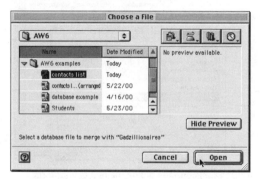

Figure 12.20 When the Choose a File dialog box appears, navigate to the database you want to use for the mail merge and click *Open*.

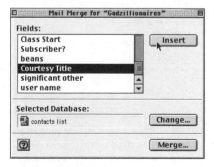

Figure 12.21 Scroll in the *Fields* list until you find the first field you want to use and click *Insert*. If you want to switch databases, click *Change*.

To create a form letter using merge fields:

1. If you only want to use some of the database records in your form letter, search and sort the database to use only those records. (For information on searches and sorts, see *Finding and Sorting Records* on page 306.) Also make sure you have defined fields for all the data you need inserted into the form letter.

2. Create a word-processing document for the form letter and begin typing until you reach the first place in the letter where you want a merge field inserted (**Figure 12.18**).

3. Choose File > Mail Merge (**Figure 12.19**).

4. When the Choose a File dialog box appears, navigate to the database you want to use for the mail merge and click *Open* (**Figure 12.20**).

5. When the Mail Merge dialog box appears, scroll until you find the first field you want to use, then click *Insert* (**Figure 12.21**).

(continued)

6. A merge field, marked by double chevrons on each side, will be inserted into the letter (**Figure 12.22**).

7. Type the rest of your form letter, adding other merge fields as needed (**Figure 12.23**). When you are done with the letter, click *Merge* in the Mail Merge dialog box.

8. When the Mail Merge Destination dialog box appears (**Figure 12.24**), choose one of the three options:

   Send documents to printer if you want to print out the form letters immediately.

   Save in a new document if you want to save all the form letters in a single word-processing document for later printing or editing.

   Save each final document on disk if you want a separate document for each form letter created.

Figure 12.22 A merge field, marked by double chevrons on each side, is inserted into the letter.

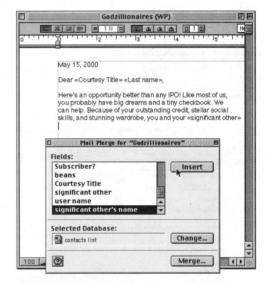

Figure 12.23 Continue typing the rest of your form letter, inserting other merge fields as needed.

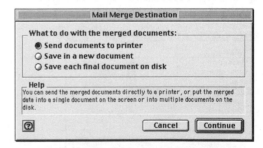

Figure 12.24 When the Mail Merge Destination dialog box appears, choose whether you want to print the form letters immediately or save them for later use.

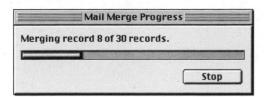

Figure 12.25 A progress bar tracks the merging of the data fields with the form letters.

9. Once you've made your choice, click *Continue* and the database data will be merged with the word-processing document (**Figure 12.25**).

10. When the progress bar disappears, the form letters will be printed or saved based on your choice.

✔ Tips

■ It's up to you whether you type out the entire form letter and then insert the needed merge fields or insert them as you go.

■ It sounds odd but make sure you close the database you want to use *before* choosing File > Mail Merge. AppleWorks of course opens it as part of the mail merge process but gets confused if it is already open.

■ In step 5, if you accidentally opened the wrong database, click the *Change* button to find the one you need instead (**Figure 12.21**).

■ In step 8, if you choose *Save in a new document* the document will be untitled so be sure to actually save it (⌘S) before you close it.

■ If you expect to frequently use the same set of sorted records for form letters, see *To create a reusable search* on page 312 and *To create a reusable sort* on page 317.

Working with Parts

In most cases, the function of the various layout parts are obvious from their names: header, body, and footer. Summary parts work a bit differently than other layout parts. Since summary fields gather information from across several records, they cannot appear within the body of an individual record. That's where the various kinds of summary parts come in by providing a way to display this cross-record data. *Grand summary* parts summarize information for all the records being browsed. *Subsummary* parts do the same for a group of records. For more information on summary fields, see *To insert a summary part* on page 286 and *Using calculation and summary fields* on page 268.

Header: The header appears at the top of each page in the database, but only in the layout to which it is added. Each layout can only contain one header. This is not the same thing as a *document* header, which appears on every page of a database, no matter which layout you use. Document headers are covered on page 140.

Leading grand summary: This part displays summary information at the *beginning* of the group of the records being browsed. It can contain one or more summary fields.

Body: Use for the bulk of your data, including graphics. The body will appear for each record in the database. Each layout can only contain one body.

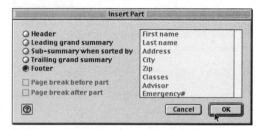

Figure 12.26 To add a part to a layout, choose Layout > Insert Part.

Figure 12.27 When the Insert Part dialog box appears, choose *Footer* from the five part types listed down the left side.

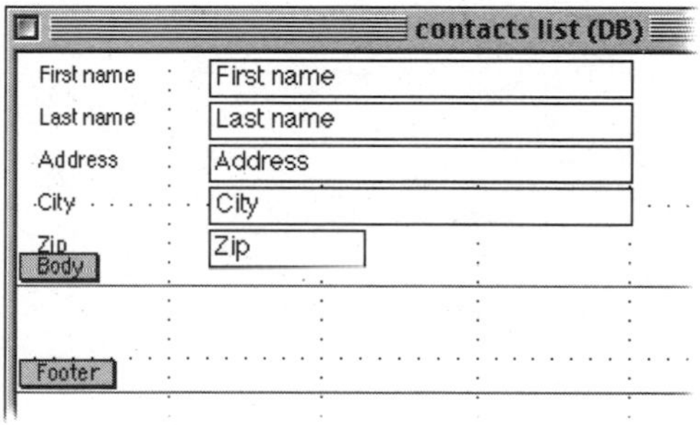

Figure 12.28 Once added to a layout, the footer can have fields placed within it.

Subsummary: Use this type of summary part to display summary information for the group of records specified by the break field. It can contain one or more summary fields.

Trailing grand summary: Use this type of summary part to display summary information at the *end* of the group of the records being browsed. It can contain one or more summary fields.

Footer: Use for dates or page numbers. The footer will appear at the bottom of the database, but only in the layout to which it is added. Each layout can contain only one footer. This is not the same thing as a *document* footer, which appears on every page of a database, no matter which layout you use. Document footers are covered on page 140.

To insert a layout header or footer:

1. Make sure you are in Layout mode by choosing Layout > Layout (Shift⌘L) and select the layout you want to change.

2. Choose Layout > Insert Part (**Figure 12.26**).

3. When the Insert Part dialog box appears, choose *Header* or *Footer* from the five part types listed down the left side (**Figure 12.27**).

4. Once you have made your choices, click *OK*. The part will be added to the layout (**Figure 12.28**).

Inserting summary parts

Inserting summary parts is the second step of a two-step process. Before you can insert a summary part, you must first define a summary field as explained in *Using calculation and summary fields* on page 268.

To insert a summary part:

1. Make sure you are in Layout mode by choosing Layout > Layout ([Shift][⌘][L]) and select the layout you want to change.

2. Choose Layout > Insert Part (**Figure 12.26**).

3. When the Insert Part dialog box appears:

    Choose *Leading grand summary* or *Trailing grand summary* from the part types listed down the left side.

    or

    Choose *Sub-summary when sorted by* and select a field in the right-side list to sort by. If you want a page break to appear, use the two checkboxes to control whether the page break will appear *before* or *after* the sub-summary (**Figure 12.29**).

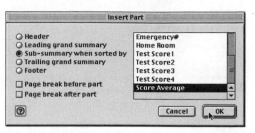

Figure 12.29 If you choose *Sub-summary*, select which field it will be sorted by. Use the checkboxes if you want a *Page break* before or after the subsummary.

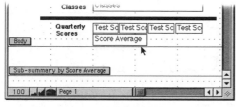

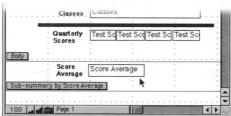

Figure 12.30 Once the summary part is inserted into the layout (top), you can drag the needed field to it (bottom).

4. Click *OK* and the summary part will be inserted into the layout (top, **Figure 12.30**).

5. Now click and drag your pre-defined summary *field* into the summary *part* (bottom, **Figure 12.30**).

6. To see the summarized information, switch to Browse mode ((Shift)(⌘)(B)) and choose Window > Page View.

✔ Tips

- If you are creating a sub-summary part, a dialog box will appear after you click *OK* in step 4 asking whether you want the sub-summary part to appear *Above* or *Below* the group of sorted records. The sub-summary part will be inserted into the layout based on your choice.

- If you insert a sub-summary part, remember to sort your records by the same field you chose in step 3. If you plan to perform this sub-summary sort repeatedly, it will jog your memory if you give the sort a name. For more information, see *To create a reusable sort* on page 317.

To resize a layout part:

1. Make sure you are in Layout mode by choosing Layout > Layout ((Shift)(⌘)(L)) and select the layout you want to change.

2. Move the cursor toward the part boundary until it becomes a double arrow. Click and drag the cursor to enlarge or shrink the part. A dotted outline will guide your progress (**Figure 12.31**).

3. Release the cursor and the part will be resized.

To delete a part:

1. Make sure you are in Layout mode by choosing Layout > Layout ((Shift)(⌘)(L)) and select the layout you want to change.

2. Move the cursor over the part boundary and when it becomes a double arrow, click and drag the cursor until the part shrinks to nothing. Release the cursor and the part will be deleted (**Figure 12.32**).

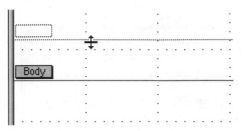

Figure 12.31 To resize a layout part, click and drag the cursor to enlarge or shrink the part. A dotted outline guides your progress.

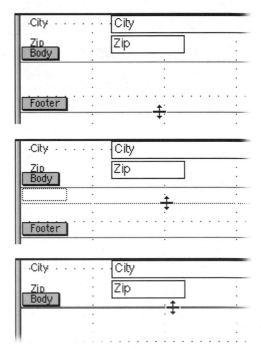

Figure 12.32 To delete a part, click and drag the cursor until the part shrinks to nothing (top to bottom).

Working with Fields in Layouts

When you're working with layouts remember: *inserting* a field into a *layout* isn't the same thing as *creating* a field for the *database*. Layouts are simply differing views of the same data. Add a layout or delete a layout—either way the database itself isn't changed. The same notion applies when inserting (sometimes called adding) a field in a layout: It's just a view of a field that's already been created within the database.

For information on how to create a brand new field, see *To define a field* on page 264. Once you've created a field, you can easily add it to a new layout directly without having to define it again. However, it's common while designing a layout to discover that you need to define a new field. Just keep straight the difference between defining fields for the database versus adding a field to a layout and you'll be fine.

To insert fields in a layout:

1. Make sure you are in Layout mode by choosing Layout > Layout ([Shift][⌘][L]).

2. Use the Layout menu or layout icon's pop-up menu to select the layout you want to use (top, **Figure 12.33**).

3. Choose Layout > Insert Field (**Figure 12.34**).

4. When the Insert Fields dialog box appears, only the fields not already in the layout will be listed. Choose a field(s) from the list and click *Insert* (**Figure 12.35**). The field(s) will be added to the layout (bottom, **Figure 12.33**).

✔ Tips

■ To select more than one field in step 4, press [Shift] as you click field names in the list.

■ If the Insert Fields dialog box is blank, all the fields are already in the layout.

■ You cannot create, that is define, fields in this step. You can only insert *existing* fields. For information on defining fields, see page 262.

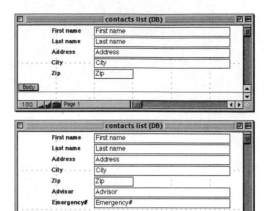

Figure 12.33 Before the fields are inserted into the layout (top) and after (bottom). The layout automatically grows to accommodate the inserted fields.

Figure 12.34 To insert fields in a layout, choose Layout > Insert Field.

Figure 12.35 Use the Insert Fields dialog box to insert fields not already in the layout.

To remove fields or field labels from a layout:

1. Make sure you are in Layout mode by choosing Layout > Layout ([Shift][⌘][L]).

2. Use the Layout menu or layout icon's pop-up menu to select the layout from which you want to remove fields.

3. Click your cursor on the fields or field labels you want to remove, or click and drag the cursor to select several items.

4. Press [Delete] and the selected fields or field labels will be removed from the layout.

✔ Tips

- If a field has a field label, be sure to select it as well in step 3.

- Since field names always appear inside blank fields, you may decide that a layout will look less cluttered or can be more compact if you remove some or all of the field *labels*.

To resize layout fields:

1. Make sure you are in Layout mode by choosing Layout > Layout (Shift ⌘ L).

2. Use the cursor to select the field(s) that you want to resize. Small black boxes (handles) will appear around the edge of the selected field(s) (top, **Figure 12.36**).

3. Click any one of the handles and drag the handle to enlarge or shrink the field. A dotted outline will guide your progress (middle, **Figure 12.36**).

4. Release the cursor and the field will be resized (bottom, **Figure 12.36**).

✔ Tip

- To select more than one field, press Shift as you click the fields. If the fields are different sizes, they will be resized relative to their original size.

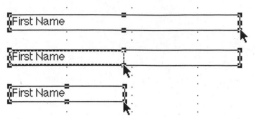

Figure 12.36 To resize layout fields, click and drag any handle to enlarge or shrink the field.

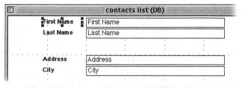

Figure 12.37 To rearrange layout fields, click the field to select it (top). Click again to drag each field or field label to its new position (bottom).

To rearrange layout fields:

1. Make sure you are in Layout mode by choosing Layout > Layout (Shift ⌘ L).

2. Use the cursor to select the field(s) that you want to rearrange. Small black boxes (handles) will appear around the edge of the selected field(s) (top, **Figure 12.37**).

3. Click any one of the handles and drag the handle to its new position. A dotted outline will guide your progress. Release the cursor and the field will move to its new position.

4. Repeat steps 2–3 until you've rearranged the layout to your liking (bottom, **Figure 12.37**).

✔ Tips

- You can use the same technique to move and rearrange anything within the layout, including added text, drawn objects, and frames.

- When you move a field, don't forget to move its label as well.

Changing the field tab order

By default, AppleWorks sets the tab order for the fields based on when the fields were created. It makes more sense, however, to set the order based on what is the most convenient sequence for entering data into records.

To set the field tab order:

1. Switch to Browse mode ([Shift][⌘][B]) or List mode ([Shift][⌘][I]).

2. Choose Layout > Tab Order (**Figure 12.38**).

3. When the Tab Order dialog box appears, click *Clear* to start a fresh *Tab Order* (top, **Figure 12.39**).

4. Select in the *Field List* the field you want at the top of the *Tab Order* and click *Move* (bottom, **Figure 12.39**).

5. Continue adding fields to the *Tab Order* until you are done, then click *OK*. The new tab order for the fields will be applied.

Figure 12.38 To set the field tab order, choose Layout > Tab Order while in Browse or List mode.

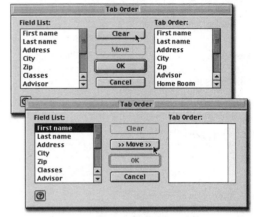

Figure 12.39 Click *Clear* to start a fresh *Tab Order* (top). Use the *Field List* and the *Move* button to create a new *Tab Order* (bottom).

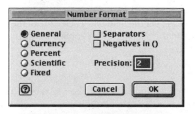

Figure 12.40 To format number, date, or time fields, select the field and choose Edit > File Info.

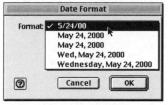

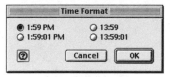

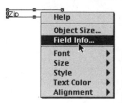

Figure 12.41 From the top: The format dialog boxes for Number, Date, and Time fields.

Figure 12.42 You also can Ctrl-click the field and choose *Field Info* from the pop-up menu.

Formatting Layout Fields

For fields already defined as number, date, or time fields, AppleWorks lets you choose a variety of formats. When formatting database field text you have two choices: changing the text for an *individual* entry or changing the text format for *every entry* in that particular field. In all cases, the formatting change only affects the selected layout.

To format number, date, or time fields:

1. Make sure you are in Layout mode (Shift ⌘ L) and choose the layout you want to change.

2. Select any field already defined as a number, date, or time field. Double-click the field or choose Edit > Field Info (**Figure 12.40**).

3. Depending on how the field is defined, a dialog box to format the number, date, or time will appear (**Figure 12.41**). Make your choices and click *OK*. The formatting will be applied to the field.

✔ Tip

■ You also can Ctrl-click the field and choose *Field Info* from the pop-up menu (**Figure 12.42**).

To format text for individual entries:

1. Use the Layout menu or layout icon's pop-up menu to select the layout you want to change.

2. Make sure you switch to *Browse* mode (⌈Shift⌉⌈⌘⌉⌈B⌉).

3. Select the field or field label you want to change (left, **Figure 12.43**).

4. Choose Format and then choose *Font*, *Size*, *Style*, or *Text Color* from the sub-menu. Once you make your choice and release the cursor, the change is applied to the selected entry only (right, **Figure 12.43**).

Figure 12.43 To format text for *individual* entries, stay in Browse mode, select the field *entry* (left), make the style change, and the change will be applied only to that entry (right).

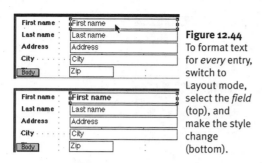

Figure 12.44
To format text for *every* entry, switch to Layout mode, select the *field* (top), and make the style change (bottom).

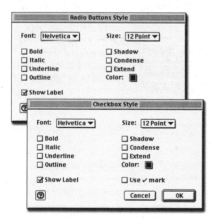

Figure 12.45 Switch to Browse mode to see how the change made in Figure 12.44 affects *every* entry in that field.

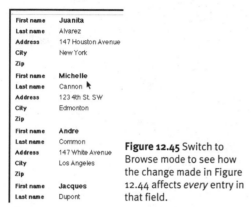

Figure 12.46 To quickly format any field while in Layout mode, double-click the field and a dialog box based on the field type will appear.

Figure 12.47 In Layout mode, you also can Ctrl-click the field and choose the appropriate text-related item from the pop-up menu.

To format text for every entry:

1. Use the Layout menu or layout icon's pop-up menu to select the layout you want to change.

2. Make sure you are in *Layout* mode ([Shift][⌘][L]).

3. Select the field or field label you want to change (top, **Figure 12.44**).

4. Choose Format and then choose *Font*, *Size*, *Style*, or *Text Color* from the submenu. Once you make your choice and release the cursor, the change is applied (bottom, **Figure 12.44**). Switch to Browse mode and you will see that the change affects every entry in that field or every field label (**Figure 12.45**).

✔ Tips

- To quickly format any field, switch to Layout mode and double-click the field. A dialog box based on the field type will appear (**Figure 12.46**). Make your choices, click *OK*, and the changes will be applied.

- You also can Ctrl-click the field and choose the appropriate item from the pop-up menu (**Figure 12.47**).

FORMATTING LAYOUT FIELDS

To format the field borders:

1. Switch to *Layout* mode (Shift⌘L) and use the Layout menu or layout icon's pop-up menu to select the layout you want to change.

2. Open the Accents Palette (⌘K) (**Figure 12.48**).

3. Select the field or field name you want to change.

4. Click the Accents Palette's *Pen* icon if it's not already highlighted (**Figure 12.49**), and then click the palette's color, line style, or pattern tab.

5. Use the palette panel that appears to change the field's border.

To format the field background:

1. Switch to *Layout* mode (Shift⌘L) and use the Layout menu or layout icon's pop-up menu to select the layout you want to change.

2. Open the Accents Palette (⌘K) (**Figure 12.48**).

3. Select the field or field name you want to change.

4. Click the Accents Palette's *Fill* icon if it's not already highlighted (**Figure 12.50**), and then click the palette's color, pattern, wallpaper, or gradient tab.

5. Use the palette panel that appears to change the field's background.

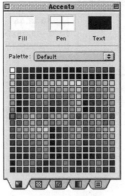

Figure 12.48 To format field borders or backgrounds, open the Accents Palette (⌘K).

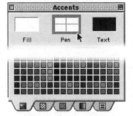

Figure 12.49 To change field borders, click the Accents Palette's *Pen* icon (top) and then choose the color, line style, or pattern tab (bottom).

Figure 12.50 To change a field background, click the Accents Palette's *Fill* icon (top) and then choose the color, pattern, wallpaper, or gradient tab (bottom).

WORKING WITH RECORDS

13

While the previous two chapters focused on building databases, this one concentrates on the business of actually entering data. In working directly with the records, you will spend most of your time adding new records, moving around within a single record, and then moving from record to record. The chapter also shows you how to use the powerful Find and Sort commands, which enable you to quickly find the data you need. AppleWorks's Button Bar automatically displays database-related icons whenever you are working in a database (**Figure 13.1**).

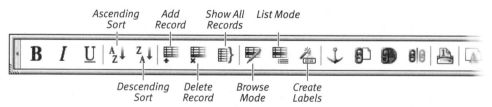

Figure 13.1 The Button Bar automatically displays database-related icons whenever you are working in a database.

Opening and Viewing Records

By default, AppleWorks displays database records in Browse mode, which makes it easy to see the overall layout of the records including their position and size. By switching to List mode, you can see more records onscreen simultaneously. List mode also makes it easier to compare the contents of different records at a glance.

To open an existing database file:

◆ Double-click any AppleWorks database file and it will open in Browse mode.

or

◆ Choose File > Open and when the Open dialog box appears, navigate to where you have stored a database file, and click *Open* (**Figure 13.2**). The file will open in Browse mode.

✔ Tip

■ AppleWorks files all use the same icon, regardless of file type. To make it easier to spot your database files, set the Open dialog box's *Document Type* pop-up menu to *Database* (**Figure 13.2**).

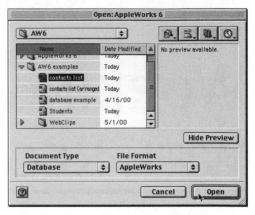

Figure 13.2 To make it easier to spot your database files, set the Open dialog box's *Document Type* pop-up menu to *Database*.

Figure 13.3 To view records with each field clearly visible, choose Layout > Browse (Shift ⌘ B).

Figure 13.4 Browse mode shows the position and size of the fields.

Figure 13.5 To view records in a spreadsheet-style list, choose Layout > List (Shift ⌘ I).

Figure 13.6 List mode displays the records in rows and columns.

To view records with their fields:

◆ To view records with each field clearly visible, choose Layout > Browse (Shift ⌘ B) (**Figure 13.3**) or click the Browse Mode icon in the button bar (**Figure 13.1**). AppleWorks will switch to Browse mode and show the position and size of the fields (**Figure 13.4**).

To view a list of records:

◆ To view records in a spreadsheet-style list, choose Layout > List (Shift ⌘ I) (**Figure 13.5**) or click the List Mode icon in the button bar (**Figure 13.1**). AppleWorks will switch to List mode and display the records in rows and columns (**Figure 13.6**).

VIEWING RECORDS

301

Adding, Duplicating, and Deleting Records

Once a database has been built, it's time to start adding records and entering data. Duplicating an existing record can save you data-entry time if most of the data is the same and only a few fields need changing. Over time, you also may need to delete out-of-date records.

To add a record:

1. Make sure you are in Browse or List mode ([Shift][⌘][B] or [Shift][⌘][I]).

2. Choose Edit > New Record ([⌘][R]) (**Figure 13.7**) or click the New Record icon in the button bar (**Figure 13.1**). A new blank record will appear.

To duplicate a record:

1. Make sure you are in Browse or List mode ([Shift][⌘][B] or [Shift][⌘][I]).

2. Click anywhere in the record you want to duplicate and choose Edit > Duplicate Record ([⌘][D]) (**Figure 13.8**). A duplicate of the selected record will appear in the database, which you can then modify as needed.

To delete a record:

1. Make sure you are in Browse or List mode ([Shift][⌘][B] or [Shift][⌘][I]).

2. Click anywhere in the record you want to delete and choose Edit > Delete Record (**Figure 13.9**) or click the Delete Record icon in the button bar (**Figure 13.1**). The selected record will be deleted.

✔ Tip

■ There is no warning box to let you change your mind, so be sure you really want to delete the record before choosing the delete command.

Figure 13.7 To add a new record, choose Edit > New Record ([⌘][R]).

Figure 13.8 To duplicate a record, click in the record you want to duplicate and choose Edit > Duplicate Record ([⌘][D]).

Figure 13.9 To delete a record, click in the record and choose Edit > Delete Record.

Moving within a Record

Getting around within a single AppleWorks record couldn't be easier, but as usual, there are several ways to do it.

Using your cursor to directly select a field works best when you need to change only a couple of items within a particular record. Using the Tab key generally works best when you're filling in new *blank* records or when you want to keep your hands on the keyboard. Both methods work in either Browse or List mode.

To move by direct selection:

◆ Click on any field you want to modify. Once the field becomes highlighted, type in your data. To reach another spot in the record, click your cursor on the desired field.

To move with the Tab key:

◆ After a record opens, press (Tab) to reach the first field. Continue pressing (Tab) until you reach the desired field. To move backward among the fields, press (Shift)(Tab).

✔ Tips

■ You can't tab to fields that contain calculations or summaries. But the contents of those fields are based on values set in other fields, so it's not really a problem. Just keep it in mind.

■ AppleWorks lets you set the tab order for all the fields in a record. Reordering the tabs is particularly handy if you need to reach only a few scattered fields within each record. For more on setting the tab order, see page 294.

MOVING WITHIN RECORDS

Navigating from Record to Record

AppleWorks offers you six ways to quickly jump from record to record within a particular file. Only the first four methods, however, work in the Browse and List views.

To move from record to record:

◆ While viewing the records, choose Organize > Go To Record (⌘G). When the Go to record dialog box appears, type in the number of the record you want, and click *OK* (**Figure 13.10**). The record will appear and become active.

or

◆ Press ⌘↓ to move forward one record at a time or press ⌘↑ to move backward. The thin bar just to the left of the records will jump to the next record, indicating that it is now the active record (**Figure 13.11**).

or

◆ Click the flipbook's pages. Click the lower page to move forward in the sequence (**Figure 13.12**); click the upper page to move back. A blank upper or lower page indicates there are no more records in that direction (**Figure 13.13**).

or

Figure 13.10 To jump straight to a particular record, choose Organize > Go To Record (left), type in the record number, and click *OK* (right).

Figure 13.11 The thin black bar just to the left of the records jumps to the next record, indicating that it is now the active record.

Figure 13.12 Click the flipbook's lower page to move forward in the records.

Figure 13.13 A blank upper or lower page in the flipbook indicates there are no more records in that direction.

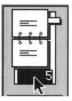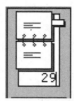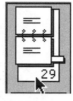

Figure 13.14 To quickly skip ahead or back within the records, click and drag the flipbook's bookmark bar.

Figure 13.15 In Browse mode, if you know the desired record's number, click the current record number at the bottom of the flipbook (left), type in the number (middle), and press [Return] or [Enter] to move to it (right).

Figure 13.16 In List mode you can click the small box next to the record (left) and it will immediately become the active record (right).

- To quickly skip ahead or back within the records, click and drag the flipbook's bookmark bar. Dragging it down will skip you ahead in the sequence (**Figure 13.14**); dragging it up moves you back.

  or

- If you know the number of a particular record, click on the current record number at the bottom of the flipbook, type in the desired number, and press [Return] or [Enter] (**Figure 13.15**). This method works only in Browse mode.

  or

- In List mode you have another navigation option: Click the small box just left of a record and it will immediately become the active record (**Figure 13.16**).

Finding and Sorting Records

Finding and sorting records are like two halves of the same process. Together, they give you the power to spotlight particular records in a particular order. With Find you can hunt down a record that needs changing without having to go through the records one by one. While records normally are displayed in the order they were created, the Sort command lets you arrange the view to what best suits your needs.

Understanding a few key terms—Find requests, along with *And* vs. *Or* searches—will make it easier to use AppleWorks's Find features.

Find Requests: What AppleWorks calls a *Find request* simply represents all the criteria entered for a particular search. Whether they're plain or fancy, all the field criteria associated with a single search represent one Find request.

The Found Set: The records returned in any search are called the *found set*. Working with a found set allows you to focus on tailoring it for sorting, printing, exporting, etc. The rest of the database's records still exist but are not displayed and make up what's called the *omitted set*. For more information, see *Omitting records* on page 314. You can return to working with the full set of records within a file at any time. To do so, choose Organize > Show All Records (Shift ⌘ A).

And vs. Or Searches: Find's features allow you to create wonderfully specific search requests but they all involve variations of two kinds of searches: the *And* search vs. the *Or* search.

Any time you create a Find request that looks for data in two or more *different* fields in a record, you're performing what's called a logical *And* search. AppleWorks also calls this a *single Find request.* If, for example, you create a Find request that asks for any records within a file where the city is San Francisco and the state is California, you're asking AppleWorks to find records that contain San Francisco *and* California. Such *And* searches tend to narrow your search since you're not just looking for records containing California but a smaller group within that group that also contains San Francisco.

Any time you create a Find request that looks for *different* values within the *same* field, you're performing what's called a logical *Or* search. AppleWorks also calls this a *multiple Find request.* If, for example, you create a Find request for all records containing California *or* Arizona, that will require AppleWorks to search the database's state field for two different values. Such *Or* queries tend to widen your search.

To make a single Find request:

1. Make sure you are using a layout that contains the field or fields you want to search, then choose Layout > Find ((Shift)(⌘)(F)) (**Figure 13.17**).

2. When a blank version of the selected layout appears, type the terms you are seeking into the layout field or fields. Click the *Find* button or press (Return) or (Enter) (**Figure 13.18**). All the records matching your search criteria will appear (**Figure 13.19**).

Figure 13.17 To start any search, switch to Find mode by choosing Layout > Find ((Shift)(⌘)(F)).

Figure 13.18 Use the blank fields to create your Find request, then click the *Find* button.

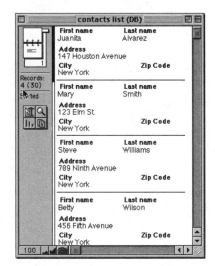

Figure 13.19 All the records matching your search will appear in a scrollable window.

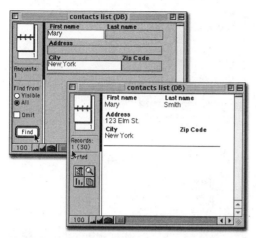

Figure 13.20 Though AppleWorks calls it a single Find request, you can search more than one field (top) to find records that meet both criteria (bottom).

Figure 13.21 If nothing in the database matches your search criteria, the flipbook will indicate that 0 records were found.

Figure 13.22 To see all the records again after performing a find, choose Organize > Show All Records ([Shift][⌘][A]).

✔ Tips

■ Though AppleWorks calls it a *single* Find request, don't let the name fool you. You can search for more than one item in the same Find request (**Figure 13.20**).

■ If nothing in the database matches your search criteria, AppleWorks will return a blank screen and the flipbook will indicate that 0 records were found (**Figure 13.21**).

■ As long as each item you're requesting appears in a *different* field, you can make such requests as specific as you like. Many times this *And* search will be all you need. To search for different values within the *same* field, you'll need to make a *multiple* Find request.

■ If you have already performed several Find requests, the visible records do not include every record in the database. Depending on your needs, you may want to choose the *All* radio button in the *Find from* section above the *Find* button (**Figure 13.18**).

■ If you want to see all your records again after performing a find request, choose Organize > Show All Records ([Shift][⌘][A]) (**Figure 13.22**). All the records in the database will reappear.

To make a multiple Find request:

1. Choose Layout > Find ([Shift][⌘][F]) and type the terms you are seeking into the layout field or fields. Do *not* hit [Return] or [Enter] just yet.

2. To add your second search item, choose Edit > New Request ([⌘][R]) (**Figure 13.23**). A duplicate set of blank fields will appear.

3. Type what you're seeking into the duplicate set of fields you used in the first request (top, **Figure 13.24**). Within the left-hand mode status area, the number of requests you've made within this set of records is displayed. If you want, you can continue to add multiple criteria by repeating this step.

4. When you're ready, click the *Find* button or press [Return] or [Enter]. The search will display all records that match any of your criteria request (bottom, **Figure 13.24**).

Figure 13.23 To add your second search item in a *multiple* Find request, choose Edit > New Request ([⌘][R]).

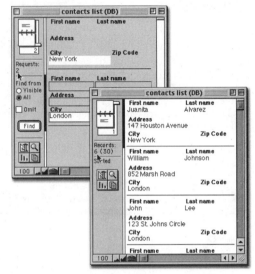

Figure 13.24 In a *multiple* Find request, you use two forms to search the same field (top) to find records that contain *either* term, in this case *New York* or *London* (bottom).

Table 13.1

USE	TO FIND	TYPE IN FIELD
	Using Operators in Searches	
<	Less than value to right of symbol	<200
<=	Less than or equal to value to right	<=200
>	Greater than value to right	>200
>=	Greater than or equal to value to right	>=200
=	Exact value in order & nothing else	= New York
<>	All values except New York	<New York>

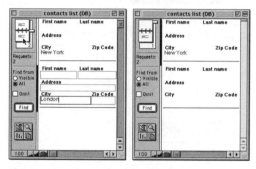

Figure 13.25 Left: The black bar and flipbook indicate that the second request (*London*) is selected. Right: After clicking the flipbook, the first request (*New York*) is selected.

Figure 13.26 After selecting one of your multiple Find requests, delete it by choosing Edit > Delete Request.

Figure 13.27 To copy and then change a complicated multiple Find request, choose Edit > Duplicate Request (⌘D).

✔ Tips

■ You also can use arithmetic operators, (such as +, <, >=) in building your Find request. For more information, see **Table 13.1**.

■ As long you are still creating a multiple Find request, you can go back and fine-tune any of the individual requests that comprise it.

■ While building a multiple Find request, you also can delete one of your requests if you want. Select the request by using the flipbook or by clicking within the request, then choose Edit > Delete Request (**Figures 13.25** and **13.26**). The selected request will be deleted.

■ You can save yourself a bit of time if you are building a complicated multiple Find request by duplicating one of the requests and then changing it as needed. Select the request and then choose Edit > Duplicate Request (⌘D) (**Figure 13.27**). Once the duplicate appears, you can change it as needed.

MAKING FIND REQUESTS

Creating a reusable search

When working with a database it's not unusual to repeatedly use the same search criteria. Instead of forcing you to rebuild the Find request again and again, AppleWorks lets you create it once, give it a name and then it will be available for reuse as needed. AppleWorks calls this reusable search a *named* search.

To create a reusable search:

1. Make sure you are in Find mode, click the search icon and choose *New Search* from the pop-up menu (top, **Figure 13.28**).

2. When the Search Name dialog box appears, type in a descriptive name for your search and click *OK* (middle, **Figure 13.28**).

3. When a blank version of the selected layout appears, create a Find request as you would normally and then click the *Store* button. The search will be saved. You can then reuse it any time by clicking the search icon and choosing the search by name from the pop-up menu (bottom, **Figure 13.28**).

To use a named search:

◆   Make sure you are in Browse or List mode, click the search icon and choose one of the saved searches from the pop-up menu (**Figure 13.29**). The requested search request will be activated.

Figure 13.28 To create a *reusable* search, click the search icon, choose *New Search* from the pop-up menu (top), and give it a name (middle). After you create the search criteria, the search will be available in the pop-up menu (bottom).

Figure 13.29 To trigger a named (reusable) search, click the search icon and choose it from the pop-up menu.

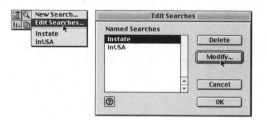

Figure 13.30 To change a named (reusable) search, choose *Edit Searches* from the pop-up menu (left), select it in the list, and click *Modify* (right).

To change a named search:

1. Click the search icon and choose *Edit Searches* from the pop-up menu (left, **Figure 13.30**).

2. When the Edit Searches dialog box appears, click in the *Named Searches* list on the search you want to change (right, **Figure 13. 30**). Click *Delete* if you want to remove the named search entirely or *Modify* if you want to change its name or search criteria.

3. If you click *Delete*, the named search will be deleted immediately, and you'll need to click *OK* to close the dialog box.

   or

   If you click *Modify*, the Search Name dialog box will appear. If you want to change the name, do so now and click *OK*. If you want to change only the search criteria, leave the name as is and click *OK*. When the search criteria appear, change them, and click *Store*. The search criteria will be updated and saved.

CREATING REUSABLE SEARCHES

Omitting records

When you perform a regular Find request, the records *not* shown are known as the *omitted records*. In that sense, omitted records are the reverse of the *found set* generated by a Find request. Sometimes it's quicker to search for these records—the ones that do *not* meet your search criteria. Used with the Find and Sort commands, the Omit command allows you to quickly make a selection and then *invert* it by finding all the records *not* in that selection.

Figure 13.31 To omit (hide) records, build a regular Find request and then check the *Omit* box just above the *Find* button.

To omit records:

1. Make sure you are using a layout that contains the field or fields you want to search, then choose Layout > Find ((Shift)(⌘)(F)).

2. When a blank version of the selected layout appears, type into the fields the terms for records you want to *omit*. You can build a single or multiple Find request.

3. When you are done creating the Find request, check the *Omit* box just above the *Find* button (**Figure 13.31**).

4. Click the *Find* button or press (Return) or (Enter). All the records *not* matching the search criteria will appear.

✔ Tip

■ To search through every record in the database—not just those still visible—in step 3 remember to chose *All* in the *Find from* section just above the *Omit* box (**Figure 13.31**). This is very useful if you have run several Find requests, and, so, have already sifted out some of the database's records.

To bring back omitted records:

◆ Omitted records are not deleted, just hidden. To bring them back, choose Organize > Show All Records ((Shift)(⌘)(A)).

OMITTING RECORDS

Table 13.2

How AppleWorks Sorts What		
CONTENT	ASCENDING	DESCENDING
Text	A to Z	Z to A
Numbers	1–100	100–1
Time	6:00–11:00	11:00–6:00
Dates	1/1/98–12/1/98	12/1/98–1/1/98
	Jan.–Dec.	Dec.–Jan.

Sorting records

AppleWorks stores records in the order they were created but that's no reason for you to work with them in that somewhat random order. Using the Sort command, you can rearrange the record to suit your needs. You may, for example, want them sorted one way for viewing and another way for printing. You sort records based on the database's fields and can fine-tune the sort by choosing whether the field contents are sorted in ascending or descending order.

Remember that while you can sort all of the database records, you may want to sort the records remaining *after* performing a series of Find requests, which enables you to zero in on a particular set of records. And if, like me, you can hardly keep right and left straight, let alone what's ascending and descending, *How AppleWorks Sorts What* (**Table 13.2**) should help.

To sort records:

1. Make sure you are in Browse or List mode and choose Organize > Sort Records (⌘ J) (**Figure 13.32**).

2. When the Sort Records dialog box appears, the database's fields will be listed in the left-side *Field List*. Click in the list on the first field you want applied to the sort and click the *Move* button (top, **Figure 13.33**). The field name will be added to the right-side *Sort Order* list.

   By default, the field will be sorted in ascending order. If you want to change the *type* of sort, first click the field name in the *Sort Order* list, then click the *Descending* radio button in the lower-right area of the Sort Records dialog box.

3. Continue adding field names and setting the type of sort as needed. When you are done building the sort, click *OK* (bottom, **Figure 13.33**). The records will be sorted based on your request.

✔ Tips

■ You also can do a quick single-field sort by clicking in the field you want sorted and then clicking the Ascending or Descending icon in the Button Bar (**Figure 13.1**).

■ It's common to apply the same sort again and again to the records in a particular database. To save a particular sort order, see *To create a reusable sort* on page 317.

■ Unfortunately, you cannot click and drag field names in the *Sort Order* list to rearrange their order. Instead, select items in the *Sort Order* and click *Move* to reshuffle the order.

Figure 13.32 To sort records, make sure you are in Browse or List mode and choose Organize > Sort Records (⌘ J).

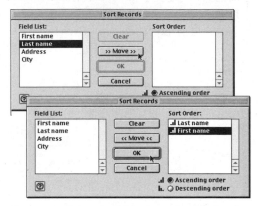

Figure 13.33 Select the fields you want applied to the sort and click the *Move* button (top). After you finish setting the sort criteria, click *OK* (bottom).

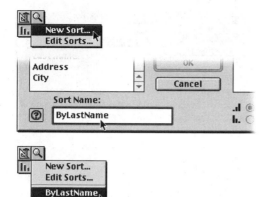

Figure 13.34 To create a *reusable* sort, click the sort icon, choose *New Sort* from the pop-up menu (top), and give it a name (middle). After you create the sort criteria, the sort will be available in the pop-up menu (bottom).

To create a reusable sort:

1. Click the sort icon and choose *New Sort* from the pop-up menu (top, **Figure 13.34**).

2. When the Sort Records dialog box appears, there will be a *Sort Name* text window at the lower-right (middle, **Figure 13.34**). Type in a descriptive name for your search, build the sort as described in *To sort records* on page 316, and click *OK*. The sort will run. You can then reuse the sort any time by clicking the sort icon and choosing the sort by name from the pop-up menu (bottom, **Figure 13.34**).

To use a named sort:

◆ Make sure you are in Browse or List mode, click the sort icon and choose one of the saved sorts from the pop-up menu (bottom, **Figure 13.34**). The requested sort will be performed.

CREATING REUSABLE SORTS

To change a named sort:

1. Click the sort icon and choose *Edit Sorts* from the pop-up menu (left, **Figure 13.35**).

2. When the Edit Sorts dialog box appears, click in the *Named Sorts* list on the search you want to change (right, **Figure 13.35**). Click *Delete* if you want to remove the named sort entirely or *Modify* if you want to change its name or sort criteria.

3. If you click *Delete*, the named sort will be deleted immediately, and you'll need to click *OK* to close the dialog box.

   or

   If you click *Modify*, the Sort Records dialog box will appear. To change the sort's name, type in the *Sort Name* text window and click *OK*. If you want to change the sort criteria, use the *Move* button to reshuffle the *Sort Order* list, and then click *OK*. The sort criteria will be updated and saved.

Figure 13.35 To change a named (reusable) sort, choose *Edit Sorts* from the pop-up menu (left), select it in the list, and click *Modify* (right).

CREATING REUSABLE SORTS

PART V

DRAWING, PAINTING, AND PRESENTATIONS

DRAWING

While the AppleWorks drawing and painting modules both let you create graphics, they do it in very different ways. Each has its pluses and minuses. Understanding a little bit about how each module works will help you know when to use which. This chapter focuses on the drawing module. For more information on the painting module, see *Painting* on page 355. The AppleWorks Button Bar, by the way, automatically displays drawing-related icons whenever you are working with a drawing document (**Figure 14.1**).

Wrap Text Around Object   *Align Objects*

Rotate Object

Figure 14.1 The Button Bar automatically displays drawing-related icons whenever you are working with a drawing document.

Drawing vs. Painting

AppleWorks's drawing tools create what are called vector-based graphics, which are mathematically generated *objects*. That means you can enlarge, say, a square and it will look just as sharp at 800 percent as it does at 100 percent (**Figure 14.2**). Because they are objects, drawn graphics also can be selected in a single click and arranged in layers.

The painting tools create what are called bit-mapped graphics, which are just a bunch of differently colored pixels. Enlarge a painted graphic and the nearly invisible pixels become increasingly jagged blocks of color (**Figure 14.3**). Since a painted graphic is composed of individual pixels, you cannot select it with a single click.

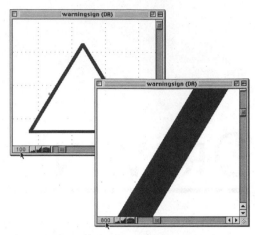

Figure 14.2 Drawing tools create *vector-based* graphics, which look just as sharp enlarged to 800 percent (bottom) as they do at 100 percent (top).

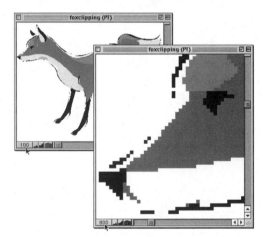

Figure 14.3 Painting tools create *bit-mapped* graphics, which look fine at normal size (top) but become jagged blocks of pixels when enlarged (bottom).

Figure 14.4 To create a drawing document, choose File > New > Drawing.

Creating Drawing Documents

Because they are built around objects, drawing documents are ideal for mixing text and graphics. While you can create a newsletter as a word-processing document and add drawing frames to it, a drawing document can accomplish the same thing more directly.

It's also easy to add drawings to other types of AppleWorks documents, even though there is no dedicated drawing frame tool. Simply select a drawing tool and draw directly in the word-processing, spreadsheet, database, painting, or presentation document. You also can select a drawing and paste it directly into the other documents.

To create a drawing document:

◆ Choose File > New > Drawing (**Figure 14.4**). A new, blank drawing document will appear.

✔ Tip

■ By default, drawing documents display a background grid of dots, which makes it easier to accurately position objects. To turn it off, choose Options > Hide Graphics Grid.

To add pages to a drawing document:

1. Open the drawing document that you want to expand.

2. Choose Format > Document (**Figure 14.5**).

3. When the Document dialog box appears, use the *Size* panel's *Pages Across* and *Pages Down* entry windows to add extra pages (**Figure 14.6**). Click *OK* and the document will be expanded.

✔ Tip

■ Depending on the size of your drawing, or if you're planning to create a newsletter, it makes sense to expand your document before you start working.

Figure 14.5 To add pages to a drawing document, choose Format > Document.

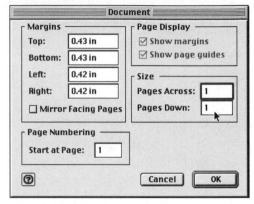

Figure 14.6 Use the *Size* panel's *Pages Across* and *Pages Down* windows to add extra pages.

Using the Drawing Tools

AppleWorks's drawing tools occupy the upper half of the Tool Tab (**Figure 14.7**). Many of the drawing tools can also be used in painting documents. Just remember that they do not create objects that can be selected, as they do in drawings, and the changes will merge with the rest of the painting.

To select a drawing tool:

◆ Make sure the Tool Tab is visible and click once on the tool you want to use. The tool will be selected, indicated by a recessed box surrounding the tool.

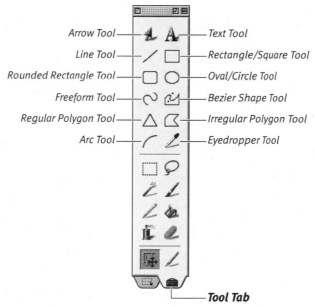

Arrow Tool — — Text Tool
Line Tool — — Rectangle/Square Tool
Rounded Rectangle Tool — — Oval/Circle Tool
Freeform Tool — — Bezier Shape Tool
Regular Polygon Tool — — Irregular Polygon Tool
Arc Tool — — Eyedropper Tool

— Tool Tab

Figure 14.7 AppleWorks's 12 drawing tools occupy the upper half of the Tool Tab.

Selecting objects with the Arrow Tool

The Arrow Tool is your main tool for selecting drawn objects. Once you select objects,
you can move them, change their attributes,
or rearrange them. For information on moving and handling objects, see page 343.

To select a single object:

◆ Click the Arrow Tool and then click on
the object in the drawing document. The
object will be selected and display small
black squares (handles) around the edges.

To select multiple objects:

◆ Click the Arrow Tool and then press [Shift]
while clicking each object. Each of the
objects will be selected and display small
black squares (handles) around the edges.

 or

◆ Click the Arrow Tool and then click and
drag the cursor. A dotted outline will
guide your progress as you select objects
(top, **Figure 14.8**). Release the cursor
and all the selected objects will display
small black squares (handles) around
their edges (bottom, **Figure 14.8**).

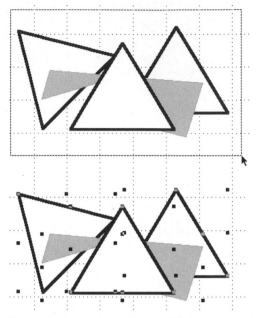

Figure 14.8 One method to select multiple objects:
Click and drag the cursor (top) and then release it to
select the objects (bottom).

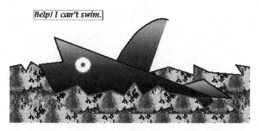

Figure 14.9 To add text to a drawing, select the Text Tool and then type directly into the text window that appears.

To add text to a drawing:

1. Select the Text Tool by clicking it in the Tool Tab.

2. Click in your drawing document where you want the text to appear. A text box will appear and the cursor will become an I-beam.

3. As you type in your text, the text box will expand as needed (**Figure 14.9**). Click outside the box when you are done and the text will be added to the drawing.

✔ Tips

■ You can change the text's font, size, style, and text color by selecting it and using the commands under the Format menu. For more information, see *Formatting Text* on page 117.

■ You can change the color and fill pattern of the text's background box with the Accents Palette. For more information, see *Using the Accents Palette* on page 340.

To draw a line:

1. Select the Line Tool by clicking it in the Tool Tab.

2. Click in your drawing document where you want the line to begin. Continue pressing the cursor while dragging to where you want the line to end (left, **Figure 14.10**).

3. Release the cursor and the line will be drawn (right, **Figure 14.10**).

✔ Tips

■ [Shift]-clicking while drawing the line will constrain it to a horizontal, vertical, or 45-degree angle.

■ You can change the width and color of the line using the Accents Palette. For more information, see *Using the Accents Palette* on page 340.

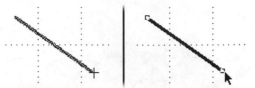

Figure 14.10 To draw a line, click where you want the line to begin and drag to the end point and release the cursor.

Figure 14.11 Click where you want the rectangle to begin and drag to the opposite corner. Release the cursor and it is filled with the current color.

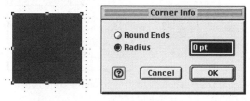

Figure 14.12 To adjust the sharpness of the corners, double-click the rectangle or square (left). A *Radius* of *0* generates a right-angle corner.

To draw a rectangle or square:

1. Select the Rectangle/Square Tool by clicking it in the Tool Tab.

2. Click in the drawing document where you want the rectangle or square to begin and then drag until it reaches the size you want (left, **Figure 14.11**).

3. Release the cursor and the rectangle or square will appear (right, **Figure 14.11**).

✔ Tips

■ (Shift)-clicking while dragging will create a perfect square.

■ To adjust the sharpness of the corners, double-click the rectangle or square. A dialog box will appear where you can enter a number to change the appearance of the corners (**Figure 14.12**). (The default value is 0, which generates a right-angle corner.)

■ Use the Accents Palette's *Fill* icon and the colors, patterns, wallpapers, or gradients tabs to set the interior of a rectangle or square. Use the *Pen* icon with the Line styles tab to set the width of the border. Use the *Pen* icon and the colors, patterns, wallpapers, or gradients tabs to set the border color. For more information, see *Using the Accents Palette* on page 340.

DRAWING RECTANGLES AND SQUARES

To draw a rounded rectangle:

1. Select the Rounded Rectangle Tool by clicking it in the Tool Tab.

2. Click in the drawing document where you want the rounded rectangle to begin and then drag until it reaches the size you want.

3. Release the cursor and the rectangle will appear.

✔ Tips

■ (Shift)-clicking while dragging will create a square with rounded corners.

■ To adjust the sharpness of the corners, double-click the rectangle. The Corner Info dialog box will appear where you can enter a number to change the appearance of the corners (**Figure 14.13**). The higher the number, the more rounded the corner, or choose *Round Ends* to completely round off the corners (**Figure 14.14**).

■ The same Accents Palette icons and tabs used for rectangles and squares also apply to rounded rectangles. For more information, see *Using the Accents Palette* on page 340.

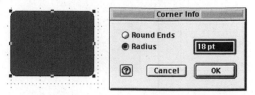

Figure 14.13 Adjust the corners of a rounded rectangle by double-clicking it (left). The higher the *Radius* value, the more rounded the corners.

Figure 14.14 To completely round off the corners of a rectangle, choose *Round Ends*.

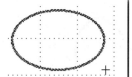

Figure 14.15 Click where you want the oval to begin and drag until it reaches the desired size (left). Release the cursor and it is filled with the Accents Palette's current fill.

To draw an oval or circle:

1. Select the Oval/Circle Tool by clicking it in the Tool Tab.

2. Click in the drawing document where you want the oval or circle to begin and then drag until it reaches the size you want (left, **Figure 14.15**).

3. Release the cursor and the oval or circle will appear (right, **Figure 14.15**).

✔ Tips

■ Shift-clicking while dragging will create a perfect circle.

■ The same Accents Palette icons and tabs used for rectangles and squares also apply to ovals and circles. For more information, see *Using the Accents Palette* on page 340.

To draw a freehand shape:

1. Select the Freehand Tool by clicking it in the Tool Tab.

2. Click and drag in your drawing document to create a line, much as you would use a pencil (left, **Figure 14.16**). (The tool is not especially useful in painting documents.)

3. Release the cursor once you have drawn the line and it will appear highlighted and ready for smoothing, as explained in the *Tips* (right, **Figure 14.16**).

✔ Tips

■ To smooth or reshape the line, select it, choose Arrange > Reshape (⌘R), and then click and drag any of the handles that appear along the line (**Figure 14.17**). Repeat until you are satisfied with the overall shape.

■ The same Accents Palette icons and tabs used for lines created with the Line Tool also apply to lines created with the Freehand Tool. For more information, see *Using the Accents Palette* on page 340.

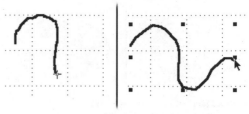

Figure 14.16 To draw a freehand shape, click and drag as you would a pencil (left). Release the cursor and the highlighted shape is ready for reshaping.

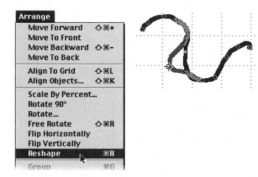

Figure 14.17 Choose Arrange > Reshape and then drag any of the handles to reshape the freehand line.

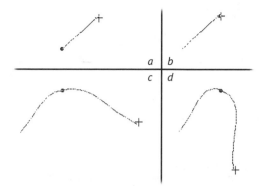

Figure 14.18 With the click-and-release method, the Bezier Shape Tool creates an anchor point (b), which lets you adjust the curve of the lines on *both* sides of the anchor (c, d).

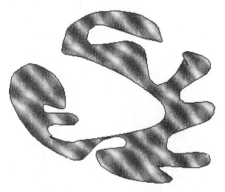

Figure 14.19 Once you close the Bezier shape, it is filled with the Accents Palette's current fill.

Using the Bezier Shape Tool

If you have never used a Bezier tool, be prepared to practice getting the hang of it. This powerful tool lets you create a shape by drawing line segments whose curves you can adjust as you go. Initially it can be tricky to control. Just to make things even more challenging, the tool offers two different methods for shaping your line segments. The best way to master the tool is just to play with it.

To create a Bezier shape (click-and-release method):

1. Select the Bezier Shape Tool by clicking it in the Tool Tab.

2. Click in the drawing document to create the shape's first anchor point, then click and release to add the second anchor point (a and b, **Figure 14.18**).

3. Release the cursor and move it around and you'll see that *both* segments of the line flex in relation to the second anchor point (c and d, **Figure 14.18**). When you get the desired curve, click to create a third anchor, which then becomes the new flex point.

4. Repeat steps 2 and 3 to add more line segments as needed for the shape.

5. When you are ready to close the shape, click again on the first point and the entire shape will become highlighted (**Figure 14.19**).

✔ Tips

- To fine-tune the shape, choose Arrange > Reshape and then drag the handles that appear.

- The same Accents Palette icons and tabs used for rectangles and squares also apply to Bezier shapes.

To create a Bezier shape (click-and-drag method):

1. Select the Bezier Shape Tool by clicking it in the Tool Tab.

2. Click in the drawing document to create the shape's first anchor point (a, **Figure 14.20**).

3. Now click again and drag in a single motion to create the second anchor point. Do *not* release the cursor (b, **Figure 14.20**).

4. As you move the cursor, a pair of handles will appear, which pivot around the second anchor and control the curve of the line segment *between the first and second anchors* (c and d, **Figure 14.20**). Once you have a curve you are satisfied with, click again. The curve will lock into place and a new anchor will appear.

5. Repeat steps 3 and 4 to add more line segments as needed for the shape.

6. When you are ready to close the shape, click again on the first point and the entire shape will become highlighted.

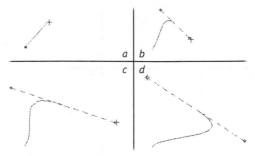

Figure 14.20 With the click-and-drag method, the Bezier Shape Tool creates an anchor point (b) with a pair of handles that control the curve of the line *between* the two anchors (c, d).

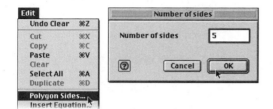

Figure 14.21 Click where you want the regular polygon to start and then drag the cursor (left). Once you have the size you want (middle), release the cursor, and the polygon is filled with the current fill color.

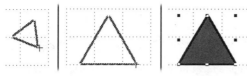

Figure 14.22 To change the regular polygon setting, choose Edit > Polygon Sides (left) and enter a new *Number of sides*.

Drawing polygons

Regular polygons have straight sides of the same length, while irregular polygons have straight sides of unequal length. By default, the Regular Polygon Tool creates a triangle but can be set to create objects with up to 40 sides. For more information, see *To change the regular polygon setting* below.

To create a regular polygon:

1. Select the Regular Polygon Tool by clicking it in the Tool Tab.

2. Click in the drawing document where you want the polygon to begin, and then drag your cursor (left, **Figure 14.21**).

3. As you drag, you can pivot the polygon around the beginning point to position it as needed (middle, **Figure 14.21**).

4. Release the cursor when the polygon reaches the size you need (right, **Figure 14.21**).

To change the regular polygon setting:

1. Choose Edit > Polygon Sides if you are working in a drawing document (left, **Figure 14.22**).

   or

   Double-click the Regular Polygon tool if you are working in a painting document.

2. When the Number of sides dialog box appears, enter a number and press *OK* (right, **Figure 14.22**). The Regular Polygon Tool will create objects with the number of sides you selected until you change the setting again.

✔ Tip

■ The same Accents Palette icons and tabs used for rectangles and squares also apply to regular polygons. For more information, see *Using the Accents Palette* on page 340.

To create an irregular polygon:

1. Select the Irregular Polygon Tool by clicking it in the Tool Tab.

2. Click in your drawing to create the shape's first anchor.

3. Continue clicking at what will be the corners of your polygon in a connect-the-dots fashion to draw the outline (left, **Figure 14.23**).

4. When you are ready to close the polygon, click again on the first point where you started (middle, **Figure 14.23**). The polygon will be selected and ready for any changes you want to make with the Accents Palette (right, **Figure 14.23**).

✔ Tip

- The same Accents Palette icons and tabs used for rectangles and squares also apply to irregular polygons. For more information, see *Using the Accents Palette* on page 340.

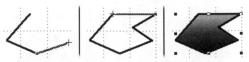

Figure 14.23 To create an irregular polygon, click each corner in a connect-the-dots fashion (left, middle). Once you close the shape, it fills with the current fill color (right).

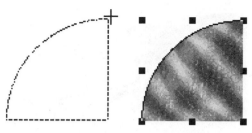

Figure 14.24 To create an arc, click where you want it to begin and drag the cursor to the opposite corner (left). Release the cursor and the arc is filled.

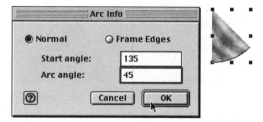

Figure 14.25 Enter new numbers for the *Start angle* or *Arc angle* (left) to change the arc's shape (right).

To create an arc:

1. Select the Arc Tool by clicking it in the Tool Tab.

2. Click and drag in the direction you want the curved portion of the arc to appear (left, **Figure 14.24**).

3. When the arc reaches the size you need, release the cursor and the arc will appear (right, **Figure 14.24**).

4. If you want to adjust where the arc begins or how many degrees it covers, double-click the completed arc.

5. When the Arc Info dialog box appears (left, **Figure 14.25**), enter a number for the *Start angle* (0 is equivalent to twelve o'clock; 180 is six o'clock). Enter a number between 0 and 360 to set the *Arc angle*. (0 will make the arc disappear.) Select *Frame Edges* if you want the two straight sides to be solid edges. Click *OK* and the changes will be applied (right, **Figure 14.25**).

✔ Tip

■ The same Accents Palette icons and tabs used for rectangles and squares also apply to arcs, though you will have to select *Frame Edges* in step 5 if you want a border on the two straight sides. For more information, see *Using the Accents Palette* on page 340.

Using the Eyedropper Tool

The Eyedropper Tool lets you quickly copy the attributes of an object or selection—color, pattern, border thickness, whatever—and apply it to another object or selection. Obviously this saves you lots of time, especially if you have objects or painted areas that you have already tweaked to perfection.

To copy a drawn object's attributes:

1. Select the Eyedropper Tool by clicking it in the Tool Tab.

2. With the Eyedropper Tool, click the object whose attributes you want to duplicate (**Figure 14.26**).

3. To apply the attributes to an existing object, press ⌘ while clicking the object with the Eyedropper tool. The attributes will be copied to the object (**Figure 14.27**).

   or

   To apply the attributes to a new object, select the appropriate drawing tool and begin to draw. The new object will have the attributes of the copied object (**Figure 14.28**).

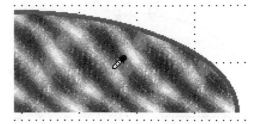

Figure 14.26 Use the Eyedropper Tool to click the object whose attributes you want to duplicate.

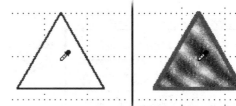

Figure 14.27 To apply the attributes to an existing object, press ⌘ while clicking the object with the Eyedropper tool (left). The attributes are copied to the object (right).

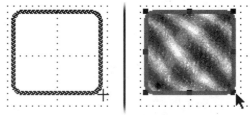

Figure 14.28 After sampling another object, you can draw a new object (left) and the other object's attributes are applied when you release the cursor (right).

Figure 14.29 To copy a painted object's color, sample it with the Eyedropper Tool (left), choose another tool (middle) and the sampled color will be applied (right).

To copy a painted selection's color:

1. Select the Eyedropper Tool by clicking it in the Tool Tab.

2. Click the Eyedropper Tool in the portion of the painting you want to copy (left, **Figure 14.29**).

3. Select a painting tool and the copied color will be used when you begin painting (middle and right, **Figure 14.29**).

✔ Tip

■ If you are copying color from a pattern, wallpaper, or gradient, zoom to 800 percent so you can accurately copy a single pixel of color.

Using the Accents Palette

The Accents Palette is your primary tool for changing the fill, lines, borders, and text color of drawn objects. Its five tabs—color, pattern, wallpaper, gradient, and line styles—offer plenty of choices for customizing the appearance of drawn objects and paint selections (**Figures 14.30–14.34**). The same steps explained on the following pages also can be used in painting documents, but only for an active selection since paintings do not contain objects. Use the Selection Rectangle, Lasso, or Magic Wand tools to select painted areas. For more information, see *Using the Painting Tools* on page 360.

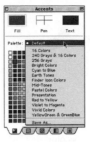

Figure 14.30 The Accents Palette's color tab controls the color of fills, lines, and text. The *Palette* pop-up menu includes 15 different color sets.

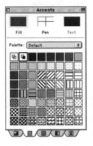

Figure 14.31 Use the Accents Palette's pattern tab to set fills for objects and selections.

Figure 14.32 Use the Accents Palette's wallpaper tab to set fills for objects and selections. The *Palette* pop-up menu includes six collections of textured backgrounds.

Figure 14.33 Use the Accents Palette's gradient tab to set fills for objects and selections. The gradient choices under the *Palette* pop-up menu are grouped by color.

Figure 14.34 Use the Accents Palette's line styles tab to set the width of object lines and borders.

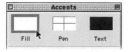

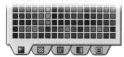

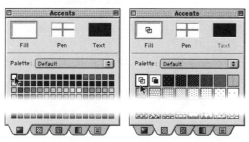

Figure 14.35 To change an object's interior, click the Accents Palette's *Fill* icon.

Figure 14.36 To reset the *Fill* window's color to white, click the top-left square in the color tab (left) or the pattern tab (right).

To change the fill for objects:

1. Open the Accents Palette (⌘K).

2. Use the Arrow Tool to select the object whose fill you want to change.

3. Click the Accents Palette's *Fill* icon if it's not already highlighted (**Figure 14.35**), and then click the palette's color, pattern, wallpaper, or gradient tab.

4. Click any of the squares in the tab that appears and the contents will be applied to the object or selection.

✔ Tips

- Be sure to experiment with the *Palette* pop-up menu in the color, wallpaper, and gradient tabs to see the variety of fill choices available (**Figures 14.30**, **14.32**, and **14.33**).

- It's easy to get confused about what is active in the Accents Palette. In general, pay attention to which *icon* you have selected (*Fill, Pen,* or *Text*) but ignore what appears *inside* the *Fill, Pen,* and *Text* windows. Instead, pay attention to which squares are selected in the bottom portions of *every* tab.

- As explained in the previous step, what appears in the *Fill* window may not be the current fill choice. If you want to make sure it's blank (white), click either the top-left square in the color or pattern tabs (**Figure 14.36**). Otherwise, you may find yourself wondering how to stop applying a previously selected sample.

To change the lines or borders of objects:

1. Open the Accents Palette (⌘K).

2. Use the Arrow Tool to select the object whose lines or borders you want to change.

3. Click the Accents Palette's *Pen* icon if it's not already highlighted (**Figure 14.37**), and then click the palette's color, pattern, or line styles tab.

4. Click any of the squares in the tab that appears and the contents will be applied to the selected line or border.

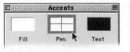

Figure 14.37 To change an object's line or borders, click the Accents Palette's *Pen* icon.

Moving and Handling Objects

Because the drawing tools create separate objects, it is easy to select them and then rearrange them. You can, for example, arrange objects in the equivalent of layers to create a three-dimensional quality. You also can resize, rotate, flip, or even reshape the objects as needed.

To move objects:

1. Select the object or objects you want to move.

2. Drag the object to move it.

   or

   Press any of the keyboard arrow keys (⬆ ⬇ ➡ ⬅).

   or

   Ctrl-click the object, choose *Object Size* from the pop-up menu, and use the left-side entry windows to set a new position. For more information, see *Using the Object Size dialog box* on page 348.

✔ Tip

- To drag an object along a horizontal, vertical, or 45-degree path, press Shift before clicking the object.

Using the Autogrid

The Autogrid, which is on by default, can make it easier to position objects more uniformly. As you move an object, it will "snap" to the nearest line in this *invisible* grid. You can turn the grid on and off as needed. If the Autogrid units are set too small, you may not even feel this snap. Adjusting the unit settings, which are based on the number of divisions in the graphics ruler, can make a big difference. The fewer divisions your ruler has, the greater the snap effect. You may have to fiddle with the ruler divisions to hit the right balance. Ruler settings, by the way, are set document by document rather than for the entire AppleWorks program.

To turn the Autogrid on and off:

◆ Depending on the current setting, choose Options > Turn Autogrid Off or Turn Autogrid On (⌘Y). The grid will be turned on or off. Repeat the command to reverse the setting.

To change the Autogrid settings:

1. Choose Format > Rulers > Ruler Settings.

2. When the Rulers dialog box appears (**Figure 14.38**), select the *Graphics* button in the *Ruler Type* panel. Then adjust the number in the *Divisions* text window.

3. Click *OK* and the new settings will be applied to the current document.

✔ Tip

■ In step 2 (**Figure 14.38**), you also can change the *Units* selection to affect the size of the *Divisions*. For example, *Points* are smaller units than *Inches*, so the same number of *Divisions* will create a much smaller "snap" distance.

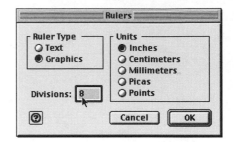

Figure 14.38 To change the Autogrid's "snap-to" distance, adjust the number of *Divisions*.

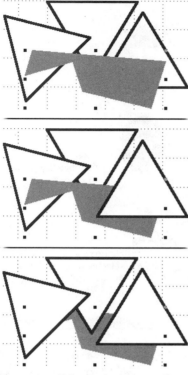

Figure 14.39 Using the Arrange menu's move commands, a selected object (top) can be sent back one level (middle) or to the back of all the objects (bottom).

Figure 14.40 To rearrange the stack order of objects, use the first four commands: Move Forward, Move To Front, Move Backward, or Move To Back.

Figure 14.41 You also can Ctrl-click an object to choose *Move* in the pop-up menu and a command from the sub-menu.

Rearranging objects

By default, AppleWorks displays drawn objects in the order they were created with the most recent atop, that is, in front of, the earlier objects. That, however, may not be the order in which you want them displayed. You can easily change what is sometimes called the stack order of the objects using a cluster of commands under the Arrange menu.

To rearrange objects:

1. Use the Arrow Tool to select an object (top, **Figure 14.39**).

2. Choose Arrange and then choose one of the first four commands: Move Forward, Move To Front, Move Backward, and Move To Back (**Figure 14.40**). The object's stack order will change (middle and bottom, **Figure 14.39**).

3. If you need to move the selected object forward or back several levels, repeat step 2 until it reaches the desired level.

✔ Tip

■ Ctrl-click the object to trigger a pop-up menu where you can choose *Move* and a command from the sub-menu (**Figure 14.41**).

To align objects:

1. Select the objects you want to align (**Figure 14.42**).

2. Choose Arrange > Align Objects (Shift ⌘ K) (**Figure 14.43**).

3. When the Align Objects dialog box appears, *None* will be selected in the *Top to Bottom* and *Left to Right* panels (**Figure 14.44**). Select a new choice in either panel, or both panels. Click *Apply* to preview your choice.

4. Once you are satisfied with your choice, click *OK* and the objects will be aligned (**Figure 14.45**).

✔ Tip

■ You also can Ctrl-click the object and choose *Align Objects* from the pop-up menu.

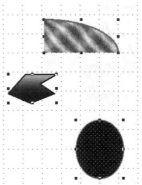

Figure 14.42 Select the objects you want to align.

Figure 14.43 To align the selected objects, choose Arrange > Align Objects (Shift ⌘ K).

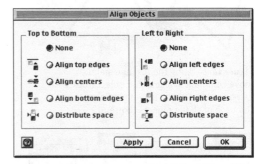

Figure 14.44 Use the Align Objects dialog box's *Top to Bottom* and *Left to Right* panels to control how the objects are aligned.

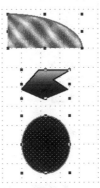

Figure 14.45 The objects in Figure 14.42 after being aligned vertically along their centers.

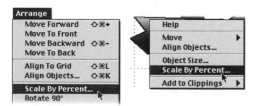

Figure 14.46 To resize objects, choose Arrange > Scale By Percent (left) or [Ctrl]-click the object and use the pop-up menu (right).

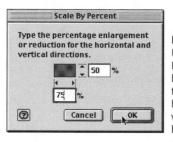

Figure 14.47 Use the Scale By Percent dialog box to resize the object horizontally, vertically, or both ways.

Figure 14.48 To quickly resize an object, click and drag one of its handles.

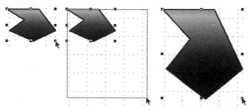

Figure 14.49 For precise resizing, [Ctrl]-click an object and choose *Object Size* from the pop-up menu.

To resize objects:

1. Select the object or objects you want to resize.

2. Choose Arrange > Scale By Percent or [Ctrl]-click the object and use the pop-up menu (**Figure 14.46**).

3. When the Scale By Percent dialog box appears (**Figure 14.47**), you can change the horizontal or vertical sizing of the object. Or, if you prefer, change both dimensions. Enter numbers in either window to enlarge (>100) or reduce (<100) the object.

4. Click *OK* and the object will be resized.

✔ Tips

- A quick, though less precise, way to resize an object is to click and drag one of its handles (**Figure 14.48**). Press [Shift] while dragging to confine the change to a horizontal, vertical, or 45-degree angle.

- For precise resizing, [Ctrl]-click an object and choose *Object Size* from the pop-up menu (**Figure 14.49**). When the Object Size dialog box appears, enter the new dimensions, close the box and the object will be resized. For more information, see *Using the Object Size dialog box* on page 348.

RESIZING OBJECTS

347

Using the Object Size dialog box

The Object Size dialog box is tiny but has a lot of power (**Figure 14.50**). With this single dialog box, you can reposition, align, resize, and rotate the selected objects. It also includes a *Name* text window, which allows you to assign a name to similar objects as a way to distinguish them when you open the dialog box in the future.

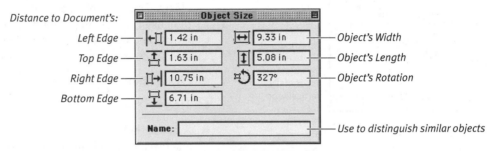

Distance to Document's:
Left Edge
Top Edge
Right Edge
Bottom Edge

Object's Width
Object's Length
Object's Rotation
Use to distinguish similar objects

Figure 14.50 The tiny Object Size dialog box packs a lot of power for changing objects.

Figure 14.51 Choose Options > Object Size to reach the Object Size dialog box.

To use the Object Size dialog box:

1. Select the object or objects you want to change.

2. Choose Options > Object Size (**Figure 14.51**) or Ctrl-click an object and choose *Object Size* from the pop-up menu.

3. When the Object Size dialog box appears (**Figure 14.50**), use the left-hand entry windows to position the object relative to the document's edge.

4. Use the width and length entry windows to resize the object.

5. Use the rotation entry window to rotate the object.

6. Press Return or Enter to preview your choices. Once you're satisfied, close the dialog box by clicking the top-left close box and the changes will be applied to the selected object or objects.

USING THE OBJECT SIZE DIALOG BOX

To rotate objects:

1. Select the object or objects you want to rotate.

2. To rotate the object exactly 90 degrees counter-clockwise, choose Arrange > Rotate 90° (**Figure 14.52**).

   or

   To rotate the object counter-clockwise by a precise amount, choose Arrange > Rotate and enter a number in the dialog box that appears (**Figure 14.53**).

   or

   To rotate the object in either direction by any amount, choose Arrange > Free Rotate ([Shift][⌘][R]) and then click and drag any of the object's handles (**Figures 14.54** and **14.55**).

✔ Tip

■ You also can rotate the object by [Ctrl]-clicking it and choosing *Object Size* from the pop-up menu. For more information, see *Using the Object Size dialog box* on page 348.

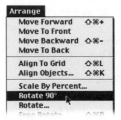

Figure 14.52 To rotate an object exactly 90 degrees counter-clockwise, choose Arrange > Rotate 90°.

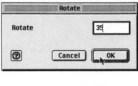

Figure 14.53 To precisely rotate an object, choose Arrange > Rotate and enter a number in the *Rotate* window.

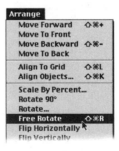

Figure 14.54 To rotate an object in either direction by any amount, choose Arrange > Free Rotate.

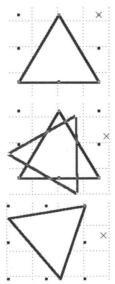

Figure 14.55 Using the free rotate options, simply click and drag any object handle.

ROTATING OBJECTS

Figure 14.56 A horizontal flip: before the flip (left) and after (right).

Figure 14.57 To flip objects horizontally, choose Arrange > Flip Horizontally.

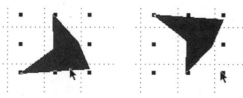

Figure 14.58 A vertical flip: before the flip (left) and after (right).

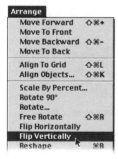

Figure 14.59 To flip objects vertically, choose Arrange > Flip Vertically.

To flip objects horizontally:

1. Select the object or objects you want to flip (left, **Figure 14.56**).

2. Choose Arrange > Flip Horizontally (**Figure 14.57**). The object will be flipped (right, **Figure 14.56**).

To flip objects vertically:

1. Select the object or objects you want to flip (left, **Figure 14.58**).

2. Choose Arrange > Flip Vertically (**Figure 14.59**). The object will be flipped (right, **Figure 14.58**).

FLIPPING OBJECTS

To reshape objects:

1. Select the object or objects you want to reshape.

2. Choose Arrange > Reshape (⌘R) (left, **Figure 14.60**).

3. When the cursor becomes a cross-hair, click and drag any of the object's handles to change its shape (right, **Figure 14.60**). Release the cursor and the object will be reshaped.

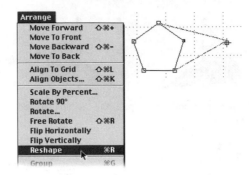

Figure 14.60 Choose Arrange > Reshape (left) and drag any handle to change the object's shape.

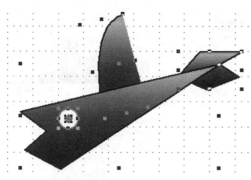

Figure 14.61 Select the individual objects that you want to turn into a single group.

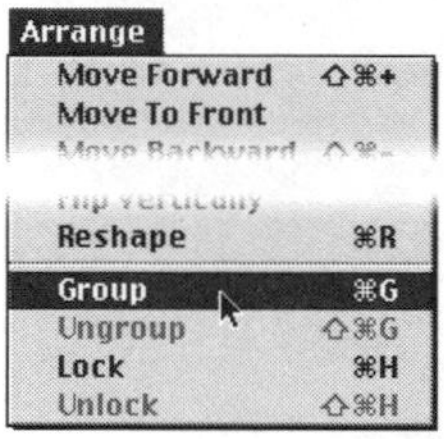

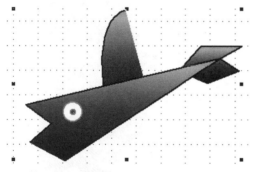

Figure 14.62 To turn the objects into a group, choose Arrange > Group (⌘G).

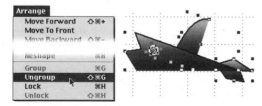

Figure 14.63 The net effect: The Group command turns a bunch of single objects into a grouper.

Figure 14.64 Choose Arrange > Ungroup to turn a single object back into individual objects.

To group and ungroup objects:

1. Select the objects you want to turn into a single group (**Figure 14.61**).

2. Choose Arrange > Group (⌘G) (**Figure 14.62**). The individual objects will become a single object, which now can be manipulated more easily (**Figure 14.63**).

✔ Tip

■ To ungroup a selected object formed of previously individual objects, choose Arrange > Ungroup (Shift⌘G) (left, **Figure 14.64**). The group's individual objects will reappear (right, **Figure 14.64**).

To lock and unlock objects:

1. Select the object or objects you want to lock so they cannot be changed.

2. Choose Arrange > Lock (⌘H) (left, **Figure 14.65**). The object's previously black handles will become gray, indicating that the object is locked (right, **Figure 14.65**).

✔ Tip

■ To unlock selected objects, choose Arrange > Unlock (Shift⌘H) and the black handles will return, indicating you can move or edit the object.

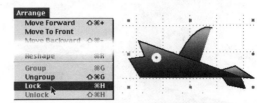

Figure 14.65 Choose Arrange > Lock (⌘H) to block any changes to an object, as indicated by the previously black handles becoming gray (right).

PAINTING

Like the drawing module, the AppleWorks painting module lets you create graphics. But the two modules work in very different ways. Understanding the difference will help you decide which module best suits your particular project. For more information, see *Drawing vs. Painting* on page 322. The Button Bar, by the way, automatically displays painting-related icons whenever you are working with a painting document (**Figure 15.1**).

Lighten Image   Tint Image   Invert Image Colors

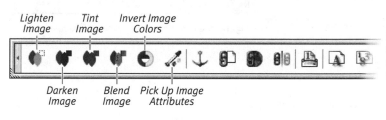

Darken Image   Blend Image   Pick Up Image Attributes

Figure 15.1 The Button Bar automatically displays painting-related icons whenever you are working with a painting document.

Creating Painting Documents

AppleWorks gives you two ways to create paintings: as separate documents or as frames inserted into other types of documents. In either case, the painting tools work identically. For general information on creating frames see *Using Frames* on page 61.

To create a painting document:

◆ Choose File > New > Painting (**Figure 15.2**). A new, blank painting document will appear.

✔ Tip

■ By default, painting documents display a background grid of dots, which makes it easier to accurately position objects. To turn it off, choose Options > Hide Graphics Grid.

To change the size of a painting document:

1. Open the painting document whose width or length you want to change.

2. Choose Format > Document (**Figure 15.3**).

3. When the Document dialog box appears, use the *Size* panel's *Pixels Across* and *Pixels Down* entry windows to change the painting's dimensions (**Figure 15.4**). Click *OK* and the document size will be changed.

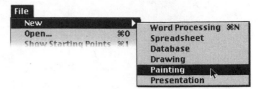

Figure 15.2 To create a painting document, choose File > New > Painting.

Figure 15.3 To change the size of a painting, choose Format > Document.

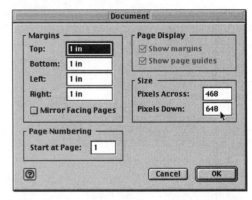

Figure 15.4 Use the *Size* panel's *Pixels Across* and *Pixels Down* entry windows to change the painting's dimensions.

Figure 15.5 To change the Autogrid settings, choose Options > Grid Size (left) and select a setting from the Painting Grid Size dialog box.

Using the Autogrid

The Autogrid, which is normally off in paintings, can make it easier to position items more uniformly. As you move an item, it will "snap" to the nearest line in this *invisible* grid. You can turn the grid on and off as needed. If the Autogrid units are set too small, you may not even feel this snap. Adjusting the painting grid settings can make a big difference in how smooth or jerky the snap feels. The larger the grid setting, the greater the snap effect. The grid controls, by the way, are set document by document rather than for the entire AppleWorks program.

To turn the Autogrid on and off:

◆ Depending on the current setting, choose Options > Turn Autogrid Off or Turn Autogrid On (⌘Y). The grid will be turned on or off. Repeat the command to reverse the setting.

To change the Autogrid settings:

1. With your painting document already open, choose Options > Grid Size (left, **Figure 15.5**).

2. When the Painting Grid Size dialog box appears, select a setting (right, **Figure 15.5**). Click *OK* and the setting will be applied to the active painting document.

Setting resolution and color depth

By default, AppleWorks creates new painting documents with a resolution of 72 dpi (dots per inch). Resolution is a measure of the detail you can see in a document. The higher the dpi, the greater the resolution and, so, the more detail you can see. An obvious example of why resolution matters is the difference between the slight graininess of a home video and the see-every-detail quality of a big-screen movie. The same principle applies to computers. Your monitor can display no more detail than 72 dpi, while most desktop color printers can produce 300 to 720 dpi. A good laser printer can produce printouts of 1,200 dpi.

If you plan to display a painting only on your computer or the Web, 72 dpi is fine because monitors can't show more detail anyway. If, however, you plan on printing out your painting, you may want to set the resolution to match your printer's resolution. Just bear in mind that higher resolution images take lots of computer memory to display and will slow your machine way down unless you have at least 32–64 MB of RAM (or more). The other drawback to high resolution paintings is that they take much longer to print.

AppleWorks also lets you change the color depth of your painting, which is a measure of the range of colors used. Most images on the Web have a color depth of 256 or fewer colors, sometimes simply called *hundreds* of colors. Photo-quality images usually contain *thousands* of colors, and high-end computer graphics contain *millions* of colors. The higher an image's color depth, the more memory required to handle the image. For that reason, your maximum color depth is controlled by how much memory (RAM) your computer has. By default, AppleWorks sets the color depth to the maximum your

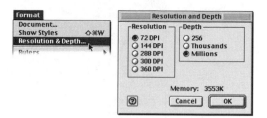

Figure 15.6 To change a *new* painting's level of detail, choose Format > Resolution & Depth (left) and select your *Resolution* and *Depth* settings.

machine can display, which for the current crop of iMacs and iBooks is *millions* of colors. In general, don't change the color depth unless you are creating images for the Web. In that case, set the depth to 256.

To set a painting document's resolution and color depth:

1. Create a new painting and choose Format > Resolution & Depth (left, **Figure 15.6**).

2. When the Resolution and Depth dialog box appears (right, **Figure 15.6**), click a button to set the *Resolution* and another button to set the *Depth*. Click *OK* to close the box and the painting document will be set to the desired resolution and color depth.

✔ Tips

- Depending on which *Depth* choice you make in step 2, the *Memory* number will change to show how much RAM you will need for that setting.

- In general, don't change the color depth unless you are creating images for the Web. In that case, set the depth to *256*.

SETTING RESOLUTION AND COLOR DEPTH

Using the Painting Tools

AppleWorks's eight painting tools occupy the lower half of the Tool Tab (**Figure 15.7**). While many of the 12 drawing tools can also be used in painting documents, their effects are not applied to objects but to your selection. Just remember that once you deselect an area, the changed area merges with the rest of the painting, making it very hard to go back and change the effect. The Arrow Tool, however, cannot be used at all in paintings. Click it and the Pencil Tool will be activated instead. That's because the Arrow Tool is for selecting *objects* and paintings have none. For information on the other drawing tools, see *Using the Drawing Tools* on page 325.

The Accents Palette and Eyedropper Tool are essential for using many of the painting tools and are covered separately. For information on the Accents Palette, see page 340. For information on the Eyedropper Tool, see page 338.

To select a painting tool:

◆ Make sure the Tool Tab is visible and click once on the tool you want to use. The tool will be selected, indicated by a recessed box surrounding the tool.

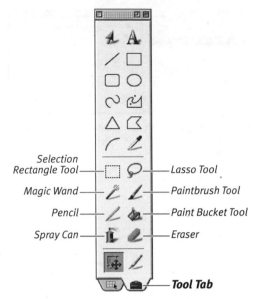

Figure 15.7 The eight painting tools occupy the lower half of the Tool Tab.

Figure 15.8 A moving dotted border marks the boundary of rectangular selections.

Figure 15.9 To select everything *except* the surrounding white areas, press ⌘ while dragging the cursor.

Using the selection tools

As explained earlier, paintings do not contain objects but are instead composed of individual pixels. That's why AppleWorks offers three separate tools to help you select exactly the pixels you want: the Selection Rectangle Tool, the Lasso Tool, and the Magic Wand Tool. Use the rectangle to select large blocks or easy to select areas. Use the lasso when you need to select an irregularly shaped area. Use the wand to select all the adjacent pixels of a single color, which can be particularly handy when editing detailed paintings.

Once you have selected an area, you can move it, copy it, delete it, or change it using the Accents Palette or AppleWorks's transformation tools. For more information, see *Using the Accents Palette* on page 340 and *Transforming Paint Selections* on page 367.

To use the Selection Rectangle Tool:

1. Select the Selection Rectangle Tool by clicking it in the Tool Tab.

2. Click in the document where you want the selection to begin and then drag until the rectangle reaches the desired size.

3. Release the cursor and the area will be selected, as indicated by a moving dotted border (**Figure 15.8**).

✔ Tip

■ To select everything *except* the surrounding white areas, press ⌘ while dragging the cursor. When you release the cursor, the selection will be confined to the areas with other colors (**Figure 15.9**).

To use the Lasso Tool:

1. Select the Lasso Tool by clicking it in the Tool Tab.

2. Click in the document where you want the selection to begin and use the tool as you would a pencil to encircle the area you want selected (left and middle, **Figure 15.10**).

3. Release the cursor and everything except the surrounding white areas will be selected (right, **Figure 15.10**).

✔ Tip

- If your initial selection contains white, the Lasso Tool will automatically exclude the white areas from the final selection. That frees you from having to exactly trace the edge of an isolated image. In every other case, however, the Lasso Tool selects exactly what you encircle.

To use the Magic Wand Tool:

1. Select the Magic Wand Tool by clicking it in the Tool Tab.

2. Click the wand on the *color* you want to select (left, **Figure 15.11**). Release the cursor and all adjacent areas of the same color will be selected (right, **Figure 15.11**).

✔ Tip

- The Magic Wand Tool will only select the color in adjacent areas, which you can see on the right in **Figure 15.11** where the color on the other side of the tree trunk was not selected.

Figure 15.10 To use the Lasso Tool, click and drag to encircle the selection area.

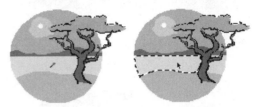

Figure 15.11 To use the Magic Wand Tool, click the wand on the *color* you want to select (left) and release the cursor (right).

Figure 15.12 To use the Paintbrush Tool, select it and then drag the cursor in the painting.

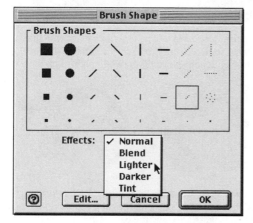

Figure 15.13 Use the Brush Shape dialog box to choose a new brush shape and to select any effects.

To use the Paintbrush Tool:

1. Select the Paintbrush Tool by clicking it in the Tool Tab.

2. Set the brush color and other attributes with the Accents Palette or the Eyedropper Tool.

3. Click in the painting where you want to begin and drag your cursor to create a brush stroke (**Figure 15.12**).

To change the brush shape:

1. Double-click the Paintbrush Tool.

2. When the Brush Shape dialog box appears, click on a new brush shape (**Figure 15.13**). Click *OK* and the new brush shape will become active.

✔ Tips

- Shift-clicking while dragging will constrain the brush stroke to a horizontal or vertical angle.

- In step 2 use the *Effects* pop-up menu if you want to use one of four special brush actions:

  Blend lightly blurs pixels without changing their color.

  Lighter adds white pixels to the brushed area, gradually lightening it.

  Darker adds black pixels to gradually darken the brushed area.

  Tint applies to the brushed area a light wash of whatever color is selected in the Accents Palette's *Fill* window.

Using the Pencil Tool

The Pencil Tool gives you pixel-by-pixel control over your painting.

To use the Pencil Tool:

1. Select the Pencil Tool by clicking it in the Tool Tab.

2. Set the pencil color with the Accents Palette or the Eyedropper Tool.

3. Click in your document where you want to begin and drag to create your line.

✔ Tips

- ▪ Shift-clicking while drawing the line will constrain it to a horizontal or vertical angle.

- ▪ To make pixel-by-pixel changes in your painting, double-click the Pencil Tool and the document will be displayed at 800 percent. To restore the 100 percent view, double-click the tool again.

- ▪ In making pixel-level changes, click once in the document to apply the current fill color or double-click to apply white (**Figure 15.14**).

To use the Paint Bucket Tool:

1. Select the Paint Bucket Tool by clicking it in the Tool Tab.

2. Set the fill color and other attributes with the Accents Palette or the Eyedropper Tool.

3. Guide the tip of the paint bucket over the color in the painting you want to change and click. The new color will be applied (**Figure 15.15**).

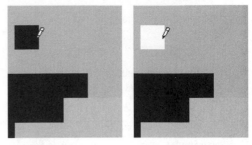

Figure 15.14 In making pixel-level changes with the Pencil Tool, click once to apply the current fill color (left) or double-click to apply white (right).

Figure 15.15 To use the Paint Bucket Tool, select it, guide the bucket's tip over the color you want to change (left). Click and the color is applied (right).

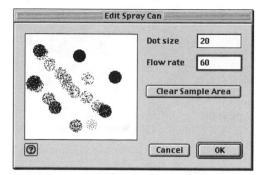

Figure 15.16 Use the Edit Spray Can dialog box to change the spray pattern's *Dot size* and *Flow rate*. Test the new pattern in the sample area.

To use the Spray Can Tool:

1. Select the Spray Can Tool by clicking it in the Tool Tab.

2. Set the fill color and other attributes with the Accents Palette or the Eyedropper Tool.

3. Click to paint a single spot in the painting or click and drag to spray a larger area.

✔ Tip

■ Just like a real spray can, the slower you drag the heavier the paint is applied.

To change the spray pattern:

1. Double-click the Spray Paint Tool.

2. When the Edit Spray Can dialog box appears, use the *Dot size* and *Flow rate* entry windows to change the spray pattern (**Figure 15.16**).

3. Click in the white square to test how the new spray pattern will appear. Click *Clear Sample Area* if you want to change the settings and test another pattern. Once you are satisfied with the pattern, click *OK* and the Spray Can Tool's setting will be changed.

✔ Tip

■ In setting the spray rate, increase the *Dot Size* number to broaden the spray pattern. Increase the *Flow rate* number to apply a heavier coat of color.

To use the Eraser Tool:

1. Select the Eraser Tool by clicking it in the Tool Tab.

2. Click once to erase a single area in the painting or click and drag to erase a larger area (**Figure 15.17**). The erased area will become white.

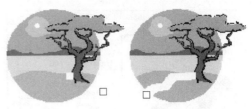

Figure 15.17 Click once to erase a single area (left) or click and drag to erase a larger area (right).

✔ Tips

■ [Shift]-clicking while using the eraser will constrain its action to a horizontal or vertical angle.

■ To erase with more precision, zoom in on your document before using the Eraser Tool.

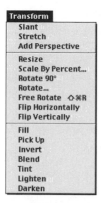

Figure 15.18 The Transform menu only appears when you are working in a painting document.

Figure 15.19 To slant a selection, choose Transform > Slant.

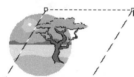

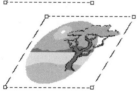

Figure 15.20 Click and drag any of the selection's handles (top and middle). Release the cursor and the selection is slanted (bottom).

Transforming Paint Selections

The Transform menu (**Figure 15.18**), which only appears when you are working in a painting document or paint frame, is packed with power. And it's plain fun when it comes to some of the commands. The first section of commands—Slant, Stretch, and Add Perspective—change the shape of your painting selection. Except for Resize, the second group of commands, from Scale by Percent through Flip Vertically, also appear under the Arrange menu when you're working in a drawing document. They behave similarly to the draw commands and are explained on pages 347–351. The big difference between using these commands in paintings vs. drawings is that you cannot easily reselect the painted area once you apply the command. The final group of commands, from Fill through Darken, all essentially change the color or the fill of a selection.

To slant a selection:

1. Select the part of the painting you want to change.

2. Choose Transform > Slant (**Figure 15.19**).

3. Click and drag any of the four squares (handles) along the edge of the selection (top and middle, **Figure 15.20**).

4. Release your cursor and the slant will be applied (bottom, **Figure 15.20**).

5. If you want to adjust the slant, click and drag the same or another handle. Once you're satisfied with the degree and angle of the slant, click anywhere outside the selection to deactivate it.

To stretch a selection:

1. Select the part of the painting you want to change.

2. Choose Transform > Stretch (**Figure 15.21**).

3. Click and drag any of the four squares (handles) along the edge of the selection (top and middle, **Figure 15.22**).

4. Release your cursor and the transformation will be applied (bottom, **Figure 15.22**).

5. If you want to adjust the effect, click and drag the same or another handle. Once you're satisfied with the effect, click anywhere outside the selection to deactivate it.

Figure 15.21 To stretch a selection, choose Transform > Stretch.

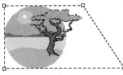

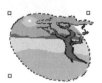

Figure 15.22 Click and drag any of the selection's handles (top and middle). Release the cursor and the selection is stretched (bottom).

Figure 15.23 To add perspective to a selection, choose Transform > Add Perspective.

Figure 15.24 Click and drag any of the selection's handles (top and middle). Release the cursor and the perspective effect is applied (bottom).

To add perspective to a selection:

1. Select the part of the painting you want to change.

2. Choose Transform > Add Perspective (**Figure 15.23**).

3. Click and drag any of the four squares (handles) along the edge of the selection (top and middle, **Figure 15.24**).

4. Release your cursor and the transformation will be applied (bottom, **Figure 15.24**).

5. If you want to adjust the effect, click and drag the same or another handle. Once you're satisfied with the effect, click anywhere outside the selection to deactivate it.

✔ Tip

■ When dragging the handles, it can be a bit tricky controlling whether the motion creates a front-to-back or side-to-side perspective shift. To get a front-to-back shift, drag your cursor *straight to the side* before you attempt to pull the selection up or down. Likewise, for side-to-side perspective shifts drag straight up or down first, then adjust your cursor sideways.

To resize a selection:

1. Select the part of the painting you want to change.

2. Choose Transform > Resize (**Figure 15.25**).

3. Click and drag any of the four squares (handles) along the edge of the selection (top and middle, **Figure 15.26**).

4. Release your cursor and the resizing will be applied (bottom, **Figure 15.26**).

5. If you want to adjust the resizing, click and drag the same or another handle. Once you're satisfied with the effect, click anywhere outside the selection to deactivate it.

✔ Tip

■ Press (Shift) while dragging to enlarge the selection by the same amount in the horizontal *and* vertical directions.

Figure 15.25 To resize a selection, choose Transform > Resize.

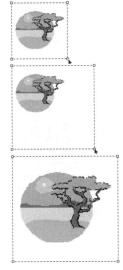

Figure 15.26 Click and drag any of the selection's handles (top and middle). Release the cursor and the selection is resized (bottom).

Figure 15.27 Select the part of the painting you want to fill with a new color, pattern, wallpaper, or gradient. In this example, all the letters are selected.

Figure 15.28 To apply a new fill to the selected area, choose Transform > Fill.

Figure 15.29 The selected area is filled immediately based on your Accents Palette choice.

Figure 15.30 While the Fill command can be simultaneously applied to multiple selections, the Paint Bucket can only fill one contiguous area at a time.

To fill selections:

1. Select the part of the painting you want to change (**Figure 15.27**).

2. Set the fill color with the Accents Palette or the Eyedropper Tool.

3. Choose Transform > Fill (**Figure 15.28**). The selected areas will be filled immediately (**Figure 15.29**).

✔ Tip

■ You might wonder what's the difference between this command and just using the Paint Bucket Tool. The Fill command can be simultaneously applied to multiple selections, while the Paint Bucket Tool fills selections one at a time (**Figure 15.30**).

Copying part of another painting

The Transform menu's Pick Up command can create some very cool effects, including fancy filled type. You're not likely to use this often, but play with it a bit and you'll soon find unexpected uses for the command.

To copy part of another painting:

1. If the painting or image you want to copy is not part of the current document, open it and position it next to the first document.

2. Select the part of your painting or image you want to change (**Figure 15.31**).

3. Drag the selection over the second image that you want to copy (**Figure 15.32**).

Figure 15.31 Select the part of your painting or image that you want to change.

Figure 15.32 Drag the selection over the image that you want to copy.

Figure 15.33 After dragging the selection, choose Transform > Pick Up.

Figure 15.34 Except for a dotted outline, the selection seems to disappear because it's filled with the underlying image's content.

4. Choose Transform > Pick Up (**Figure 15.33**). The selection will seem to disappear as it is filled with the underlying image's content (**Figure 15.34**).

5. Now drag the selection to where you want it to appear (in either the first document or the second) (**Figure 15.35**).

6. Once you're satisfied with the positioning, click anywhere outside the selection to deactivate it.

✔ Tip

- While the Eyedropper Tool can only pick up one color, this trick lets you copy broad areas of even the most complicated images.

Figure 15.35 Drag the selection where you want it to appear in either the first or, in this case, the second image.

To invert colors:

1. Select the part of the painting you want to invert (**Figure 15.36**).

2. Choose Transform > Invert or click the Invert icon in the Button Bar (**Figure 15.37**). The selected areas will be inverted immediately to their color opposites, creating an effect similar to a photographic negative (**Figure 15.38**).

Figure 15.36 Select the part of the painting you want to invert.

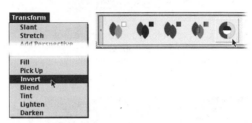

Figure 15.37 Choose Transform > Invert or click the Invert icon in the Button Bar.

Figure 15.38 The inverted selection takes on the look of a photographic negative.

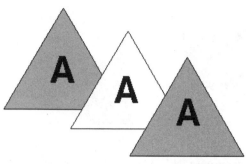

Figure 15.39 Before applying the blend, the selection is sharp and clear.

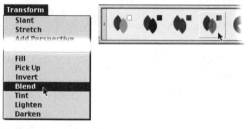

Figure 15.40 To apply the blend, choose Transform > Blend or click the Blend icon in the Button Bar.

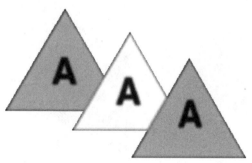

Figure 15.41 Because the blend effect is subtle, it was applied five times to the selection.

To blend a selection:

1. Select the part of the painting you want to blend (**Figure 15.39**).

2. Choose Transform > Blend (**Figure 15.40**) or click the Blend icon in the Button Bar. The selected areas immediately will be slightly softened (**Figure 15.41**). Repeat the command or click the icon again until you're satisfied with the effect.

To tint a selection:

1. Select the part of the painting you want to tint (**Figure 15.42**).

2. Use the Accents Palette or Eyedropper Tool to pick a fill color, a pale tint of which will be applied to the selection in the next step.

3. Choose Transform > Tint or click the Tint icon in the Button Bar (**Figure 15.43**). The selected areas will be tinted immediately (**Figure 15.44**). Because the tint effect is subtle, you may need to repeat the command or click the icon several times before you're satisfied with the effect.

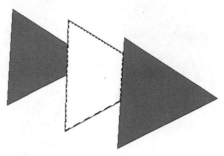

Figure 15.42 Select the part of the painting you want to tint, in this case the center triangle.

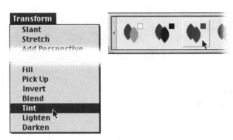

Figure 15.43 After picking a fill color, choose Transform > Tint or click the Tint icon in the Button Bar.

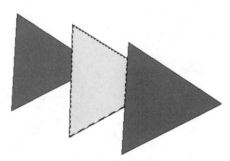

Figure 15.44 Because the blend effect is subtle, it was applied twice to the center triangle.

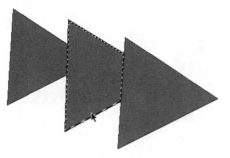

Figure 15.45 Select the part of the painting you want to lighten or darken, in this case the center triangle.

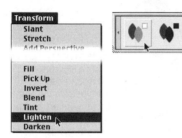

Figure 15.46 To lighten the selection, choose Transform > Lighten or click the Lighter icon in the Button Bar.

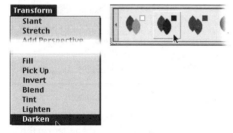

Figure 15.47 To darken the selection, choose Transform > Darken or click the Darker icon in the Button Bar.

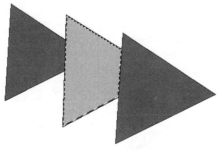

Figure 15.48 Because the lighten effect is subtle, it was applied five times in this case.

To lighten or darken a selection:

1. Select the part of the painting you want to change (**Figure 15.45**).

2. Choose Transform > Lighten or click the Lighter icon in the Button Bar (**Figure 15.46**).

   or

   Choose Transform > Darken or click the Darker icon in the Button Bar (**Figure 15.47**).

3. The selected areas will be lightened or darkened immediately (**Figures 15.48** and **15.49**). Because the effect is subtle, you may need to repeat the command or click the icon several times before you're satisfied.

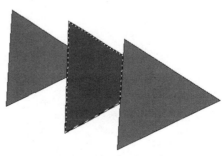

Figure 15.49 Because the darken effect is subtle, it was applied four times in this case.

LIGHTENING, DARKENING SELECTIONS

Switching painting modes

By default, AppleWorks operates in the opaque painting mode in which any new color applied covers up the existing colors. The transparent and tint modes, however, let you apply a color so that the underlying, existing colors remain partially visible. The transparent mode depends on using a pattern from the Accents Palette that contains white areas, which become transparent. The tint mode simply applies a pale wash that lightens any underlying colors. For example, red will become light red, blue will become light blue, and white (which has no color to lighten) will remain white.

To use the transparent mode:

1. Open the painting in which you want to use the transparent mode (**Figure 15.50**).

2. Use the color tab in the Accents Palette to pick a fill color.

3. Switch to the Accents Palette's pattern tab and choose a pattern (**Figure 15.51**). Use any pattern except the solid white or the solid fill (the first two at the left end of the first row). The more white in the pattern square, the greater the transparent effect will be.

4. Choose Options > Paint Mode (left, **Figure 15.52**).

5. When the Paint Mode dialog box appears, select *Transparent pattern* and click *OK* (right, **Figure 15.52**).

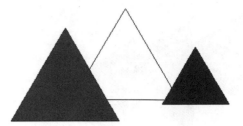

Figure 15.50 Open the painting in which you want to apply the Transparent or Tint mode.

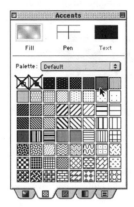

Figure 15.51 After choosing a fill color, switch to the Accents Palette's pattern tab and choose any square except the first two (crossed out here for clarity). The more white in the pattern square, the greater the transparent effect.

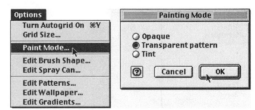

Figure 15.52 Switch modes by choosing Options > Paint Mode and selecting *Transparent pattern* in the Painting Mode dialog box.

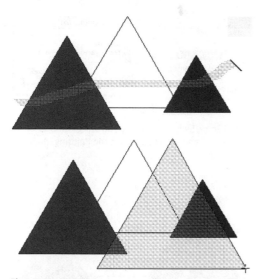

Figure 15.53 A semi-transparent brush shape applied to the painting (top) and a shape created in the same mode (bottom).

6. Select a shape from the top half of the Tool Tab or the Paintbrush Tool or Spray Can Tool from the bottom half of the tab.

7. Apply the shape or tool to your painting. The white areas in your selected pattern will be transparent, letting the underlying image be partially visible (**Figure 15.53**).

8. When you are done, return to the normal opaque painting mode by choosing Options > Paint Mode again, selecting *Opaque*, and clicking *OK*.

✔ Tip

■ If you don't pick a pattern in step 5, this effect simply won't work. That's why the mode is called transparent *pattern*.

To use the tint mode:

1. Open the painting in which you want to use the tint mode (**Figure 15.50**).

2. Use the color tab in the Accents Palette to pick a fill color.

3. Choose Options > Paint Mode (left, **Figure 15.54**).

4. When the Paint Mode dialog box appears, select *Tint* and click *OK* (right, **Figure 15.54**).

5. Select the Paintbrush Tool in the Tool Tab.

6. As you brush over the painting, a pale wash will be applied to whatever is the underlying color (**Figure 15.55**).

7. When you are done, return to the normal opaque painting mode by choosing Options > Paint Mode again, selecting *Opaque*, and clicking *OK*.

✔ Tip

■ To make switching painting modes less cumbersome, customize your Button Bar by adding the icons for the three painting modes (**Figure 15.56**). For information on customizing the Button Bar, see page 35.

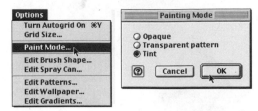

Figure 15.54 Switch modes by choosing Options > Paint Mode and selecting *Tint* in the Painting Mode dialog box.

Figure 15.55 Brushing over the painting in Tint mode applies a pale wash to the underlying colors. The middle triangle and background show no brush stroke because you cannot tint an area that's already white.

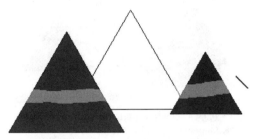

Figure 15.56 To make switching painting modes easier, you can add the mode icons to your Button Bar.

CREATING PRESENTATIONS

Start Slide Show

Figure 16.1 The Button Bar displays presentation-related icons when you work with a presentation document.

Presentation documents are built with individual slides, which you can arrange in any order to create a slide show. The slide show can be displayed on your computer or a digital projector, or printed out for overhead projector transparencies or as hard copies for the audience.

Each slide is the equivalent of a page in your presentation document. The dimensions of slides always are 640 by 480 pixels. The Button Bar, by the way, automatically displays presentation-related icons whenever you are working with a presentation document (**Figure 16.1**).

The presentation Controls Palette includes all the tools you need to create, edit, and delete slides (**Figure 16.2**). The window also lets you arrange the order of your slides and hide slides you do not want to use in a particular presentation.

The presentation module is a bit memory hungry, so you may want to boost the amount of memory (RAM) devoted to AppleWorks. For information on increasing the memory, see page 452.

To open or close the presentation controls:

◆ Choose Window > Show Presentation Controls to open the Controls Palette (left, **Figure 16.3**). To close the palette, choose Window > Hide Presentation Controls (right, **Figure 16.3**). Or click the Show/Hide Presentation Controls icon in the Button Bar.

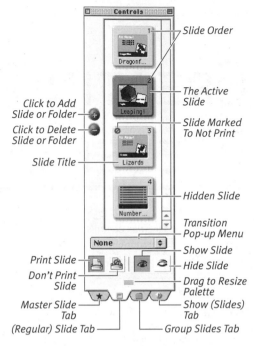

Figure 16.2 The presentation Controls Palette includes all the tools you need to create, edit, delete, and reorder slides.

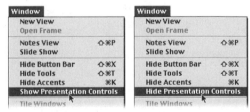

Figure 16.3 Choose Window > Show Presentation Controls to open the Controls Palette (left). To close it, choose Window > Hide Presentation Controls (right).

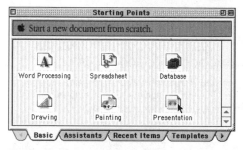

Figure 16.4 To create a presentation document, choose File > New > Presentation (top) or click the Presentation icon in the Starting Points Palette's Basic tab (bottom).

Figure 16.5 When a new presentation document appears, it contains one blank, untitled slide.

Creating Presentation Documents

When creating presentation slides, you can start from scratch with a new, blank slide or you can get a jump start by using the slides in one of AppleWorks's five presentation templates.

To create a presentation document:

1. Choose File > New > Presentation or click the Basic tab of the Starting Points Palette and then click the Presentation icon (**Figure 16.4**). A new, blank presentation document will appear, along with the Controls Palette. By default, the new document contains one blank, untitled slide (**Figure 16.5**).

2. Be sure to save the document (⌘S) and give it a distinctive name that identifies its purpose. For information on adding slides to your document, see *Creating Slides* on page 385.

To use a presentation template:

1. Open the Starting Points Palette by choosing File > Show Starting Points (⌘ 1).

2. Click the palette's Templates tab, Ctrl-click inside the palette's main window, and choose Sort > by Kind (**Figure 16.6**). Scroll down the window and you will find all five of the presentation templates near the bottom (**Figure 16. 7**).

3. Double-click any one of the five templates and the first slide of the template will appear along with the Controls Palette (**Figure 16.8**).

4. Open each presentation template in turn to see which one best suits your needs at the moment.

5. Once you settle on a particular presentation, click each of the thumbnails in the master slide and (regular) slide tabs of the Controls Palette. When you find a thumbnail on which to base your own slide, you can begin customizing its appearance but first you need to save the template under a new name to avoid overwriting the original.

6. Choose File > Save As (Shift ⌘ S).

7. When the Save dialog box appears, type in a new name, navigate to where you want to save the document, and click *Save*. The document will be saved and now you're ready to begin adding slides to your document. See *Creating Slides* on the next page.

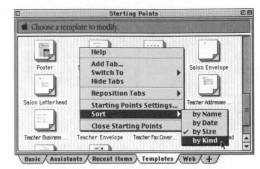

Figure 16.6 To find AppleWorks's presentation templates, Ctrl-click inside the Templates tab's main window, and choose Sort > by Kind.

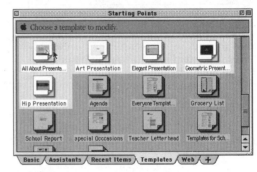

Figure 16.7 After sorting, all five of the presentation templates appear together in the Templates tab's main window.

Figure 16.8 The All About Presentations template, one of five presentation templates included with AppleWorks.

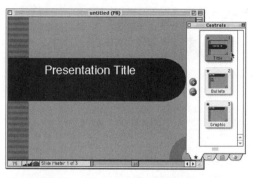

Figure 16.9 If you are working from a template to create a master slide, the ★ tab will include at least one master slide.

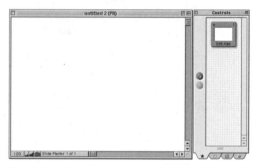

Figure 16.10 If you use a new presentation document, the master slide tab will contain one blank, untitled master slide.

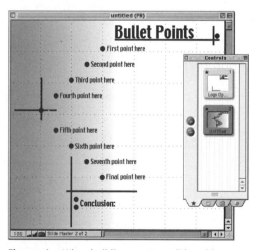

Figure 16.11 When building a master slide, add *general* elements, such as placeholder text and bullets, since the master slide acts as a template for your later individual slides.

Creating Slides

The Controls Palette lets you create two different kinds of slides: regular slides or master slides. In general, it's best to create master slides first and then base your subsequent regular slides on the masters. That way you can establish a consistent look in the master slides and then easily replicate it in the regular slides. In that sense, master slides work a bit like templates.

To create a master slide:

1. Either open a template presentation or a new, blank presentation document.

2. Click the ★ (master slide) tab in the Controls Palette. If you are working from a template, the ★ tab already will include at least one master slide (**Figure 16.9**). If you're working from a new presentation document, the master slide tab will contain one blank, untitled master slide, marked by a star in the upper left (**Figure 16.10**).

3. Click in the main document window to begin creating the slide's content.

4. If you're working from a presentation template, modify the slide's general elements to suit your needs. If you are working with a blank master slide, add the general elements you need, such as placeholder text and bullets, and a background image (**Figure 16.11**). Do not add specific text since the master slide acts as a general template for individual slides, which you will create separately. For information on background images, see page 387.

(continued)

5. Once you have edited the first master slide to your satisfaction, give it a name by clicking the word *Untitled* in the slide thumbnail (left, **Figure 16.12**). Type in a name, press Return or Enter, and the slide will be named (middle and right, **Figure 16.12**).

Figure 16.12 To name a slide, click the word *Untitled* in the thumbnail (left), type in a name (middle), press Return or Enter, and the slide will be named (right).

6. At this point, you can stay in the ★ (master slide) tab and create additional master slides by clicking the **+** button (**Figure 16.13**).

or

Use the master slide you just created as the basis for an individual slide. For more information, see *To create a regular slide* on page 389.

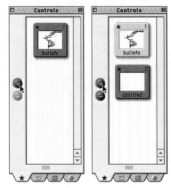

Figure 16.13 To add more untitled master slides, stay in the ★ (master slide) tab and click the **+** button.

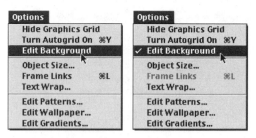

Figure 16.14 To create a master background image for all the document's slides, choose Options > Edit Background (left). Once you're done, close it by choosing Options > Edit Background again (right).

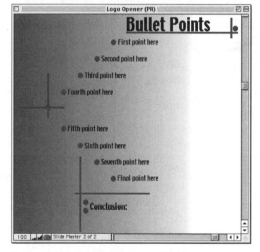

Figure 16.15 A background image (in this case a light gradient) appears behind every slide in the presentation document.

To create a master background:

1. Click the ★ (master slide) tab in the Controls Palette and select any slide.

2. Choose Options > Edit Background (left, **Figure 16.14**).

3. The main presentation window will become blank as all but the slide's background is hidden. Use any of the draw, text, clippings, or Accents Palette choices to create a background.

4. When you are satisfied with the background image, choose Options > Edit Background again (right, **Figure 16.14**). Your background image will appear behind the master slide's content and the content of every other slide based on this document (**Figure 16.15**).

✔ Tips

■ To preserve the legibility of your slide's main content, the background needs to be fairly light, such as the Accents Palette gradient applied in Figure 16.15.

■ To change or delete the background image, choose Options > Edit Background again and make your changes to the image.

To edit a master slide:

1. Click the ★ (master slide) tab in the Controls Palette.

2. Select one of the master slide thumbnails and when it appears in the main presentation window, make your changes.

3. When you are done, be sure to save the changes (⌘ S).

To delete a master slide:

1. Click the ★ (master slide) tab in the Controls Palette.

2. Select the thumbnail of the master slide you want to delete and press the – button. The slide will be deleted from the Controls Palette (**Figure 16.16**).

✔ Tip

■ There's no way to undo deleting a master slide. To avoid losing all the work put into creating that master, just be sure you no longer need it before deleting it.

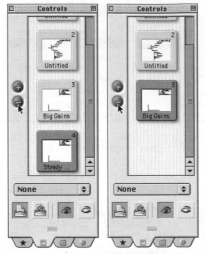

Figure 16.16 To delete a slide, select its thumbnail and press the – button.

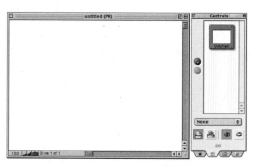

Figure 16.17 To create a regular slide, click the (regular) slide tab and a blank, untitled slide will appear in the Controls Palette and the main document window.

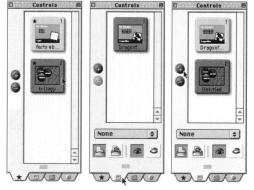

Figure 16.18 To create a slide based on a master slide, click the ★ tab and select the master slide (left). Then click the (regular) slide tab (middle), click the + button, and a duplicate of the master will appear (right).

Figure 16.19 Work in the main document window to add the text, graphics, and other elements you need to create a slide.

To create a regular slide:

1. If you want to create a slide not based on a master slide, click the (regular) slide tab and a new, untitled slide will appear in the Controls Palette and the main document window (**Figure 16.17**).

   or

   If you want to base your regular slide on a master slide, click the ★ (master slide) tab in the Controls Palette and select the master slide on which you'll base the regular slide (left, **Figure 16.18**). Now click the (regular) slide tab, click the + button, and a duplicate of the master will appear for customizing (middle and right, **Figure 16.18**)

2. Click in the main window to add the text, graphics, and other elements you need for the slide (**Figure 16.19**).

3. Once you have created the first regular slide to your satisfaction, give it a name by clicking the word *Untitled* in the slide thumbnail. Type in a name, press Return or Enter, and the slide will be named.

4. At this point, you can switch back to the ★ (master slide) tab, select another master slide, switch back to the (regular) slide tab, and repeat steps 1–3.

   or

   Stay in the (regular) slide tab and create additional slides by clicking the + button and repeating steps 1–3.

To add a regular slide:

◆ Click the (regular) slide tab in the Controls Palette, then click the + button. A new, untitled slide will appear in the palette.

To change a slide's name:

1. Click the slide's name in the Controls Palette thumbnail.

2. Type in a new name for the slide, press ⎵Return⎵ or ⎵Enter⎵, and the slide name will be changed.

To edit a regular slide:

1. Click the (regular) slide tab in the Controls Palette and select the slide you want to change.

2. Make your changes in the main window using any of AppleWorks's tools, then save the changes (⌘S).

To delete a regular slide:

1. Click the (regular) slide tab in the Controls Palette.

2. Select the thumbnail of the slide you want to delete.

3. Press the – button and the slide will be deleted from the Controls Palette.

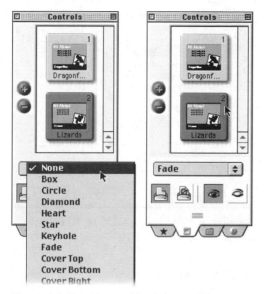

Figure 16.20 To add a transition between slides, select a thumbnail, click the pop-up menu, and select an effect.

Adding Transitions, Movies, and Sounds

The Controls Palette includes 26 different transition effects—enough screen wipes, swirling shapes, and cross fades to make your own television sportscast. Don't let all that variety tempt you into creating a dizzying mess. To keep the focus on the content of your slides, use the simpler transitions (such as Fade) and use as few as possible.

Likewise, movies and sounds can add excitement to a presentation—if used with restraint. Movies, particularly, increase the size of your presentation document and can slow down older Macs.

To add a transition between slides:

1. Click the slide tab in the Controls Palette and select a slide thumbnail.

2. Click the pop-up menu and select a transition effect (left, **Figure 16.20**). The transition will be applied to the slide, indicated by the effect being listed in the pop-up menu whenever you select the slide thumbnail (right, **Figure 16.20**).

✔ Tip

■ To see the actual transition in motion, you will need to start the slide show. For information on running the slides, see *Running the Slide Show* on page 398.

ADDING TRANSITIONS, MOVIES, AND SOUNDS

To add a movie or sound:

1. Click in the slide where you want the movie or sound to reside.

2. Choose File > Insert.

3. When the Open dialog box appears, use the *File Format* pop-up menu to choose *All Available*, then navigate to where the movie or sound file is stored (**Figure 16.21**). Click *Insert* and the movie or sound will be added to the slide.

4. If necessary, drag the movie frame to reposition it within the slide.

5. Click the Controls Palette's show tab and use the *Movies & Sounds* panel to set controls for the inserted movie or sound (**Figure 16.22**). In most cases, leave *Show controls* unchecked and check *Play automatically*.

6. Click the big triangular play button at the bottom of the show tab panel to preview the movie or sound (**Figure 16.23**).

✔ Tip

■ AppleWorks will support most major movie and sound file formats. Because more formats are added regularly, visit the AppleWorks Web site (`www.apple.com/appleworks`) for a complete list.

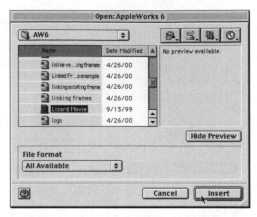

Figure 16.21 To add a movie or sound, use the Open dialog box to navigate to where the movie or sound file is stored, and click *Insert*.

Figure 16.22 Click the show tab and use the *Movies & Sounds* panel to set controls for the inserted movie or sound.

Figure 16.23 To preview your movie, you'll have to play the slide show.

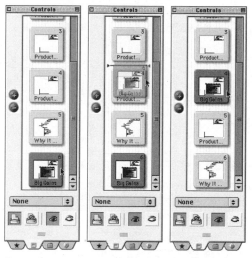

Figure 16.24 To change the slide order, click the slide you want to move (left) and drag it to its new spot in the order (middle). Release the cursor and all the slides will be renumbered (right).

Arranging Slides

AppleWorks lets you arrange your slides in two ways: the slide-by-slide sequence and in larger groupings of folders. The folders approach is great for breaking a long presentation into separate sections, which you can then include or exclude from your show as needed. There may be times, for example, when one audience wants to see all the details and another just a short overview. By grouping the slides topically and using the hide feature, you can quickly switch your slide show to match the audience. For information on hiding slides, see *To hide slides in a show* on page 396.

To change the slide order:

1. Click the slide tab in the Controls Palette and select the slide you want to move to another place in the order (left, **Figure 16.24**).

2. While pressing the cursor, drag the selected slide to its new spot in the order. As you do so, a semi-transparent image of the slide will mark your progress. A thin blue line will appear to mark the slide's destination (middle, **Figure 16.24**).

3. Release the cursor and the selected slide will move to the new spot and the slides will be renumbered to reflect the new order (right, **Figure 16.24**).

✔ Tips

- Before you start shuffling your slides, be sure you have given all of them distinctive names or you'll lose track of which is which.

- Unfortunately, you cannot select multiple slides when rearranging them. Instead, you will have to click and drag the slides one by one.

ARRANGING SLIDES

To group slides:

1. Click the group slides tab, which when first opened displays a single untitled folder. Click the triangle left of the name and you'll see that all of your slides reside in that folder (**Figure 16.25**).

2. Click the **+** button and a new untitled folder will appear (**Figure 16.26**).

3. Select the new folder and type in a distinctive name for it (left, **Figure 16.27**).

4. Now that you have a second folder, you can click and drag individual slides from the first folder into the new folder. You also can click and drag the folders to rearrange their order (right, **Figure 16.27**).

5. Continue adding, naming, and moving folders and reordering the slides within them until you are satisfied with the order. You can control which slides appear in your final slide show by using the Hide and Don't Print buttons in the (regular) slide tab. For more information, see *To hide slides in a show* on page 396 and *To not print certain slides* on page 400.

✔ Tip

■ Before you can reorder the *folders*, you have to close them by clicking the triangle beside each folder's name.

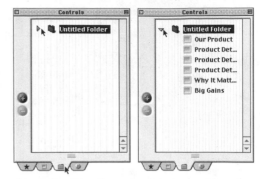

Figure 16.25 When first opened, the group slides tab displays a single untitled folder. Click the triangle (left) and you can see all the slides in the folder (right).

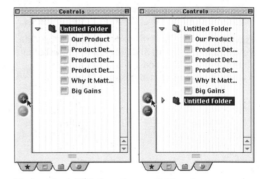

Figure 16.26 Click the **+** button (left) and a new untitled folder will appear.

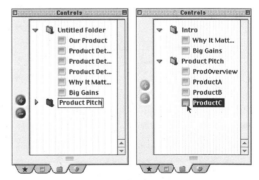

Figure 16.27 Name the new folder (left), then drag slides to the folders and rearrange them to suit your needs (right).

To delete a folder:

1. Click the group slides tab, then click the folder you want to delete.

2. Click the – button and the folder will be deleted—along with all the slides inside it.

✔ Tip

- There's no warning and no going back when you delete a folder and its slides, so be sure you no longer need them before clicking that – button. For that very reason, make a habit before you delete a folder to open it and see which slides are inside.

Controlling Which Slides Appear

AppleWorks gives you precise control over which slides actually appear in your slide show. This lets you tailor a slide show to your audience—without having to create a whole new set of slides. By default, all slides are set to appear unless you follow these steps. You have the same selective control over which slides print. For more information, see *Printing Presentations* on page 400.

To hide slides in a show:

1. Click the (regular) slide tab and select the slide you want to hide.

2. Once you have selected the slide, click the Hide Slide button at the bottom of the Controls Palette (left, **Figure 16.28**). A closed set of shades will appear in the slide's thumbnail, indicating that it will not be visible in the slide show (right, **Figure 16.28**).

3. Continue selecting slides that you want to hide and clicking the Hide Slide button until you have finished hiding all the slides you do not want to appear in the slide show.

✔ Tip

■ Because the presentation module offers no way to select multiple slides, you have to select and hide slides one by one.

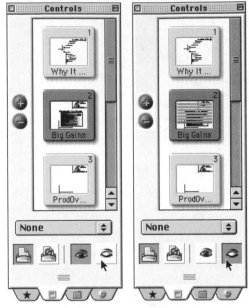

Figure 16.28 Select a slide and click the Hide Slide button (left). A closed set of shades appears to indicate that the slide will not appear in the slide show (right).

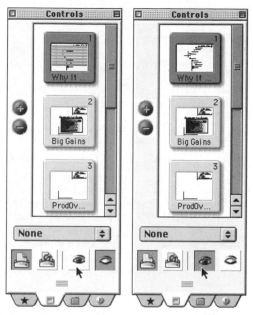

Figure 16.29 To show a hidden slide, select it and click the Show Slide button (left). The shades will disappear from the slide to indicate that it now will appear in the slide show (right).

To show hidden slides:

1. Click the (regular) slide tab and select a hidden slide that you now want to appear in the slide show. (Hidden slides are marked by a closed set of shades.)

2. Click the Show Slide button and the shades will disappear from the slide, indicating that it will now appear in the slide show (**Figure 16.29**).

3. Continue selecting hidden slides that you now want to appear in the slide show and clicking the Show Slide button until you are finished.

Running the Slide Show

You're almost ready to unveil your presentation to others, but a few crucial steps remain. By fine-tuning the settings for your show first and then playing it through, you'll spot any glitches before show time.

To fine-tune the show settings:

1. Click the Controls Palette's show tab to fine-tune the slide show's settings (**Figure 16.30**).

2. Use the *Slide Options* panel to set whether the slides *Auto-advance* and how many *seconds* each slide stays on the screen. You also can choose *Play show continuously*, a great option for a conference or trade show booth. Check *Show cursor* if you want to use your cursor during the slide show to highlight items. For information on the *Movies & Sounds* panel, see *To add a movie or sound* on page 392.

3. Once you are done choosing the settings, you can click the play button or click another Controls Palette tab.

Figure 16.30 Click the Controls Palette's show tab to fine-tune the slide show's settings with the *Slide Options* panel.

Figure 16.31 To run a slide show, choose Window > Slide Show (left) or click the play button in the Button Bar (right).

Table 16.1

Moving Through Slides

TO MOVE TO	PRESS
Next slide	→, ↓, Return, Tab or press cursor or Spacebar
Previous slide	←, ↑, Shift Return, Shift Tab, or Shift Spacebar
End of slides	End
Start of slides	Home

To preview or run a slide show:

1. Choose Window > Slide Show (left, **Figure 16.31**).

   or

   Click the play button in the Button Bar (right, **Figure 16.31**).

   or

   Click the show slides tab in the Controls Palette and press the big, triangular play button.

   The menus and desktop of your Mac will disappear and be replaced by a full-screen version of the slide show.

2. Unless you set the slide show to automatically move from slide to slide, click the cursor or press Return or Tab to move to the next slide. For more on controlling the show, see **Table 16.1**.

3. To stop the show and return to AppleWorks's normal mode, press Esc, Q, or ⌘.

✔ Tip

■ Normally, AppleWorks switches to a lower screen resolution before starting the slide show. If you want the show to use your computer screen's present resolution, press Option while choosing the Slide Show command or clicking the play button.

Printing Presentations

Providing hard copies of your presentation to the audience can help people follow along during the show, or remember key points afterward. By default, every slide in the show will print out, but AppleWorks lets you exclude from the print order any slides you choose. The presentation module also lets you create personal notes, and then print them out, to guide you through your presentation.

To not print certain slides:

1. Click the (regular) slide tab and select the slide you do not want printed.

2. Click the Don't Print Slide button and a circle-and-slash icon will be added to the upper left of the selected slide's thumbnail image to indicate that it will not be printed (**Figure 16.32**).

3. Continue selecting slides that you do not want to print and clicking the Don't Print Slide button until you have finished.

To turn off print blocking for slides:

1. Click the (regular) slide tab and select a slide that you now want to include in your printouts. (Slides blocked from printing have a circle-and-slash icon in the upper left of the thumbnail image.)

2. Click the Print Slide button and the circle-and-slash icon will disappear from the slide, indicating that it will be printed (**Figure 16.33**).

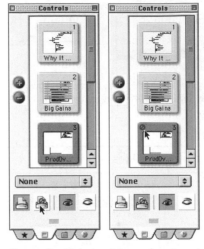

Figure 16.32 Select a slide you do not want printed, click the Don't Print Slide button (left) and a circle-and-slash icon will appear in the thumbnail (right).

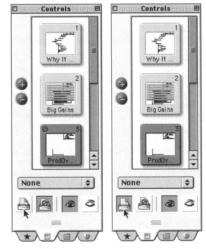

Figure 16.33 Select a slide that you now want to print and click the Print Slide button (left). The circle-and-slash icon will disappear from the thumbnail, indicating the slide will be printed (right).

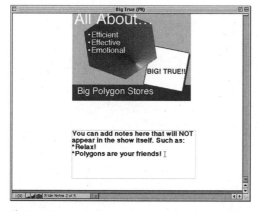

Figure 16.34 To add slide notes, choose Window > Notes View (⇧⌘P) (left). To switch out of notes view (indicated by the check), choose the command again (right).

Figure 16.35 In notes view, an area around the slide becomes available for typing notes to yourself about the slide.

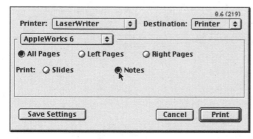

Figure 16.36 To print slide notes, choose *AppleWorks 6* from the pop-up menu in the Print dialog box and then select the *Notes* button.

To create slide notes:

1. Click the (regular) slide tab in the Controls Palette and select a slide.

2. Choose Window > Notes View (⇧⌘P) (left, **Figure 16.34**).

3. The view of the selected slide will zoom out and display an area outside its normal margin where you can type any notes you might want to make (**Figure 16.35**). These notes will not appear in the slide show itself.

4. Use the Controls Palette to select any other slides to which you want to add notes.

5. To switch from notes view back to the regular view, choose Window > Notes View (⇧⌘P) again (right, **Figure 16.34**).

✔ Tip

■ To print your slide notes, print as you would any document (⌘P). When the Print dialog box appears, choose *AppleWorks 6* from the pop-up menu and then select the *Notes* button (**Figure 16.36**).

401

PART VI

EXTENDING APPLEWORKS

CREATING
LINKS AND
WEB PAGES

17

Perhaps the World Wide Web's most powerful feature is its hyperlinks, which enable users to jump from file to file anywhere on the Internet. Taking its cue from the Web, AppleWorks 6 brings the power of links to its own documents. Using a similar system of anchors and file addresses, the program enables you to place links in your text, images, or tables. For more information, see *Creating Anchors and Links* on the following page.

Converting AppleWorks documents to full-fledged Web pages is a relatively painless operation, thanks to the built-in translation filter. The process isn't perfect but it's close enough for most of your projects. For more information, see *Saving Documents for the Web* on page 419.

Creating Anchors and Links

If you have ever surfed the Web, the linking features of AppleWorks will seem immediately familiar. Adding links to AppleWorks documents is a two-step process. To link to your own AppleWorks documents, you first define targets, known as anchors, within the documents. You then create links that point to these AppleWorks anchors or to pages on the Web. The Button Bar, by the way, displays link-related icons no matter which module you are using (**Figure 17.1**).

To open the Links window:

◆ Make sure you have a document open, then choose Format > Show Links Window ([Shift][⌘][M]) (left, **Figure 17.2**). When the Links window appears, click the appropriate tab: Anchor, Document, or Internet (**Figure 17.3**).

To close the Links window:

◆ Choose Format > Hide Links Window ([Shift][⌘][M]) (right, **Figure 17.2**) or click the close box in the upper-left corner of the Links window.

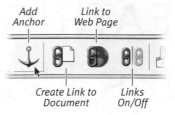

Figure 17.1 The Button Bar displays link-related icons no matter which module you are using.

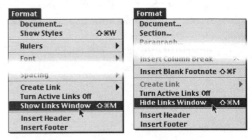

Figure 17.2 To open the Links window, choose Format > Show Links Window ([Shift][⌘][M]) (left). To close it, choose Format > Hide Links Window (right).

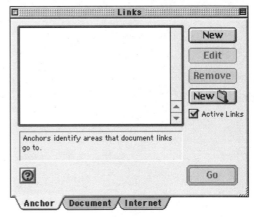

Figure 17.3 The Links window is used to create anchors and links to AppleWorks documents or to Web pages.

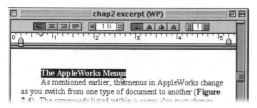

Figure 17.4 To define an anchor, first select the item you want to use as the anchor.

Figure 17.5
To create an anchor, click the Anchor tab if it's not already visible and then click the *New* button.

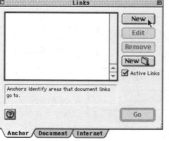

Figure 17.6
Use the New Anchor dialog box to name your anchor.

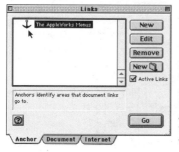

Figure 17.7
Once created, an anchor is listed in the Anchor tab of the Links window.

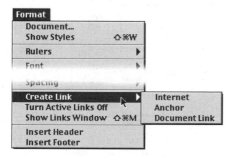

Figure 17.8 Choose Format > Create Link and an item from the submenu as a shortcut.

Defining anchors

Anchors define places in a document to which you want to link. In that sense, anchors are the targets of links. AppleWorks lets you define anchors not only for text selections, but also drawn objects, painted images, spreadsheet cells, or frames. Once you define an anchor, you can create links that point to the anchor.

To define an anchor:

1. Select the item you want to use as the anchor, that is, the *target* of a link (**Figure 17.4**).

2. Choose Format > Show Links Window (⇧⌘M) (left, **Figure 17.2**).

3. When the Links window appears, click the Anchor tab if it's not already visible and then click the *New* button (**Figure 17.5**).

4. If you selected text in step 1, when the New Anchor dialog box appears, it will automatically name the anchor based on that selection (**Figure 17.6**). Enter a new name if you like and click *OK*. The new anchor will be listed in the Links window (**Figure 17.7**). You can now create a link to the anchor. For more information, see *Adding links* on page 411.

✔ Tip

■ To jump straight to the New Anchor dialog box after selecting your item in step 1, you also can choose Format > Create Link > Anchor (**Figure 17.8**) or click the Anchor icon in the Button Bar (**Figure 17.9**).

Figure 17.9 You also can jump straight to the New Anchor dialog box by clicking the Anchor icon in the Button Bar.

DEFINING ANCHORS

To change an anchor name:

1. If the Links window is not open, choose Format > Show Links Window and click the Anchor tab when the window appears.

2. In the tab's main window, click the anchor whose name you want to change, and then click the *Edit* button (**Figure 17.10**).

3. When the Edit Anchor dialog box appears, type in a new name and click *OK* (**Figure 17.11**). The new name will be listed in the main window of the Anchor tab (**Figure 17.12**).

To delete an anchor:

1. If the Links window is not open, choose Format > Show Links Window and click the Anchor tab when the window appears.

2. In the tab's main window, click the anchor you want to delete, and then click the *Remove* button. The anchor will be deleted from the list of anchors (**Figure 17.13**).

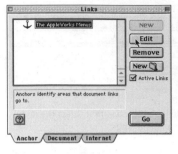

Figure 17.10
To change an anchor name, select it in the Links window and click the *Edit* button.

Figure 17.11
When the Edit Anchor dialog box appears (top), type in a new name (bottom), and click *OK*.

Figure 17.12
The new name will be listed in the Anchor tab of the Links window.

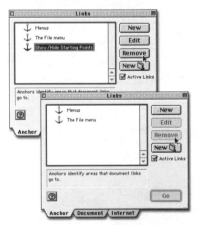

Figure 17.13 Click the anchor you want to delete, and then click the *Remove* button (top). The anchor will be deleted from the list of anchors (bottom).

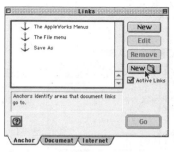

Figure 17.14
To organize anchors, click the *New* (folder) button in the Anchor tab.

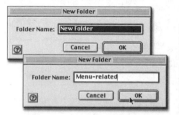

Figure 17.15
When the New Folder dialog box appears, type in a new name and click *OK*.

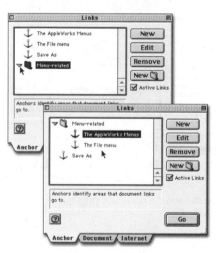

Figure 17.16 Click the triangle to open the new folder in the Anchor tab of the Links window (top). Click and drag to rearrange the folders and anchors as needed (bottom).

To organize anchors:

1. If the Links window is not open, choose Format > Show Links Window and click the Anchor tab when the window appears.

2. Click the *New* (folder) button (**Figure 17.14**).

3. When the New Folder dialog box appears, type in a new name and click *OK* (**Figure 17.15**). The new folder's name will be listed in the main window of the Anchor tab (top, **Figure 17.16**).

4. Click and drag the folder to where you want it in the list of anchors and then click and drag anchors into the folder (bottom, **Figure 17.16**).

5. Repeat steps 2–4 until you have created as many folders as you need and have organized the anchors to your satisfaction.

To reach an anchor:

1. With the document open, choose Format > Show Links Window and click the Anchor tab when the window appears.

2. Double-click any anchor listed in the Links window (**Figure 17.17**). The document will scroll to the selected anchor's location (**Figure 17.18**).

✔ Tip

■ Obviously you also can jump to a location by clicking any item that's been linked to the anchor.

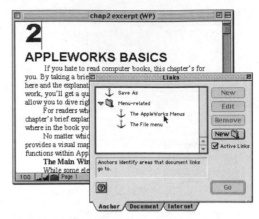

Figure 17.17 Double-click any anchor listed in the Links window...

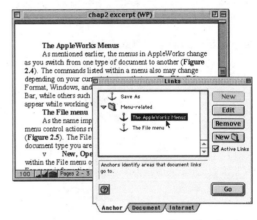

Figure 17.18 ...and the document will scroll to display the anchor.

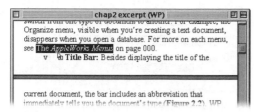

Figure 17.19 To create a document link, first select the item that you want to serve as the link.

Figure 17.20 When the Links window appears, click the Document tab and then click the *New* button.

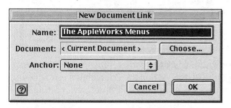

Figure 17.21 When the New Document Link dialog box appears, you can enter a new name for the link.

Adding links

If you have used a Web browser to jump from place to place, the links notion is a familiar one. AppleWorks lets you add two types of links to your documents: document links and Internet links. Clicking a document link takes you to a pre-defined (anchored) spot in the same AppleWorks document or another AppleWorks document. Internet links use Web addresses (URLs) to take you to a Web page.

To add a document link:

1. Open the document in which you want to place a link. Select the text, object, image, spreadsheet cell, or frame that you want to serve as the link (**Figure 17.19**).

2. Choose Format > Show Links Window.

3. When the Links window appears, click the Document tab if it's not already visible and then click the *New* button (**Figure 17.20**).

4. If you selected text in step 1, when the New Document Link dialog box appears, it will automatically name the link based on that text (**Figure 17.21**). Enter a new name if you like.

(continued)

ADDING LINKS

5. If you want to link to an anchor in the *current document*, use the *Anchor* pop-up menu to pick an anchor you've already defined (**Figure 17.22**).

or

If you want to link to an anchor in *another AppleWorks document*, click *Choose* and when the Open dialog box appears, navigate to the document and click *Open* (**Figure 17.23**). The selected document's name will appear in the *Document* text window (**Figure 17.24**).

Figure 17.22 Use the *Anchor* pop-up menu to pick an anchor you've already defined in the current document.

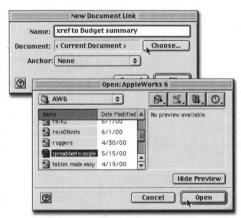

Figure 17.23 To link to *another AppleWorks document*, click *Choose* (top). When the Open dialog box appears, navigate to the document and click *Open* (bottom).

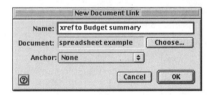

Figure 17.24 The selected document's name will appear in the *Document* text window.

Figure 17.25 The new link will be listed in the Links window's Document tab.

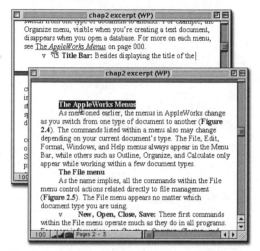

Figure 17.26 Clicking the link in the document (top), takes you to the targeted anchor (bottom).

Figure 17.27 To jump straight to the New Document Link dialog box, click the Document icon in the Button Bar.

6. Click *OK* in the New Document Link dialog box and the new link will be listed in the Links window's Document tab (**Figure 17.25**). The selected text in the document will be underlined and if clicked will jump to the anchor (**Figure 17.26**).

✔ Tips

- Because AppleWorks automatically names links and anchors based on the selected text, it's easy to wind up with links and anchors named the same thing. To avoid confusion, it's best to give each a distinctive name.

- To jump straight to the New Document Link dialog box after selecting your item in step 1, you also can choose Format > Create Link > Document Link or click the Document icon in the Button Bar (**Figure 17.27**).

To add an Internet link:

1. Open the document in which you want to place an Internet link. Select the text, object, image, spreadsheet cell, or frame that you want to serve as the link (**Figure 17.28**).

2. Choose Format > Show Links Window.

3. When the Links window appears, click the Internet tab if it's not already visible and then click the *New* button (**Figure 17.29**).

4. When the New Internet Link dialog box appears, it will automatically name the link based on the text selected in step 1. Enter a new *Name* if you like and type in the Internet address in the *URL* window (**Figure 17.30**).

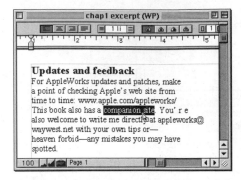

Figure 17.28 To create an Internet link, first select the item you want to serve as the link.

Figure 17.29 When the Links window appears, click the Internet tab and then click the *New* button.

Figure 17.30 When the New Internet Link dialog box appears, give the link a *Name* and type the Internet address into the *URL* window.

Figure 17.31
The new link
will be listed in
the Links
window's
Internet tab.

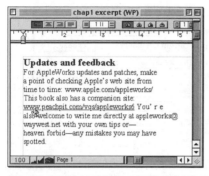

Figure 17.32 The selected text in the document
will be underlined to mark it as an Internet link.

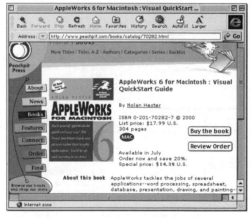

Figure 17.33 If you are online, click an Internet link
and your browser will take you to the Web page.

Figure 17.34 To jump to the New Internet
Link dialog box, click the Web page icon.

5. Click *OK* in the New Internet Link dialog
box and the new link will be listed in the
Links window's Internet tab (**Figure
17.31**). The selected text in the document will be underlined to mark it as an
Internet link (**Figure 17.32**).

6. If you want to check the link and have an
always-on Internet connection, you can
click the link and your Web browser will
launch and take you to the Web page
(**Figure 17.33**). If you rely on a dial-up
connection, however, connect to the
Internet *before* you click the link.

✔ Tip

■ To jump straight to the New Internet
Link dialog box after selecting your
item in step 1, you also can choose
Format > Create Link > Internet or
click the Web page icon in the Button
Bar (**Figure 17.34**).

ADDING LINKS

To change a link:

1. If the Links window is not open, choose Format > Show Links Window and when the window appears, depending on the type of link you want to change, click either the Document or Internet tab.

2. Select the link in the listing and click the Edit button (**Figure 17.35**).

3. When the Edit Link dialog box appears, type in a new name and click *OK* or use the *Choose* button *or Anchor* pop-up menu to change the link destination. Click *OK* and the link will be changed (**Figure 17.36**).

To delete a link:

1. If the Links window is not open, choose Format > Show Links Window. When the window appears, depending on the type of link you want to delete, click either the Document or Internet tab.

2. In the tab's main window, click the link you want to delete, and then click the *Remove* button (top, **Figure 17.37**). The link will be deleted from the list (bottom, **Figure 17.37**).

Figure 17.35 To change a link, select it and click the *Edit* button.

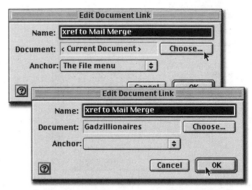

Figure 17.36 When the Edit Link dialog box appears, click *Choose* or use the *Anchor* pop-up menu (top) to pick a new *Document* (bottom).

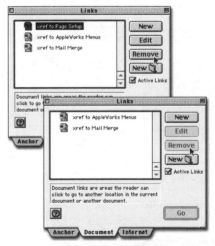

Figure 17.37 Select the link you want to delete, click the *Remove* button (top), and it will be removed (bottom).

Figure 17.38
To organize your links, click the *New* (folder) button in either the Document or Internet tabs.

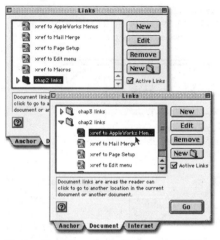

Figure 17.39 After creating one or more folders (top), you can rearrange the folders and links as needed (bottom).

To organize links:

1. If the Links window is not open, choose Format > Show Links Window. When the window appears, depending on which links you want to organize, click the Document or Internet tab.

2. Click the *New* (folder) button (**Figure 17.38**).

3. When the New Folder dialog box appears, type in a new name and click *OK*. The new folder's name will be listed in the main window of the Document or Internet tab.

4. Click and drag the new folder to where you want it in the list of links. If you wish, click and drag links into the folder. Repeat until you have organized the links and folders to your satisfaction (**Figure 17.39**).

ORGANIZING LINKS

Turning off links

If you want to change the text or item that you selected for your link, you will have to turn off the link first. If you don't, you will wind up activating the link and jumping to the anchor.

To turn off links for editing:

◆ Open the document you want to edit and choose Format > Turn Active Links Off (left, **Figure 17.40**). You also can uncheck the *Active Links* box in the Links window (right, **Figure 17.40**). You can then make your changes without triggering a link.

✔ Tip

■ You also can click the Links On/Off icon in the Button Bar (**Figure 17.41**).

To turn links back on after editing:

◆ After you make your changes in a document, choose Format > Turn Active Links On (left, **Figure 17.42**). You also can check the *Active Links* box in the Links window (right, **Figure 17. 42**). The links in the document will be reactivated.

✔ Tip

■ You also can click the Links On/Off icon in the Button Bar (**Figure 17.41**).

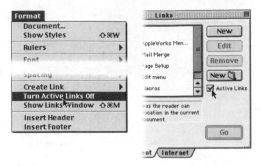

Figure 17.40 To turn off links for editing, choose Format > Turn Active Links Off (left) or uncheck *Active Links* in the Links window (right).

Figure 17.41 You also can use the Links On/Off icon in the Button Bar to activate or deactivate links.

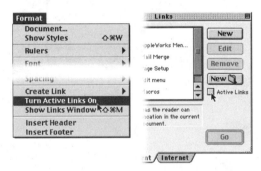

Figure 17.42 To turn links back on after editing, choose Format > Turn Active Links On (left) or check the *Active Links* box in the Links window (right).

Figure 17.43 Save your document in AppleWorks before converting it to HTML.

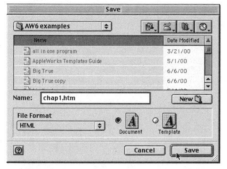

Figure 17.44 When the Save dialog box appears, choose *HTML* from the *File Format* pop-up menu and add *.htm* to the end of the file name.

Figure 17.45 Use your Web browser to check the accuracy of the document's conversion to HTML.

Saving Documents for the Web

It's fairly easy to convert AppleWorks files to HTML (HyperText Markup Language), which is the format used by Web pages. However, the matchup between AppleWorks's formatting and the Web is not always perfect. For example, AppleWorks's floating frames and objects cannot be translated into HTML. Instead, they are aligned with the document's left or right margin, depending on which is closer. For help in preparing your AppleWorks documents for Web conversion, see **Table 17.1** on page 420.

To save documents as Web pages:

1. First save the document in the AppleWorks format (**Figure 17.43**), then choose File > Save As ([Shift][⌘][S]).

2. When the Save dialog box appears, choose *HTML* from the *File Format* pop-up menu, navigate to where you want to store the file, and give it a name with *.htm* added to the end (**Figure 17.44**). Click *Save* and the AppleWorks document will be saved as an HTML document, which can be previewed in any Web browser (**Figure 17.45**).

3. If you're not satisfied with how the document appears in your browser, switch back to the original AppleWorks document, make your adjustments and save the document again in HTML.

(continued)

✔ Tips

■ When naming your HTML document, do not leave any spaces in the name. Since HTML is case sensitive, use names that are entirely lowercase or entirely uppercase.

■ If you need to make changes later, edit the original AppleWorks document and save it again in HTML. Unless you're completely comfortable coding in HTML, do not try to change the HTML document itself.

■ By default, AppleWorks saves any graphics in your HTML document as JPEG files and saves them in the same folder as the document (**Figure 17.46**). The files are given numerical names based on the document's name. For example, if the HTML file *chap1.htm* has two graphics, they will be named *chap11.jpg* and *chap12.jpg*.

■ By default, the HTML document's coding assumes any graphics will be kept in the same folder. If you move the HTML document, be sure to move any related graphic files to the same folder.

■ AppleWorks cannot post your Web pages to the Internet. Contact your Internet Service Provider for information on how to publish your pages to the Web.

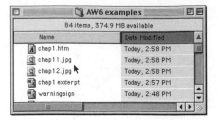

Figure 17.46 Any graphics are saved as JPEG files and placed in the same folder as the HTML document.

Table 17.1

Not a perfect match: HTML and AppleWorks	
To correctly display in HTML	Do this in AppleWorks
Text font, size, style, or color	Choose Text menu and Font, Size, Style, or Text Color in submenu
Text alignment	Use alignment icons in text ruler (Justified becomes left-aligned)
Bulleted list	Choose Outline > Label Style and Bullet, Diamond, or Checkbox in submenu
Numbered list	Choose Outline > Label Style and Numeric or Harvard in submenu
Superscript text or footnotes	Choose Format > Insert Blank Footnote
Text in columns or rows	Create a spreadsheet frame, not a table frame
Table	Create a spreadsheet frame or a table frame
Horizontal rules	Choose Format > Insert Page Break or Insert Section Break
Anchors and document links	Choose Format > Create Link > Anchor or Document Link
Hyperlinks to Web pages	Choose Format > Create Link > Internet

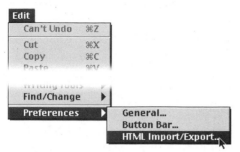

Figure 17.47 To change AppleWorks's default Web graphics format, choose Edit > Preferences > HTML Import/Export.

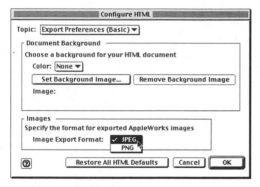

Figure 17.48 Use the *Image Export Format* pop-up menu to choose between the *JPEG* (the default) and *PNG* formats.

To change the Web graphics format:

1. Choose Edit > Preferences > HTML Import/Export (**Figure 17.47**).

2. When the Configure HTML dialog box appears, the *Image Export Format* in the *Images* panel will by default be set to *JPEG* (**Figure 17.48**). Use the pop-up menu to choose *PNG*.

3. Click *OK* and any graphics exported to HTML will use the selected format.

The GIF Tiff

When saving graphics for the Web, AppleWorks gives you just two format choices: JPG (or JPEG) and PNG. But the most common Web graphics format, GIF (CompuServe's Graphical Interchange Format), is nowhere to be found. The reason is an ongoing dispute over GIF rights. CompuServe, which owns GIF, wants companies like Apple to pay licensing fees if their software generates GIF files. The upshot: no GIF in AppleWorks.

Of the two choices you do have, JPEG (short for the Joint Photographic Experts Group, a standards-setting organization) is best for photographs. PNG (Portable Network Graphics) is better suited for illustrations, logos, or any graphic with solid areas of color. But PNG is not supported by all Web browsers, which means that some folks won't be able to see your PNG files. To be safe, stick with the JPEG default.

MACROS, SCRIPTS, AND PRINTING

18

Macros, which are built into AppleWorks, make it easy to automate simple repetitive steps. Like macros, scripts help automate your work. While scripts use AppleScript, another Apple program that comes with your Macintosh, AppleWorks has made them easy to use. That's because the program includes a group of scripts designed especially for AppleWorks.

Printing is simple in AppleWorks. Because of AppleWorks's multiple modules, however, printing offers a variety of options tailored to particular modules.

Creating Macros

Much of what you do on the computer involves performing a few basic actions again and again. AppleWorks's macros let you record those actions and trigger them with a keyboard command or custom button. Unfortunately, macros are not cross-platform: a macro created on a Macintosh will not run on a Windows machine and vice versa. Also, any macros you created in version 5 of AppleWorks must be recreated from scratch in version 6.

To create a macro:

1. If the action involves a particular document, open it first.

2. Choose File > Macros >Record Macro ([Shift][⌘][J]) (**Figure 18.1**).

3. When the Record Macro dialog box appears, the macro will be untitled (top, **Figure 18.2**). Type in a *Name* that will help you remember the macro's purpose.

4. Assign a keyboard command by selecting either the *Function Key* button or the *Option*+[⌘]+*Key* button.

5. If you want the macro to include any idle time between specific actions, check *Play Pauses* in the *Options* panel. If you want the macro to apply to just the active document, check *Document Specific*.

6. Use the *Play In* panel choices to set whether the macro will be applied to only certain types of AppleWorks documents or every AppleWorks document (*All Environments*).

7. Once you've made your choices and you are ready to create the macro, click *Record* (bottom, **Figure 18.2**).

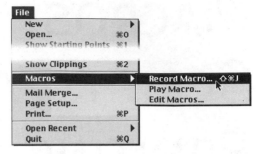

Figure 18.1 To begin creating a macro, choose File > Macros >Record Macro ([Shift][⌘][J]).

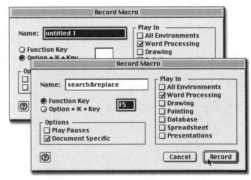

Figure 18.2 When the Record Macro dialog box appears, the macro will be untitled (top). Give it a name, choose a key to trigger it, and decide what modules it will play in (bottom).

Figure 18.3 While you are in record mode, the Apple icon in the menu bar is replaced by a flashing, tape-recorder style icon.

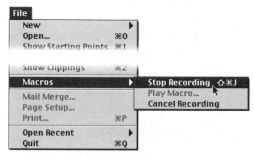

Figure 18.4 When you are done recording the macro, choose File > Macros > Stop Recording (Shift ⌘ J).

Table 18.1

Creating Automatic Macros	
NAME YOUR MACRO:	**AND IT WILL RUN WHENEVER YOU:**
Auto-Startup	Launch AppleWorks
Auto-Open WP	Open an *existing* word-processing document
Auto-Open DR	Open an *existing* drawing document
Auto-Open PT	Open an *existing* painting document
Auto-Open SS	Open an *existing* spreadsheet document
Auto-Open DB	Open an *existing* database document
Auto-Open PR	Open an *existing* presentation document
Auto-New WP	Open a *new* word-processing document
Auto-New DR	Open a *new* drawing document
Auto-New PT	Open a *new* painting document
Auto-New SS	Open a *new* spreadsheet document
Auto-New DB	Open a *new* database document
Auto-New PR	Open a *new* presentation document

8. Immediately begin performing the actions that you want included in the macro. The Apple icon in the menu bar will be replaced by a tape-recorder style icon as long as you remain in record mode (**Figure 18.3**).

9. When you are done recording the macro actions, choose File > Macros > Stop Recording (Shift ⌘ J) (**Figure 18.4**). AppleWorks will switch out of record mode.

✔ Tips

- Try to avoid assigning a macro to a key command combination already being used by another of your programs. Often the easiest-to-remember combinations will already be claimed by one of your utility programs, so be creative. Or assign the macro to a custom icon in the Button Bar. For more information, see *To add Button Bar icons* on page 35.

- By assigning certain preset names to your macros, you can create macros that run automatically whenever a certain type of new or existing document opens. You will still have to define what the macro does by recording your actions, but this is a major time-saver if, for example, you typi-cally apply the same set of formatting commands to every word-processing document. For details see **Table 18.1**.

To play a macro:

◆ Press the key command combination you assigned to the macro and the macro will run.

or

◆ Choose File > Macros> Play Macro (**Figure 18.5**). When the Play Macro dialog box appears, select a macro from the list and press *Play* (**Figure 18.6**). The macro will perform its action and stop.

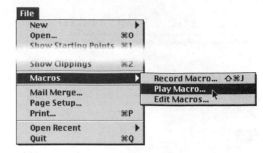

Figure 18.5 If you cannot remember the macro's triggering key, choose File > Macro > Play Macro.

Figure 18.6 When the Play Macro dialog box appears, select a macro from the list and press *Play*.

Figure 18.7 To edit or delete a macro, choose File > Macros > Edit Macros.

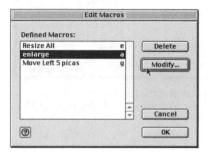

Figure 18.8 Select in the *Defined Macros* list the macro you want to change and click *Modify*.

Figure 18.9 Use the Edit Macro dialog box to change the macro's name, assigned key, or which documents it will run in.

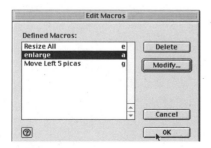

Figure 18.10 When the Edit Macros dialog box reappears, click *OK* again and the changes will be made.

Editing macros

It's too bad but the most obvious thing you would want to edit—the actions of the macro itself—cannot be changed directly. Instead, you have to record the macro all over again. AppleWorks's ability to edit macros is limited to changing the macro's name, assigned key, or the module in which it operates.

To edit a macro:

1. Choose File > Macros > Edit Macros (**Figure 18.7**).

2. When the Edit Macros dialog box appears, select in the *Defined Macros* list the macro you want to change and click *Modify* (**Figure 18.8**).

3. When the Edit Macro dialog box appears, change the *Name*, the assigned key, its *Options*, or which documents it will *Play In* (**Figure 18.9**). When you're done making your changes, click *OK*.

4. When the Edit Macros dialog box reappears, click *OK* again and the changes will be made (**Figure 18.10**).

To delete a macro:

1. Choose File > Macros > Edit Macros (**Figure 18.7**).

2. When the Edit Macros dialog box appears, select in the *Defined Macros* list the macro you want to remove and click *Delete* (top, **Figure 18.11**). The macro will be removed from the list (bottom, **Figure 18.11**).

3. Unless you want to delete or edit another macro, click *OK* and the dialog box will close.

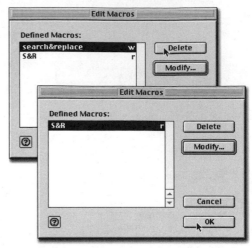

Figure 18.11 Select in the *Defined Macros* list the macro you want to remove, click *Delete* (top), and it will be removed (bottom).

Sharing macros

It's easy to share your macros with other AppleWorks 6 users—as long as you assign the macro to a specific document. You can then send others that AppleWorks document.

To share a macro:

1. Open the document to which you want the macro applied.

2. Choose File > Macros > Edit Macros.

3. When the Edit Macros dialog box appears, select in the *Defined Macros* list the macro you want to share and click *Modify* (**Figure 18.8**).

4. When the Edit Macro dialog box appears, be sure that the *Document Specific* box is checked. Check *OK*.

5. When the Edit Macros dialog box reappears, click *OK* again.

6. Now send the AppleWorks document to other people by disk, over a network, or as an email attachment.

7. When other people receive the AppleWorks document, they should open it and choose File > Macros > Edit Macros. The macro you created will be listed. They can then edit it if they wish so that the macro is no longer tied to that specific document.

Using Scripts

As you've seen, AppleWorks's macros have limited powers. However, AppleWorks also comes with a bundle of high-powered scripts created in Apple's Macintosh-native AppleScript. Unlike AppleWorks's macros, AppleScript allows you to edit the individual actions included in the scripts. The scripts can be found under the Scripts menu, that scroll-shaped icon in the menu bar between Window and Help (**Figure 18.12**).

Of the bundled AppleScripts, 14 were created by T&B Consulting, an Australian company. For a small shareware fee, they also offer a larger enhancement pack of 40 scripts for AppleWorks. For more information, visit their Web site: www.tanb.com.au/appleworks and take a look around. Explaining the ins and outs of AppleScript is beyond the scope of this book. For more information, switch to the Finder, press ⌘? and type AppleScript into the *Search* text window when it appears. Or visit the Web site: www.apple.com/applescript.

The scripts found under the Scripts menu are grouped loosely by module. For example, the Drawing menu contains two items—Join Prism Corners and Text Along Arc—that only can be used if you are working in a drawing document. However, the Universal menu item contains scripts that will work in any AppleWorks mode. Some of these scripts are definitely one trick ponies but when you need that pony, it does the job. Here's a quick rundown of the included scripts:

Open Scripts Folder: This script opens the Scripts folder, which is stored inside the AppleWorks's Essentials folder. By adding and deleting items in the subfolders, you can add and delete items from the Scripts menu.

About AppleWorks Scripts: This script opens a document that explains all the details of these scripts.

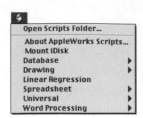

Figure 18.12
AppleWorks includes a bundle of high-powered scripts, which are found under the Scripts menu.

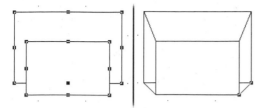

Figure 18.13 The Join Prism Corners script automatically creates a 3-D box by joining the corners of two selected rectangles.

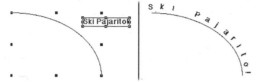

Figure 18.14 The Text Along Arc script automatically places selected text along a selected arc.

Mount iDisk: This script can be useful but comes with a lot of "ifs." If you are using Mac OS 9, if you have signed up for the iDisk service at www.apple.com, and if you are connected to the Internet, this script will automatically mount the iDisk on your desktop. In effect, the iDisk is like having an off-site hard drive. The service, which is free, enables you to store up to 20MB of data on a remote Apple server and share it with other users.

Database > Duplicate Record Multiple: If you have a database document open, this script automatically duplicates the current record. It's handy if you are creating a group of records in which most of the field data is the same.

Drawing > Join Prism Corners: This script will create a 3-D box by joining the corners of two rectangles (**Figure 18.13**). You must first open a drawing document, draw, and then select the rectangles.

Drawing > Text Along Arc: This script lets you create an effect usually limited to fancy illustration programs by placing text along the edge of an arc (**Figure 18.14**). Before running the script, open a draw document, draw an arc, type out a line of text, and then select the arc and text. The script will then automatically place the letters along the arc.

Linear Regression: Apply this script to a selected set of spreadsheet cells to calculate the slope and intercept of a line based on a series of data points. The linear regression analyzes how a single dependent variable is affected by one or more independent variables.

Spreadsheet > Draw Cell Borders: This script applies a thin, black border to selected cells in a spreadsheet.

Spreadsheet > Negative Cells Red: This script changes the text of any spreadsheet cell with a negative value to red.

Universal > Copy File's Path: This script copies the file path of the current document to the Clipboard, which can be handy when you need to tell someone where to find a document on a server.

Universal > Reveal in Finder: This script switches you from AppleWorks to the Finder and selects the icon of the current AppleWorks document. This is very handy when you're not quite sure which folder or hard drive the document's stored on.

Word Processing > Extract Containing: This script, which works only for word-processing documents, allows you to search for a phrase. Every paragraph containing the phrase will be copied to a new document. It's great for compiling references and notes.

Word Processing > Find Repeated Words: This word-processing–only script will find things that spell checking programs may miss, such as the common mistake of having "the the" in your document. An automatic dialog box then gives you the option of skipping or deleting the repeated word.

Word Processing > Small Caps: This script, which works only for word-processing documents, will change the selected text to small caps.

Word Processing > Title Caps: This word-processing–only script will capitalize every word in the selected text except for articles and prepositions.

Word Processing > Word Caps: This script, which works only for word-processing documents, will capitalize every word, including articles and prepositions, in the selected text.

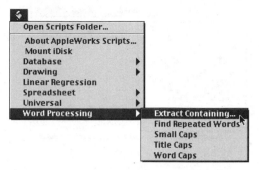

Figure 18.15 To activate an AppleScript, click the Scripts menu and make a choice from the submenu.

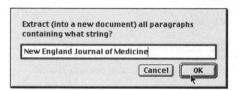

Figure 18.16 Once a script launches, it will automatically display the necessary dialog boxes for you to fill in. This example shows the dialog box that appears for the word-processing-only script Extract Containing.

To activate an AppleScript in AppleWorks:

1. If the script works only in a particular AppleWorks module, first open a document of that type.

2. Click the Scripts menu and make a choice from the submenu (**Figure 18.15**). Release your cursor and the script will launch and present you with any related dialog boxes that need to be filled out for the script to do its job (**Figure 18.16**).

Printing AppleWorks Documents

In general, printing in AppleWorks is not too different from printing in your applications. But there are a few twists worth considering, so read on.

To select a printer and print options:

1. Unless you change it, AppleWorks will use your regular printer and its default settings. If you want to use a *different* printer for AppleWorks files, select Chooser from the Apple menu.

2. When the Chooser dialog box appears, make your new selection (**Figure 18.17**). Click the close box in the upper-left corner of the title bar.

3. Now choose File > Page Setup (**Figure 18.18**).

4. When the printer dialog box appears (**Figure 18.19**), choose the document's *Orientation* and *Paper* type. When you are done, click *OK* and the options will be activated.

Figure 18.17 Use the Chooser dialog box to select a printer.

Figure 18.18 To set other print options, choose File > Page Setup.

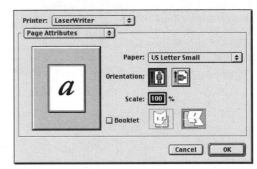

Figure 18.19 Use the printer dialog box to choose the document's *Orientation* and *Paper* type.

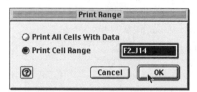

Figure 18.20 Select the spreadsheet cells you want to print and choose Options > Set Print Range.

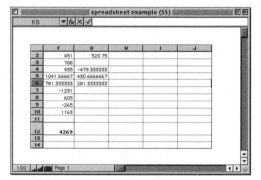

Figure 18.21 Use the Print Range dialog box to adjust the *Print Cell Range* and click *OK*.

Figure 18.22 If you have specified a print range for a spreadsheet, the page view will display only that range.

Specifying a spreadsheet printout range

It's not uncommon for spreadsheets to cover pages and pages. Most of the time, you will not want to print out all the pages, just those of immediate interest. AppleWorks lets you specify the print range to do just that.

To specify a spreadsheet printout range:

1. Select the cells in the spreadsheet that you want to print.

2. Choose Options > Set Print Range (**Figure 18.20**).

3. When the Print Range dialog box appears, the selected range will be highlighted in the *Print Cell Range* text window (**Figure 18.21**). Adjust the range if necessary. Once the range is correct, click *OK*. When you print the spreadsheet, only the specified range will be printed.

✔ Tip

■ If you have specified a print range, the page view will display only that range (**Figure 18.22**). If you want to see the entire spreadsheet—and print it all out—choose Options > Set Print Range and when the Print Range dialog box appears, select *Print All Cells With Data*, and click *OK*.

To set page margins:

1. Open the document you want to print, then choose Format > Document (**Figure 18.23**).

2. When the Document dialog box appears (**Figure 18.24**), set your *Margins* using the *Top*, *Bottom*, *Left*, and *Right* text windows. Click *OK* to close the dialog box.

✔ Tip

■ For more information on setting the *Margins* and *Page Display* options in **Figure 18.24**, see page 101. For more information on *Page Numbering*, see page 113. For more information on the *Footnotes* options, see page 145.

Figure 18.23 To set your page margins, choose Format > Document.

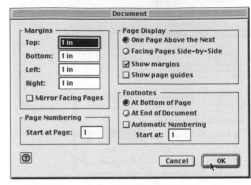

Figure 18.24 Use the Document dialog box to set your *Margins* with the *Top*, *Bottom*, *Left*, and *Right* text windows.

Figure 18.25 To preview a printout, choose Window > Page View ([Shift][⌘][P]).

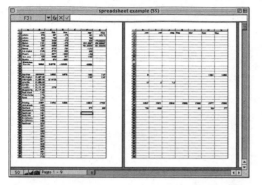

Figure 18.26 Depending on what you print, you may need to use the zoom controls to check the page view.

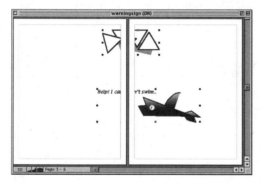

Figure 18.27 Here's why you should always preview a document before printing it.

Previewing a printout

If you are working with a word-processing or presentation document, what you see on the screen is what you'll get in the printout. In the other modules—spreadsheets, databases, drawings, and paintings—you'll want to preview the document to spot potentially overlooked problems before printing it out.

To preview a printout:

1. Choose Window > Page View ([Shift][⌘][P]) (**Figure 18.25**).

2. When the page view of your document appears, you may need to use the zoom controls to see how the document falls across the pages (**Figures 18.26** and **18.27**). If you are satisfied with the document, you can switch out of page view by again choosing Window > Page View ([Shift][⌘][P]).

To print an AppleWorks document:

1. Choose File > Print (⌘P) (**Figure 18.28**).

2. When the printer dialog box appears (**Figure 18.29**), choose how many copies you want to print and set any other printer-specific settings.

3. Set your AppleWorks-specific settings by using the pop-up menu to select *AppleWorks 6* (**Figure 18.30**). The setting choices will depend on the type of AppleWorks document you are printing. For more information, see the *Tips* on the next page.

4. Once you have made your choices, click *Print*. The document will be printed.

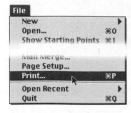

Figure 18.28 To print a document, choose File > Print (⌘P).

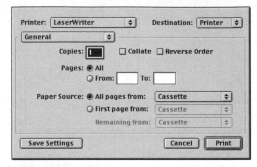

Figure 18.29 Use the printer dialog box to choose how many copies you want to print and set any other printer-specific settings.

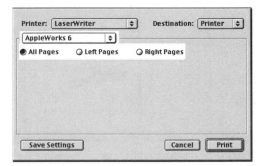

Figure 18.30 Set your AppleWorks-specific settings by using the pop-up menu to select *AppleWorks 6*. (Some printers will display the settings in the main dialog box.)

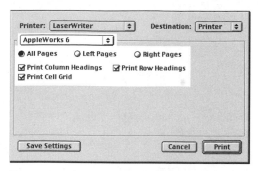

Figure 18.31 When printing out a spreadsheet, the AppleWorks options offer spreadsheet-related choices.

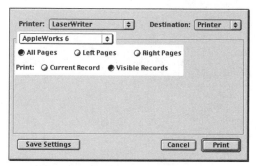

Figure 18.32 When printing out a database, the AppleWorks options offer database-related choices.

Figure 18.33 To print out a single copy based on your printer's default settings, click the Button Bar's Print icon.

✔ Tips

■ In step 3, the dialog box for some printers will not contain a pop-up menu but instead will display the AppleWorks options at the bottom of the main dialog box.

■ When printing out a spreadsheet, the AppleWorks options let you choose whether you want to *Print Column Headings*, *Print Row Headings*, and *Print Cell Grid* (**Figure 18.31**).

■ When printing out a database, the AppleWorks options let you choose whether you want to print just the *Current Record* or all the *Visible Records* (**Figure 18.32**).

■ To print out a single copy based on your printer's default settings, click the Print icon in the Button Bar (**Figure 18.33**).

PRINTING AN APPLEWORKS DOCUMENT

PART VII

APPENDIX
& INDEX

INSTALLING APPLEWORKS

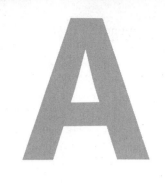

If you bought an iMac or iBook anytime after May 2000, AppleWorks 6 came pre-installed on your machine. But because the original version of AppleWorks 6 had some significant flaws, you should check to make sure you have at least version 6.04. If not, you will definitely want to download the AppleWorks updater, which includes RTF (Rich Text Format) translation. RTF is essential if you need to move word-processing documents between Microsoft Word and AppleWorks. For more information, see *To check which version of AppleWorks 6 you're using* on page 448 and *To update AppleWorks 6* on page 449.

For everyone else, this appendix shows you step-by-step how to install AppleWorks 6 from the CD and then how to update your version if necessary. Upgrading from AppleWorks 5, by the way, is relatively painless: AppleWorks 6 will be installed in its own folder, leaving your version 5 files intact. For information on using your AppleWorks 5 libraries in version 6, see page 81. To import an AppleWorks 5 dictionary, see page 191. Macros created in AppleWorks 5, unfortunately, cannot be used in version 6. Instead, you must recreate them from scratch in version 6.

Once you've installed AppleWorks 6, it's tempting to get straight to work using your new program. However, there are a few extra steps you may want to take to configure AppleWorks to your needs, such as installing extra fonts found on the CD, reallocating memory for the program, and setting some preferences to match your work style. For information on installing the fonts, see page 451. You'll find the details on memory on page 452 and information on setting your preferences beginning on page 453.

To install AppleWorks 6:

1. Turn off any anti-virus program you may have running in the background. Such programs sometimes cause problems when installing new software.

2. Put the AppleWorks 6 disc into your CD drive.

3. Once the CD launches, you may need to double-click its icon to see the contents of the AppleWorks 6 CD (**Figure A.1**). Depending on your country, double-click either *Install–US/Canada* or *Install–All Other Countries*.

4. When the AppleWorks 6 splash screen appears, click *Continue* (**Figure A.2**) and click *Accept* when the License Agreement window appears.

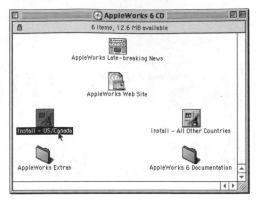

Figure A.1 To install AppleWorks 6, double-click one of the two *Install* icons.

Figure A.2 To get started, click *Continue* when the AppleWorks 6 splash screen appears.

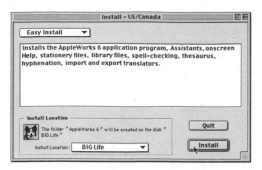

Figure A.3 *Easy Install* will be selected when the installation screen first appears. If necessary, use the *Install Location* pop-up menu to select a hard drive.

Figure A.4 When the alert dialog box asks if you want to quit all your other applications, click *Continue*.

Figure A.5 The installation process takes a minute or so to complete.

Figure A.6 Once the installation is complete, click *Restart*.

5. By default, *Easy Install* will be selected when the installation screen appears (**Figure A.3**). If you have multiple hard drives or partitions, use the *Install Location* pop-up menu to select one for the installation. Click *Install*.

6. When the alert dialog box asks if you want to quit all your other applications, click *Continue* (**Figure A.4**). The installation process, which takes a minute or so, will begin (**Figure A.5**).

7. Once the installation is complete, an alert dialog box will appear, suggesting that you restart (**Figure A.6**). Click *Restart* and your machine will shut down and then restart.

(continued)

8. Once your machine has restarted, the AppleWorks 6 folder will automatically open on your desktop (**Figure A.7**). Double-click the *AppleWorks 6* icon to launch the program.

9. Fill out the registration text windows that appear and click *OK* (**Figure A.8**). AppleWorks will open to the Starting Points palette's Recent Items tab, which will be blank (**Figure A.9**). While you can now begin working, you should make sure you are not using the crash-prone version 6.0. For more information, see *To check which version you're using* on page 448.

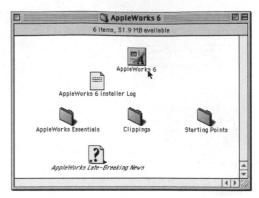

Figure A.7 When the newly installed AppleWorks 6 folder appears on your desktop, double-click the *AppleWorks 6* icon to launch the program.

Figure A.8 Fill out the registration text windows that appear and click *OK*.

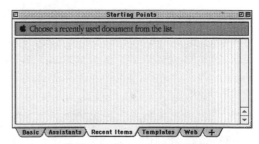

Figure A.9 When it first launches, AppleWorks will display the Starting Points Palette's Recent Items tab, which will be blank.

Figure A.10 Choose *Custom Install* if you are short on hard drive space, then check the files you need.

Figure A.11 if you're not sure about an item, click the Ⓘ icon for information on its purpose.

✔ Tips

- If you do not have enough hard drive space to install all the AppleWorks files, click the *Easy Install* pop-up menu and choose *Custom Install* and a list of the program's individual components will appear (**Figure A.10**). You can then check only the files you need. The *Approximate disk space needed* figure in the window's lower right will change as you check or uncheck items, helping you to decide how many AppleWorks items to install.

  The *Custom Install* requires less space than *Easy Install* but also restricts what you can do with AppleWorks. Consider tidying up your hard drive to make room for the *Easy Install*.

- In making a Custom Install, if you're not sure which items you truly need, click on the Ⓘ to the right of any item for more information on its purpose (**Figure A.11**).

To check which version of AppleWorks 6 you're using:

1. Double-click the AppleWorks icon to launch the program, then choose Apple menu > About AppleWorks (**Figure A.12**).

2. When the AppleWorks splash screen appears, look for the version number in the bottom third (**Figure A.13**). It should be at least 6.04. If it says 6.0 or 6.03 (there was no 6.01 or 6.02), then you need to update AppleWorks or you will spend your days fighting bugs and crashes. See *To update AppleWorks 6* on the following page.

Figure A.12 To check which version of AppleWorks 6 you're using, choose Apple menu > About AppleWorks.

Figure A.13 The version number in the bottom third of the AppleWorks splash screen should be at least 6.04.

Figure A.14 After downloading the updater, double-click the .smi file (top) and then double-click the updater file that appears on your desktop (bottom).

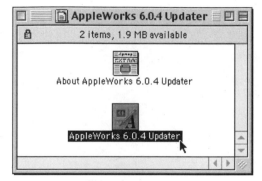

Figure A.15 When the updater folder appears, double-click the main AppleWorks icon to begin a process similar to the original installation.

To update AppleWorks 6:

1. Point your Web browser to www.apple.com/appleworks to find the latest update and download it to your hard drive.

2. Once the download is complete, double-click the self-mounting .smi file (top, **Figure A.14**). (The file's name will vary depending on what is the latest version of the updater.) Double-click the file and when, after a moment, it places the actual updater file on your desktop, double-click that as well (bottom, **Figure A.14**).

3. When the updater folder appears on your desktop, double-click the main AppleWorks icon (**Figure A.15**).

4. At this point, the installation process will be very similar to the original installation process with a series of screens asking you to accept the license agreement, choose an installation screen, close your other applications, and restart your machine. When the updated AppleWorks folder finally appears on your screen, double-click the AppleWorks 6 icon and you're set—except for two final details.

(continued)

UPDATING APPLEWORKS 6

5. The first detail: Your original AppleWorks 6 program will be automatically placed in the trash. To free up the 7.3 MB of space it claims on your hard drive (**Figure A.16**), empty the trash by choosing Special > Empty Trash.

6. The last detail: Save yourself a great deal of later frustration by taking a moment to configure AppleWorks to your needs. See *Setting Preferences* on page 453.

✔ Tip

■ The AppleWorks updater also updates the CarbonLib extension to the latest, and most stable, version. Thanks to this extension, you will be able to run AppleWorks 6 with the upcoming Mac OS X without missing a beat. If you are still running Mac OS 8 or 8.5, by the way, AppleWorks updates them respectively to 8.1 or 8.6, both of which are more stable than the earlier versions.

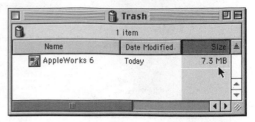

Figure A.16 The now-replaced original AppleWorks 6 program is put in the trash, which you should empty to free up space on your hard drive.

Figure A.17
To find the extra AppleWorks fonts, open the CD's *AppleWorks Extras* folder.

Figure A.18 To install any of the extra fonts, click and drag them to your *System Folder*.

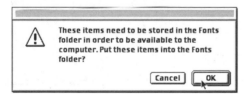

Figure A.19 Click *OK* when the alert dialog box asks to place the fonts in the Fonts folder.

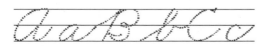

Figure A.20 The extra AppleWorks fonts include Schoolhouse Cursive for teaching handwriting.

Installing Additional AppleWorks Fonts

The AppleWorks CD includes more than 50 fonts. To keep from loading up your System folder (and overtaxing your Mac), most of the fonts are not automatically installed when you install AppleWorks 6. Some teachers, however, may find the Schoolhouse fonts of particular interest for teaching handwriting.

To install additional fonts:

1. Quit *all* of your programs (not just AppleWorks) and insert the AppleWorks 6 CD into your CD drive.

2. To find the AppleWorks fonts, open the CD's *AppleWorks Extras* folder (**Figure A.17**). The *ITC Fonts* folder contains 24 fonts and the *School Fonts* folder has two cursive and two print fonts.

3. To install any of the fonts, click and drag them to your *System Folder* (**Figure A.18**).

4. When an alert dialog box appears, asking for permission to place the fonts in the Fonts folder, click *OK* (**Figure A.19**).

5. Relaunch AppleWorks and the added fonts will be available for use by choosing Text > Font (**Figure A.20**).

Allocating Memory

AppleWorks needs at least 3.5MB of RAM (Random Access Memory) and prefers to have 5MB (10.4MB if Virtual Memory is off). But if you are running presentations or working frequently with lots of clippings, AppleWorks will run more smoothly if you can allocate even more memory for it. How much more? You may not have much to spare if your Mac only has 32MB and you run memory-hungry applications. But if you can manage it, try to bump AppleWorks's allocation to at least 8MB (13MB if Virtual Memory is off).

To allocate more memory to AppleWorks:

1. Quit AppleWorks (⌘Q).

2. Open the AppleWorks 6 folder and select the AppleWorks 6 icon (**Figure A.21**).

3. Now press ⌘I and when the AppleWorks 6 Info dialog box appears, use the *Show* pop-up menu to select *Memory* (**Figure A.22**).

4. Increase the *Preferred Size* number to at least 8000 (8MB), or 13000 (13MB) if Virtual Memory is off.

5. Click the close box in the upper-left corner of the dialog box. The new memory setting will take effect the next time you start AppleWorks.

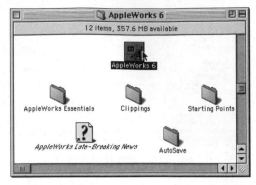

Figure A.21 To allocate more memory, quit AppleWorks, select its icon and press ⌘I.

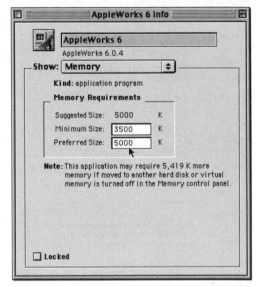

Figure A.22 Select *Memory* in the *Show* pop-up menu, then increase the *Preferred Size* entry to at least 8000.

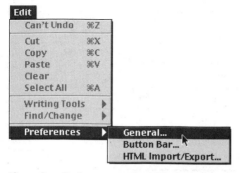

Figure A.23 To change your AppleWorks preferences, choose Edit > Preferences > General.

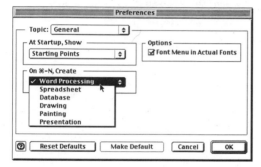

Figure A.24 Use the *Topic* pop-up menu to select *General*, then use the *On ⌘–N, Create* pop-up menu to choose which type of AppleWorks document you want the command to create.

Setting Preferences

You don't need to change most of AppleWorks preferences because the defaults will serve you perfectly well. You may want to consider changing the ones highlighted here, however, to reduce your later frustration or simply to better match your working style.

Changing the new document command default

By default, pressing ⌘N creates a new word-processing document. You can, however, change the preference so that the keyboard command creates whatever type of AppleWorks document you use most frequently.

To change the new document command:

1. Choose Edit > Preferences > General (**Figure A.23**).

2. When the Preferences dialog box appears, use the *Topic* pop-up menu to select *General* (**Figure A.24**).

3. In the *On ⌘–N, Create* panel, use the pop-up menu to choose which type of AppleWorks document you want the command to create. (The default is *Word Processing*.) Once you've made your choice, click *OK* and the change will take effect.

To change the Auto-Save interval:

1. Make sure to close all of your AppleWorks documents, then choose Edit > Preferences > General (**Figure A.23**).

2. When the Preferences dialog box appears, use the *Topic* pop-up menu to select *Files* (**Figure A.25**).

3. The *Auto-Save* panel shows that, by default, your open AppleWorks documents will be saved every *5 Minutes*. If that's too long for your own comfort, enter a new number in the text window and use the pop-up menu to choose *Seconds*, *Minutes*, or *Hours*. Once you've made your choice, click *OK* and the change will take effect.

✔ Tip

■ If you have a document open when you set the interval, the interval setting will only apply to that document rather than AppleWorks in general.

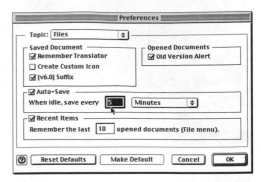

Figure A.25 Use the *Topic* pop-up menu to select *Files*, then enter a new number in the *Auto-Save* text window and use the pop-up menu to choose *Seconds*, *Minutes*, or *Hours*.

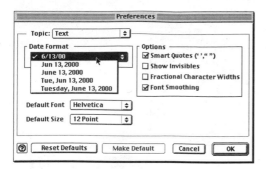

Figure A.26 Use the *Topic* pop-up menu to select *Text*, then use the *Date Format* pop-up menu to choose a format.

To change the date format:

1. Choose Edit > Preferences > General (**Figure A.23**).

2. When the Preferences dialog box appears, use the *Topic* pop-up menu to select *Text* (**Figure A.26**).

3. Use the *Date Format* pop-up menu to choose the format you want used whenever you choose Edit > Insert Date. Once you've made your choice, click *OK* and the format will take effect.

Changing how HTML is translated

If you plan on using a lot of Web documents or saving AppleWorks documents for the Web, you can control how HTML files are translated to AppleWorks and vice versa. In general AppleWorks's HTML Translation Filter does a pretty good job. But if you have specific HTML tags that you want handled a particular way, AppleWorks gives you that control. If you're not completely comfortable coding in HTML, however, leave these settings alone. The HTML Export settings control how AppleWorks's own formatting is translated into HTML. The HTML Import settings control how Web page coding is translated into AppleWorks formatting.

To change AppleWorks-to-HTML translation:

1. Choose Edit > Preferences > HTML Import/Export (**Figure A.27**).

2. When the Configure HTML dialog box appears, use the *Topic* pop-up menu to select *HTML Export (Advanced)* (**Figure A.28**).

3. Scroll through the list of *AppleWorks Attributes* to see the *Start Tag* and *End Tag* coding that AppleWorks will generate when you save an AppleWorks document as HTML.

4. When you find an AppleWorks attribute–HTML tag matchup that you want to change, just enter the new coding in either the *Start Tag* or *End Tag* text windows.

5. When you are done tweaking the tag coding, click *OK* and the changes will be used the next time you save an AppleWorks document as HTML.

✔ Tip

■ To return to the default tags, click the *Restore All HTML Defaults* button.

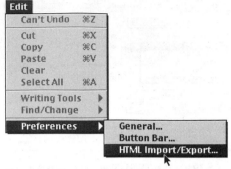

Figure A.27 To change how HTML is translated, choose Edit > Preferences > HTML Import/Export.

Figure A.28 Use the *Topic* pop-up menu to select *HTML Export (Advanced)* and then scroll the list of *AppleWorks Attributes* to see the equivalent *Start Tag* and *End Tag* codes.

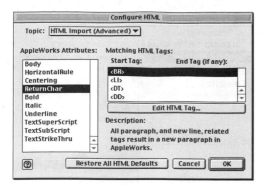

Figure A.29 Use the *Topic* pop-up menu to select *HTML Import (Advanced)* to see which HTML tags are paired with AppleWorks attributes.

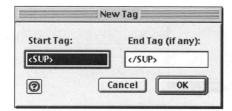

Figure A.30 Use the New Tag dialog box to change individual HTML tags.

To change HTML-to- AppleWorks translation:

1. Choose Edit > Preferences > HTML Import/Export (**Figure A.27**).

2. When the Configure HTML dialog box appears, use the *Topic* pop-up menu to select *HTML Import (Advanced)* (**Figure A.29**).

3. Scroll through the list of *AppleWorks Attributes* to see which HTML tag has been paired with that attribute. In many cases, the *Matching HTML Tags* window will list several possible tags for that attribute. If you see one you would rather use, click on it to select it.

4. If you want to further change a tag, select it in the *Matching HTML Tags* window, then click the *Edit HTML Tag* button. When the New Tag dialog box appears (**Figure A.30**), change the code and click *OK* to return to the Configure HTML dialog box.

5. When you are done changing the tag matchups, click *OK* and the changes will be used the next time you import an HTML document into AppleWorks.

✔ Tip

■ You can return to the default tags at any time by clicking the *Restore All HTML Defaults* button.

SETTING PREFERENCES

Changing the TCP/IP Setting

If you have an always-on Internet connection (DSL, cable, or dedicated network), you may want to change your TCP/IP settings. This change makes it possible to download Web clippings and templates from the AppleWorks Web site without launching your Web browser. However, as explained in *No browser necessary?* on page 86, you should *not* do this if you use a dial-up modem. In that case, leave these settings alone.

To change the TCP/IP settings:

1. Choose Apple menu > Control Panels > TCP/IP (**Figure A.31**).

2. When the TCP/IP dialog box appears, choose Edit > User Mode (⌘U) (**Figure A.32**).

3. Within the User Mode dialog box select *Advanced* and click *OK* (**Figure A.33**).

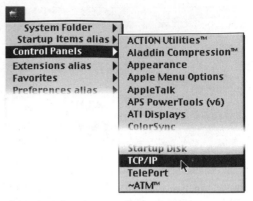

Figure A.31 If you have an always-on Internet connection, choose Apple menu > Control Panels > TCP/IP.

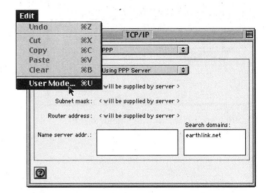

Figure A.32 When the TCP/IP dialog box appears, choose Edit > User Mode (⌘U).

Figure A.33 Select *Advanced* in the User Mode dialog box and click *OK*.

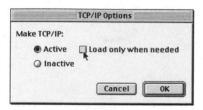

Figure A.34 Click the *Options* button in the TCP/IP dialog box.

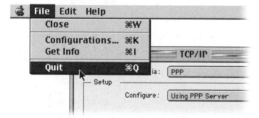

Figure A.35 Within the TCP/IP Options dialog box, select *Active* and uncheck *Load only when needed*.

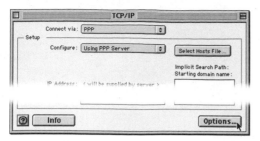

Figure A.36 When the TCP/IP dialog box reappears, choose File > Quit (⌘Q) and the TCP/IP settings will be changed.

4. Back in the TCP/IP dialog box, click the *Options* button (**Figure A.34**).

5. Within the TCP/IP Options dialog box, select *Active* and uncheck *Load only when needed* (**Figure A.35**). Click *OK* to close the TCP/IP Options dialog box.

6. When the TCP/IP dialog box reappears, choose File > Quit (⌘Q) (**Figure A.36**). The dialog box will close and the TCP/IP settings will be changed.

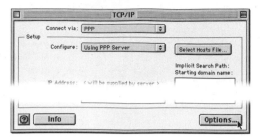

Figure A.34 Click the *Options* button in the TCP/IP dialog box.

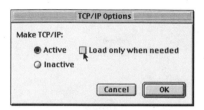

Figure A.35 Within the TCP/IP Options dialog box, select *Active* and uncheck *Load only when needed*.

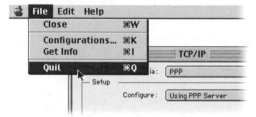

Figure A.36 When the TCP/IP dialog box reappears, choose File > Quit (⌘Q) and the TCP/IP settings will be changed.

4. Back in the TCP/IP dialog box, click the *Options* button (**Figure A.34**).

5. Within the TCP/IP Options dialog box, select *Active* and uncheck *Load only when needed* (**Figure A.35**). Click *OK* to close the TCP/IP Options dialog box.

6. When the TCP/IP dialog box reappears, choose File > Quit (⌘Q) (**Figure A.36**). The dialog box will close and the TCP/IP settings will be changed.

CHANGING TCP/IP SETTINGS

Index

Symbols

M

INDEX

INDEX